P9-BYH-201

Trefoil Round the World

'In a world fraught with uncertainty and fear our Movement shines out as a golden chain against a dark background. The links in the chain are forged out of the finest gold, our Promise and Law. Each has its special and individual decoration, its national characteristics, to enrich and beautify the whole. The chain is getting longer with each new link and stronger as each country increases in spirit and in numbers.'

Olave, Lady Baden-Powell
World Chief Guide

World Association
of Girl Guides and Girl Scouts
The World Bureau, 132 Ebury Street
London S.W.1, England

First Edition June 1958
Second Edition March 1959
Third Edition January 1961
Fourth Edition March 1964
Fifth Edition August 1967
Sixth Edition 1973
Seventh Edition 1977
Reprinted 1979 with Supplement

ISBN 0 900827 36 X

Notes

1 Where no submission has been received from a Member Organization in time for inclusion and where no other information is available, laws, promises, mottoes, badges have been reprinted from the 6th Edition of *Trefoil Round the World*.

2 In the case of Member Organizations in countries where English is not the mother tongue, the English version of the Promise and Law is a translation of the text adopted by the National Organization; it should be noted that without knowledge of the language or culture of the country it is often difficult to comprehend fully the true meaning and significance of the words chosen by an Association.

3 Since 1966 Tenderfoot Members have been known as Associate Members.

We offer our sincere thanks to the Girl Scouts of the U.S.A., whose idea it was that this book should replace HANDS AROUND THE WORLD, *published in the United States of America in 1949*

Printed in Great Britain
by Jarrold & Sons Ltd, Norwich

Contents

* Indicates associate membership.

Member Organizations of the World Association *continued*

Supplement

* Indicates associate membership.

Our grateful thanks to all those who contributed information and to the Member Organizations of the World Association of Girl Guides and Girl Scouts, whose co-operation has been invaluable in the preparation of this book.

How It All Began

The Founder

Strange as it may now seem, B-P's own generation would have connected his name more with Mafeking than with Scouting, yet today millions of boys and girls all over the world refer to him lovingly as 'The Founder'.

Born in London in 1857 and educated at Charterhouse, a famous English public school, he was by inclination not an academic, and so it was characteristic that he should found a Movement which provided young people with an out-of-school education, a 'wisdom of the woods' and an ability to survive by their own resources. It is perhaps noteworthy that 'Environment' has now become one of the major preoccupations of people all over the world.

B-P's army experiences in India and Africa convinced him of the viability and usefulness of a Scout Movement for boys. The Movement officially began in 1908; in 1909 B-P took the salute at a great Boy Scout rally held at the Crystal Palace in London where 11,000 boys appeared on parade. Scouting was intended for boys, so B-P was somewhat taken aback to see that a number of girls, calling themselves 'Girl Scouts' and adamant about joining the Movement, had turned up. He decided that if they were to join the Movement they needed to have a name of their own and a programme suited to the needs of girls. 'A scheme for Girl Guides – A suggestion for Character Training for Girls' appeared in 1909. In 1910 the Girl Guides Association was officially founded under the presidency of B-P's sister, Agnes Baden-Powell. With B-P she set about writing the first handbook for Girl Guides. This handbook was soon to be used by girls everywhere interested in becoming part of this new Movement.

In 1910 B-P, now Sir Robert Baden-Powell, retired from the Army to devote his full time to the Guide and Scout Movements. He attended camps, rallies and Jamborees all over the world, a job which was soon to be shared by his young wife Olave whom he met and married in 1912. In 1920 he was elected Chief Scout of the world, and in 1929 Sir Robert became Lord Baden-Powell of Gilwell.

In an age of restricted mass media, B-P managed to keep in close touch with Guides, Scouts and other members of the Movements through his writings. In them they found the encouragement, advice and inspiration which they needed. Always he reminded his Guiders and Scouters: 'Don't let the technical outweigh the moral – the end is CHARACTER – character with a purpose.'

Conscious of the great future of the Scout and Guide Movements, as early as 1910 B-P was writing on the subject of co-operation with other organizations. 'The Great Aim of a Movement like ours,' he wrote, 'is not only the practice of give-and-take with our own members, but also with other organizations working to the same end. In a big Movement we have to sink minor ideas and link arms in a big combine to deal effectively with the whole.'

In the 1938 edition of his handbook *Girl Guiding* he spoke of how one of the good things to come out of the First World War was the recognition of women in their own right. They had placed themselves, he said, 'on a new plane in the social order, and it is up to them now to carry the service they gave to the country in time of war into the wide field which has opened to them for developing peace and prosperity'.

Baden Powell of Gilwell

Olave Baden-Powell

In 1922 he had said that the test of success in education is not what a child knows after examination on leaving school, but what he or she is doing ten years later. Similarly, the work accomplished by the Founder in his lifetime was only the beginning – the rest depends on each of us.

The World Chief Guide

The Founder's glorious and active career was in direct contrast to the quiet and unadventurous life which Olave St. Clair Soames led up to the time of her marriage with B-P. This, however, was very soon to change completely and in later life she would exclaim: 'So little time, so little done and so much still to do!'

Born in 1889 near Chesterfield, England, Olave's early life was spent surrounded by family and friends, enjoying music and country pursuits. Her first trip abroad was when as a young woman in 1912 she accompanied her father on a cruise to Jamaica. This marked the time of her 'waking up and being a person', for it was on this journey that she met B-P. Although thirty-two years separated them in age, they were united by mutual interests, a similar attitude to life and a common birthday (22 February, now Thinking Day). In October of that same year Lt. General Sir Robert Baden-Powell and Olave St. Clair Soames were married quietly in Dorset, England. They had three children: Peter, born in 1913; Heather, in 1915; and another daughter, Betty, in 1917.

Olave's involvement in Guiding dates from 1916 when, following an offer to 'help out', she was made County Commissioner for Sussex. In 1918 she was appointed British Chief Guide and in 1919 she formed the International Council which later became the World Association of Girl Guides and Girl Scouts (WAGGGS).

The next ten years were extremely busy ones, spent attending rallies, camps, meetings, conferences and addressing Girl Guides/Girl Scouts and Boy Scouts all over the world. Looking back on them she said: 'The late twenties and early thirties really saw us reach the peak of our work together as husband and wife in the service of our brother and sister Movements.' In 1930 Lady Baden-Powell was appointed World Chief Guide. At that time she made a life-long promise – 'to do my best to help everybody all the time'.

In 1931 Girl Guiding/Girl Scouting and Boy Scouting were having a phenomenal success all round the globe. The Chiefs undertook a World Tour in that year, and were delighted at the progress they saw in every country they visited. In 1932 Lady B-P was created Dame Grand Cross of the Order of the British Empire and in the same year had the pleasure of seeing 'Our Chalet' officially opened in Switzerland.

In 1933 the famous Guide and Scout cruises began. As they gained in popularity, the Chief Guide remarked, 'I consider the cruises one of my triumphs – they were my own idea entirely.' The Chiefs celebrated their Silver Wedding anniversary in 1937, but by that time the Founder's health was giving cause for concern.

From the time of the Founder's death in 1941 until she gave up travelling in 1970, the World Chief Guide worked untiringly for the Girl Guide/Girl Scout Movement, covering many thousands of miles in order to encourage and inspire girls and young women all over the world. Her warmth and concern are known everywhere. In Australia, a group of Guiders, disappointed at having seen so little of Lady Baden-Powell during the day, seated themselves as close as possible to her V.I.P. table at dinner. When Lady Baden-Powell arrived with her party, she saw them there and exclaimed: 'Oh, how lovely! You have all come to join us for dinner!' and insisted that the whole dining room be reorganized so that she and her party could sit with the Guiders. Children warmed to her immediately; a Brownie who met her in 1967 was heard to claim: 'I've got a secret with Lady B-P now!'

The World Chief Guide's work has been recognized in the numerous honours and decorations awarded to her by heads of state, kings, queens, presidents and mayors of cities all over the world. Her most recent award was the FAO Ceres medal for 1973, presented to her in 1974 by Mrs. Helvi Sipilä, Assistant Secretary General of the United Nations for Social Development and Humanitarian Affairs. In accepting it on behalf of the whole Girl Guide/Girl Scout Movement, the World Chief Guide paid tribute to the Leaders 'who are keeping the Movement alive and growing'.

In her autobiography, *Window on my Heart*, she leaves us this message: 'Discipline yourself daily by having a plan . . . not just vague, wishful thinking. Commit yourself daily to doing something however small, for somebody else, for by making other people happy you will find true happiness yourself.'

As this edition of Trefoil Round the World *went to press we received the sad news that Olave, Lady Baden-Powell, World Chief Guide, had died peacefully in her sleep on 25 June 1977. All members past and present of the Girl Guide/Girl Scout Movement will remember her life and work with love and thanksgiving.*

World Association of Girl Guides and Girl Scouts (WAGGGS)

The World Association of Girl Guides and Girl Scouts (WAGGGS) is a world-wide organization which aims to provide girls with opportunities for self-training in the development of character and responsible citizenship and service to the community. WAGGGS is composed of individual National Organizations,[1] through which girls and women are offered an ideal and a spirit; they are brought together in a Movement which stresses voluntary membership open to all, self-government and political independence.[2] They are provided with learning opportunities through programmes adapted to each age-group, using a method based on the Promise and Law, team-work (the patrol system), etc.; they are offered the support of an organized structure for administration, training, research and other activities.

WAGGGS promotes unity of purpose and common understanding in the fundamental principles of the Movement, and encourages international friendship and understanding.

[1]There were 98 National Organizations in 1978 with a total of 7·5 million members.
[2] Read *The Essential Elements of Girl Guiding/Girl Scouting*, published by WAGGGS and available through your National Headquarters.

History

From the beginning girls were determined to be included. B-P's attention was particularly drawn to this fact at the time of the great Boy Scout Rally at the Crystal Palace in 1909, when a number of determined girls showed up. B-P recognized the need for an organization for the girls; he also realized that they must have a programme designed specifically for their needs; so he asked his sister, Agnes Baden-Powell, to help organize a Movement for girls. After his marriage, his wife took over this role, as the Movement rapidly spread around the world. So, from the earliest days, there have been two separate and independent organizations.

Women involved in Guiding in Britain at that time corresponded with friends abroad, in order to find out in which countries Girl Guiding/Girl Scouting already existed. In 1919 the true internationality of the Movement was realized when Lady Baden-Powell formed the International Council; she then arranged the first International Conference (Oxford, 1920).[1] Forty countries were represented at the first World Camp, which was held in 1924.

In 1928 the International Council was replaced by the World Association of Girl Guides and Girl Scouts. (*See* Appendix A for the Founder Members of WAGGGS.)

The first World Committee was formed and International Conferences became World Conferences. The Constitution of WAGGGS was formally adopted at the 9th World Conference (Sweden, 1936).

Membership

Membership of WAGGGS can only be acquired by a National Organization as a whole.

WAGGGS continues to expand. Every three years at each World Conference, new Full and Associate[2] Members are recognized.

Every National Organization wishing to be a member of WAGGGS must adhere to the fundamental principles of the original Promise and Law laid down by the Founder; the wording may be adjusted by National Organizations to make them more suitable for their own country. Membership in the Movement must be voluntary and open to all girls without distinction of race, creed, colour, or any other circumstance. The organization must be self-governing and independent of any political party.

As well as adhering to the principles of membership a National Organization must abide by the *Constitution and Bye-Laws* of WAGGGS; must have a Constitution of its own, approved by the World Committee; must incorporate a Trefoil in its badge; pay an annual quota (a sum of money determined on a proportional basis); and send an annual report of its work to the World Bureau.

There are two categories of membership, Full and Associate. This enables National Associations to be accepted initially into the Movement while they continue to work on their programme.

[1] See *Basics*, Appendix B (WAGGGS, London, 1976), for the full list of places and dates of World Conferences.

[2] Name changed from 'Tenderfoot' by decision of the 19th World Conference (Japan, 1966).

World Conference

The authority of WAGGGS is exercised at a World Conference through the two delegates representing each Member Organization. A limited number of visitors are also welcomed. These are individuals from within WAGGGS and specially invited representatives of other international organizations.

The Conference is held every three years in a different area of the world.

The World Conference is the policy-making body of WAGGGS. It sets the standards of the Association and formulates the general policy to be followed between its meetings. The World Committee follows up the decisions made by a World Conference; the World Bureau helps to put these decisions into action.

World Committee

The World Committee consists of twelve members from different areas of the world, elected at a World Conference. They do not represent their own National Organizations, but use their experience for the benefit of the World Association as a whole. Members serve a nine-year term in office; the terms overlap, with three members completing their term, and three new members being elected at each World Conference.

Committee Members wear the grey-blue World Uniform and the World Association pin to show that they represent WAGGGS.

Subcommittees

The World Committee appoints its own Subcommittees after consideration of the candidates submitted by National Organizations.

At present there are Subcommittees for Promotion, Constitutions and Finance. In addition each of the four World Centres (Our Chalet, Olave House, Our Cabaña and Sangam) has its own Subcommittee and there are Regional Subcommittees for Africa, Asia Pacific, Europe and Western Hemisphere Regions and the Arab Regional Group.

World Bureau

The World Bureau was first set up in London in 1928, and in 1958 moved to its present premises at 132 Ebury Street. It serves as the Secretariat of WAGGGS, assisting each National Organization to play a full role within the World Association; it acts as a link among the ninety-four Member Associations; it co-ordinates the work of the World Committee and the Subcommittees; it assists with the overall planning and organization of World Conferences, World Committee meetings, WAGGGS events and for WAGGGS representation at meetings of the UN and its Agencies.

Through the World Bureau, decisions taken at World Conferences and other meetings are implemented. It is also responsible for receiving Quota payments and contributions to the Thinking Day Fund.

Within the Bureau there are several departments: Administration, Central Office, Communications, Constitutions, Finance, Promotion and Translators.

The World Bureau staff is truly international, with a dozen or more nationalities represented at any one time. The working languages of the Bureau are English, French and Spanish – WAGGGS' three official languages.

The workload of the World Bureau, which has increased over the years, has happily not decreased the welcome which members of the Movement receive when they drop in for a visit.

Symbols of Unity

World Trefoil

The World Trefoil is the symbol of the World Association of Girl Guides and Girl Scouts (WAGGGS). Every part has a meaning. The gold colour of the Trefoil represents the sun shining over all the children in the world; the three leaves represent the three-fold Promise originally laid down by the Founder; the base of the stalk is a copy of the heraldic *feu*, representing the flame of the love of mankind; the vein pointing upwards through the centre of the Trefoil represents the compass needle, pointing the way; the two stars represent the Promise and the Law. The World Trefoil, used also on the World Flag and the World Badge, is the unifying symbol.

World Badge

- Adopted at the 11th World Conference (France, 1946).
- A gold trefoil on blue background. (See above, 'World Trefoil', for symbolism.)
- Worn by all members, girls and adults, of the World Association, in or out of uniform.
- Adopted by certain Associations as their Promise Badge. May also be used as the Promise Badge by members of International Units registered at the World Bureau.

World Brownie Badge

- Adopted at the 15th World Conference (The Netherlands, 1954).
- Depicts the Brownie Sign, two fingers raised in salute, in World Association colours (gold on a bright blue background).
- Worn in or out of uniform; may also be used as a Promise Badge by members of Brownie International Units registered with the World Bureau. National Organizations decide whether their youngest members will wear it or whether they also will wear the World Badge.

World Association Badge

- Adopted at the 7th World Conference (Poland, 1932).
- Same design as World Badge, but with light blue trefoil and silver stars and compass needle.
- Worn by members of World Committee, Subcommittees, World Bureau staff, Guiders-in-Charge of World Centres, and others who carry out special duties for the World Association.

World Flag

- Adopted at the 6th World Conference (U.K., 1930).
- Consists of the World Trefoil in gold on a bright blue background.
- Flown at the World Centres, at the World Bureau and at all World Association

gatherings and international events run by Member Organizations. Troops and companies may carry the World Flag in addition to their own national flag.

Good Turn

This is a phrase which symbolizes the service given by all members of the Movement. The youngest girls will think of ways in which they can do a good turn every day. The older girls develop this feature into Service Projects at local, national and international levels.

The Left Handshake

This special handshake is used as a greeting between members of the Movement.

The Founder knew that secret signs had a great appeal for young people. The left hand is the one nearest the heart, and so signifies friendship. B-P told another story when asked to explain its origin. While living in West Africa he heard of the legend of two hostile neighbouring tribes, who were continually at war; one day they decided it would be better to live in peace, so they flung down their shields, which they carried on the left arm and advanced unprotected, holding out their left hands in trust and friendship.

Motto – 'Be Prepared'

The motto matches the initials of the Founder, and is another unifying link. It was first adopted by the men of the South African Constabulary, the mounted police force which B-P raised in 1901.

The Sign or Salute

When Girl Guides/Girl Scouts greet one another they can give the sign or salute – three fingers of the right hand raised as a reminder of the three-fold Promise.

The World Song

The World Song, first published in Denmark in 1952, and based on a March by Sibelius, constitutes an important link for Girl Guides and Girl Scouts all over the world.

World Centres

Four World Centres,[1] each in a different area of the world, have been acquired by WAGGGS over the years. Our Chalet in Switzerland, Olave House in the U.K., Our Cabaña in Mexico and Sangam in India – all are familiar names to members of the Movement.

Any member, girl or adult, may stay in any of the World Centres. At a World Centre the visitor will meet others in the Movement from countries all round the world – an unusual opportunity for international education. Both groups and individuals are welcome to participate in conferences, seminars and training courses – or simply to have an enjoyable and different holiday.

Each centre has its own special characteristics which influence the activities held there. These include special sightseeing expeditions and sessions to learn the crafts of the area. In this way, each centre takes full advantage of its unique location to broaden the education and understanding of visitors.

[1] See *Story of the Four World Centres*, WAGGGS, London, 1976 for further information. Available through your National Headquarters.

A Subcommittee of the World Committee exists for each of the centres to supervise administration and devise programmes in co-operation with the Guider-in-Charge.

While staying in a World Centre the visitor is both guest and hostess – for the centres belong to all of us.

Our Chalet near Adelboden, Switzerland, was the first World Centre, opened in 1932. The gift of a leading member of the Girl Scouts of the U.S.A. and former World Committee Chairman, Mrs. Helen Storrow, it is set in idyllic surroundings on a mountain slope. There are excellent facilities for skiing, climbing and walking.

Olave House in London, England, provides a comfortable base in the centre of this fascinating city. There has been a WAGGGS' World Centre in London since 1939. The present location of Olave House in Earls Court offers many advantages – proximity to art galleries, museums, theatres and shops. Visitors are welcome whether they are in transit or staying for a longer time.

Our Cabaña in Cuernavaca, Mexico was opened in 1957. Generous donations from friends around the world, especially in the Western Hemisphere, made possible the acquisition of this beautiful property. A well-equipped crafts room and a swimming pool are two of its appealing features. There are also study-sessions on the crafts and history of Mexico.

Sangam, youngest of the four World Centres, was opened by Olave, Lady Baden-Powell, World Chief Guide, in October 1966. Situated at Poona in Maharastra State, Sangam combines the beauty of ancient India with the more practical aspects connected with a WAGGGS' World Centre. Sangam (which in Sanskrit means 'going together') has been hostess to a number of important international conferences and seminars. It also offers Girl Guides and Girl Scouts a unique opportunity to study the arts and crafts of India.

Thinking Day

The idea for a special day each year on which Girl Guides/Girl Scouts around the world think of each other with love and friendship originated at the 4th International Conference (U.S.A., 1926). The date chosen was 22 February – an obvious choice, since it was the joint birthday of the Founder, Lord Robert Baden-Powell, and Olave, Lady Baden-Powell, the World Chief Guide. This idea was further developed at the 7th World Conference (Poland, 1932); a Belgian delegate suggested that Girl Guides/Girl Scouts give 'a penny with their thoughts'. The suggestion caught on quickly and the Thinking Day Fund was established for the promotion of Girl Guiding/Girl Scouting wherever the need was greatest.

The sum of one penny, or its equivalent, is symbolic today; all girls are encouraged to give as much as they can. Through this concept of anonymous loving giving, girls and women can promote Girl Guiding/Girl Scouting in underprivileged areas or isolated communities; help with leadership training; contribute to the printing or translating of handbooks; encourage international exchanges; and support a wide variety of Girl Guide/Girl Scout projects that deal with the problems of malnutrition, illiteracy, the handicapped, and those in need of home care.

Support for the Thinking Day Fund demonstrates that each of us is personally involved in our World Association and shares in the responsibility for seeing that its work continues to expand.

Thinking Day Symbol

In 1975 a Thinking Day Symbol was introduced. The World Trefoil in the centre represents the World Association (WAGGGS). The arrows pointing towards the Trefoil represent *action* and give direction for that action. The arrows may also represent the ways and means in which WAGGGS can be helped by all its members. The round shape of the design represents the worldwide aspect of the Movement.

The symbol can be used in Thinking Day celebrations and in promoting the Thinking Day Fund.

Girl Guide/Girl Scout and Boy Scout Relationships[1]

The World Association of Girl Guides and Girl Scouts (WAGGGS) and the **World Organization of the Scout Movement** (WOSM) are two separate and independent organizations, having in common the same Founder and the same fundamental principles laid down by him and based on their respective Promises and Laws.

Girl Guides/Girl Scouts and Boy Scouts collaborate at all levels – local, national and international. This collaboration takes many different forms:

- At **international level** there is a Girl Guide/Girl Scout and Boy Scout Consultative Committee set up by the two world organizations.
- At **national and local level** Joint Activities are often arranged, that is jointly planned and undertaken by Girl Guides/Girl Scouts and Boy Scouts.

There are two different types of structure that can be implemented when Girl Guide/Girl Scout and Boy Scout National Organizations are collaborating on a permanent basis:

- **A Joint Organization** – with separate Girl Guide/Girl Scout and Boy Scout sections.
- **A Merged Organization** – where there is only one structure for both Girl Guides/Girl Scouts and Boy Scouts.

[1] For further information see statement on Relationships between the Girl Guide/Girl Scout and Boy Scout Movements (WAGGGS/WOSM, 1973).

Present and Future

The meaning of the original Promise and Law is still valid today. Many countries have changed the words to suit their own circumstances, for over the years WAGGGS has developed with flexibility and respect for all its Member Organizations. With members in almost every area of the world, there is a rich diversity of cultures, traditions and religions. Uniforms, badges and especially programmes have been altered in order to be suitable in and have meaning for a particular country.

It was the Founder who emphasized that this is a *Movement*, not a static body. The sound Fundamental Principles always remain relevant in a tremendous variety of cultural and geographical settings, to meet the needs of each new generation.

A Long-Term Planning Group, appointed by the World Committee from within its members, considers the future goals of WAGGGS. This group initiates studies which can give direction for the future.

Since change is the only constant with which we live, it is essential for each member, each group, each National Organization regularly to re-examine and re-assess ways of work, in order that 'the girl' may be better served.

Select Bibliography

Census For membership figures see the most recent *Triennial Report* (WAGGGS, London), published prior to each World Conference.

Games and Recipes See *Guide Games and Recipes* (WAGGGS, London, 1967).

Membership of the World Association For list of Member countries, giving years of attaining Associate and Full Membership, see *Basics*, Appendix B (WAGGGS, London, 1976).

Olave, Lady Baden-Powell, World Chief Guide See *Window on My Heart*, her autobiography, written with Mary Drewery (Hodder & Stoughton, London, 1973); and *Olave Baden-Powell*, Elizabeth Hartley (WAGGGS, London, 1975).

Quota and Donations to the Thinking Day Fund See the *Triennial Report*.

Uniforms For colour illustrations of the Guide uniforms of all member organizations, see *Uniform Charts* (set of four) (WAGGGS, London, revised 1975). For Brownie uniforms see *Brownie Painting Books* (1–6) (WAGGGS, London, 1975).

WAGGGS publications Each National Organization is supplied with *WAGGGS World Bureau Catalogue*, which lists all items published by WAGGGS. For further information contact your National Headquarters.

World Centres See *Story of the Four World Centres*, which gives the story of each centre, with photos. (WAGGGS, London, revised 1976.)

World Conferences For list of places and dates see *Basics*, Appendix A (WAGGGS, London, 1976); a *World Conference Report* is published after each Conference; the issue of *Council Fire*, your world journal, following each Conference has the Conference as its theme.

Member Organizations of the World Association

Argentina

Asociación Guías Argentinas

GUIDE

Promesa	Promise
Por mi honor y con la gracia de Dios prometo hacer todo lo posible para cumplir mis deberes para con Dios y mi Patria, ayudar al prójimo en todas las circunstancias y observar la Ley Guía.	On my honour and with the help of God I promise to do my best to do my duty to God and my country, to help other people at all times and to obey the Guide Law.

Ley	Law
1 La guía es digna de toda confianza.	A Guide is worthy of being trusted.
2 La guía es leal y responsable.	A Guide is loyal and responsible.
3 La guía sirve y ayuda al prójimo sin esperar recompensas ni alabanzas.	A Guide serves and helps her neighbour without expecting reward or praise.
4 La guía considera a todos como hermanos.	A Guide considers everyone as brothers.
5 La guía es cortés.	A Guide is courteous.
6 La guía ve en la naturaleza la obra de Dios y la respeta.	A Guide sees in nature God's work and she respects it.
7 La guía es obediente y disciplinada y nada hace a medias.	A Guide is obedient and disciplined and leaves nothing half done.
8 La guía es alegre y enfrenta las dificultades con serenidad.	A Guide is always cheerful and faces difficulties serenely.
9 La guía es económica y respeta el bien ajeno.	A Guide is thrifty and respects other people's property.
10 La guía es pura en pensamiento palabras y obras.	A Guide is pure in thought, word and deed.

Motto

Siempre lista (en Caravana)	Always prepared
Siempre adelante (del Sol)	Always forward

BROWNIE

Brownie Promise

Prometo hacer todo lo posible para cumplir mis deberes para con Dios, mi Patria, mis Padres y observar la Ley de la Ronda.	I promise to do my best in fulfilling my duties towards God, my country, my parents and to observe the Brownie Law.

Brownie Law

La Alita es activa y observadora.	The Brownie is active and observant.
La Alita está limpia y bien arreglada.	The Brownie is clean and tidy.
La Alita es alegre.	The Brownie is gay.
La Alita dice la verdad.	The Brownie tells the truth.
La Alita piensa simpre en los demás.	The Brownie always thinks of others.

Brownie Motto

Siempre mejor	Always better

Age Groups

Guía Mayor	Ranger	16–19
Guia del Sol	Guide (Sun)	13–15
Guía en Caravana	Guide (Caravan)	10–12
Alita	Little Wing	7–9

Girl Guiding began in Argentina in 1915, although it was at first confined to English schools whose companies and packs were registered with the U.K. Girl Guides Association. During the next forty years the development of the Movement was hindered by many difficulties, including a governmental ban after 1939 on all uniformed groups of foreign origin. The situation changed for the better in 1953 when Sra Nair F. B. de Gowland started an autonomous Guide Movement and the *Asociación Guías Argentinas* was officially founded in October 1953. It was granted legal status by the Government in 1956 and by decision of the 16th World Conference (Brazil, 1957) became an Associate Member of the World Association in 1958. The Association achieved Full Membership of the World Association at the 18th World Conference (Denmark, 1963). The Headquarters of the Association has been located in Buenos Aires since 1960.

PROGRAMME

Since the early 1970s a new programme has been in force, stressing the need for efficient service to the community; Rangers regularly hold successful service camps.

The Association has increasingly put stress on the strengthening of Guiding in the provinces, and is constantly on the lookout for Leaders who can work in rural or low-income areas. The aim of this drive is to emphasize the aspects of Guiding which confirm it as a factor in the development of people and communities, and to establish permanent training at all levels. In April 1976 a seminar for Group Leaders in Rural Areas was held in Buenos Aires with financial help provided by UNESCO. The main objective of this seminar was to analyse specific problems of isolated groups and to look for common solutions.

TRAINING

Training courses, including correspondence courses, are organized throughout the country. Leaders are trained in groups and by means of regional courses held in their own environment. Increasing responsibility has been given to young Leaders and Senior Guides who are taught how to take a more personal and direct part in the campaign for development. A deeper knowledge of Guiding has been achieved as a consequence of the generalization of the concept 'The Guider is an educator'. National Training Camps and Gatherings are held for Senior Guides and for Trainers; they are usually attended by delegates from neighbouring countries. Groups of Senior Guides from South American countries and from the U.S.A. attend international camps held in Argentina.

ATTENDANCE AT INTERNATIONAL AND WORLD EVENTS

The Association was represented at the Western Hemisphere Regional Conference (Lima, 1973) 'Guiding, a Contribution to the Development of

Peoples and of Communities', the results of which have given rise to new activities within the Association. Girl Guides have also represented the National Organization at various gatherings at Our Cabaña; delegates from Argentina attended WAGGGS' 22nd World Conference (U.K., 1975).

SERVICE

Service is an important part of the Girl Guide Programme in Argentina. Among the various and imaginative service projects organized by the Association is one aimed at stimulating public interest in education. Within the scope of this project, children with learning problems are helped through Literacy classes, non-school educational activities and organized recreation centres.

The Guides' work with underprivileged girls has resulted in the setting up of nursing courses for the girls, enabling them to receive a 'nursing-aid' certificate on successful completion of the course.

Australia

Girl Guides Association of Australia

GUIDE

Promise

I promise that I will do my best:
To do my duty to God;
To serve the Queen and help other people; and
To keep the Guide Law.

Law

1 A Guide is loyal and can be trusted.
2 A Guide is helpful.
3 A Guide is polite and considerate.
4 A Guide is friendly and a sister to all Guides.
5 A Guide is kind to animals and respects all living things.
6 A Guide is obedient.
7 A Guide has courage and is cheerful in all difficulties.
8 A Guide makes good use of her time.
9 A Guide takes care of her own possessions and those of other people.
10 A Guide is self-controlled in all she thinks, says and does.

Motto

Be Prepared

BROWNIE

Brownie Guide Promise

I promise that I will do my best:
To do my duty to God;
To serve the Queen, and help other people; and
To keep the Brownie Guide Law.

Brownie Guide Law

A Brownie Guide thinks of others
before herself and does a good turn
every day.

Brownie Guide Motto

Lend a Hand

Age Groups

Brownie Guide	7–11
Guide	10½–16
Ranger Guide	14–21

News of Guiding spread as swiftly in the New World as in the Old, and many Guide companies were already established in Australia before the First World War. Soon after the war, the various states acquired their own headquarters and, from 1926, they were drawn together in the Girl Guides Association of Australia (the State Guiding Associations remain autonomous). In 1928 Australia became a Founder Member of the World Association of Girl Guides and Girl Scouts.

With the independence in 1975 of Papua New Guinea, the local Girl Guide Association ceased to be a member of the Australian Association, but Christmas Island, Nauru, Norfolk Island, the Bass Strait Islands and the Torres Strait Islands continue to be part of Australian Guiding.

The Australian Executive Committee, consisting of the Chief Commissioner for Australia, Assistant Chief Commissioner and the six State Commissioners, who direct the policy of the Movement for Australia, meets regularly; Australian Office-bearers attend these meetings as required. The Australian Assembly is held every three years.

GUIDING – AUSTRALIAN STYLE

Most members of the Movement live in or near cities or towns and have regular meetings; for those unable to be members of active companies or packs there is the opportunity to be one of the 'Lones', and some are lucky enough to be 'Brownies of the Air', meeting their Guiders (and each other) in their own radio sessions.

A national development scheme which was commenced in 1970 has been extended to include urban and city high-rise building areas. The scheme has further expanded to bring Girl Guiding to the mining areas of northern and western Queensland, isolated villages in Tasmania, and Aboriginal settlements in Western Australia.

Australian Guides, like Girl Guides/Girl Scouts all over the world, enjoy camping and other outdoor activities; their Thinking Day, for instance, is likely to be very hot, so that this celebration is usually held early in the morning or in the evening. Often it is impossible to light a proper camp fire in summer, because of the danger of bush fires, and in some parts of the country camping must be done on hard ground for lack of grass, but none of this takes from the fun of a camp or a hike.

LEADERSHIP TRAINING

In September 1969 the eight-point programme – similar to that used in the United Kingdom – was introduced for Guides, Brownies and Rangers. Following this, there was a need for a more comprehensive training programme for adult Leaders to be used throughout Australia. The Australian Leadership Training Plan was launched in 1973 giving guidelines for a national training scheme for adult Leaders. This includes a Leaders' workbook in which each adult may assess her own ability and plan her own course of training. Training for potential trainers has become more regularized with emphasis on audio-visual material and the establishment of learning centres.

The Association has organized a workshop 'Look at Leadership' to which representatives of youth organizations which provide training for adult Leaders were invited. The event gave an opportunity for better understanding and an exchange of each other's aims and training needs.

SERVICE

Australia as a country is sometimes subject to violent climatic conditions, and when natural disasters occur Guides take immediate steps to give help to the victims. For example, after the cyclone which razed the city of Darwin on Christmas Day 1974 members of the Movement throughout Australia were involved in various aspects of Darwin Relief. A Guide company in Queensland received the Walter Donald Ross Trophy for its part in rescue operations during the floods in Brisbane early in 1974.

Many Guide service projects focus on ecology, and conservation has always been emphasized in the programme. In 1975 thousands of flowering trees, shrubs and bushes were planted by members of the Movement as their contribution to the beautification of the country.

NATIONAL AND INTERNATIONAL ACTION

Australian Guides have maintained their particular interest in international contacts through travel and the Post Box. During the nine months between July 1974 and March 1975, 384 Guide personnel travelled abroad to seminars, camps and conferences; and 679 Post Box contacts were linked with 28 countries.

National Gatherings have featured prominently in Guide activities and included Patrol Leaders' camps/conferences in 1972 and 1975, Australian Link-Up camps and the Australian Festival of Song.

The Australian Girl Guides Association is a member of the National Committee for UNICEF and was on the United Nations Association of Australia International Women's Year Committee. Individuals and Units have continued to support the UNESCO Gift Coupon Scheme together with the Australian Freedom From Hunger Campaign and other schemes for assisting those in need at home and abroad.

The Trefoil Guild increases in strength and a large number of representatives attended both the 1973 and 1975 General Assemblies in Austria and Denmark.

One of the important events in the recent history of Australian Guiding has been the election in 1975 of the former Chief Commissioner, Mrs. J. R. Price, O.B.E. (now Lady Price) as Chairman of the World Committee of WAGGGS.

Austria

Pfadfinder Und Pfadfinderinnen Österreichs

GUIDE

Versprechen	**Promise**
Ich will mich bemühen, meinem Land zu dienen, nach dem Gesetz der Pfadfinderinnen zu leben, und bitte Gott, mir dabei zu helfen.	I will endeavour to serve my Country, to live according to the Girl Guide Law, and ask God's help in this task.

Gesetz	**Law**
1 Suche den Weg zu Gott.	Find your way to God.
2 Sei aufrichtig.	Be sincere.
3 Hilf, wo Du kannst.	Help where you can.
4 Uberwinde Schwierigkeiten.	Vanquish difficulties.
5 Wähle, und setze Dich ein.	Choose and pledge yourself.
6 Sei zuverlässig.	Be reliable.
7 Schütze die Natur.	Protect Nature.
8 Suche und bringe Freude.	Seek and convey joy.
9 Verstehe and achte.	Understand and pay heed.

These nine clauses set out the Law which is common to all. A Girl Guide may, when she makes or renews her Promise, add a personal Law of her own choice.

Motto

Allzeit bereit	Be Prepared

BROWNIE

Brownie Promise

Ich verspreche, so gut ich kann Gott, den Eltern und dem Gesetz der Wichtel treu zu sein und täglich jemandem eine Freude zu bereiten.	I promise as well as I can to be faithful to God, my parents and the Brownie Law and bring joy to somebody daily.

Brownie Law

Das Wichtel gehorcht den Eltern und der Führerin.	The Brownie obeys her parents and her Leader.
Das Wichtel hilft freudig wo es kann.	The Brownie helps whenever she can.

Brownie Motto

Freudig Helfen	To help with joy

Age Groups

Ranger	Ranger	16–19
Pfadfinderin	Guide	12–15
Wichtel	Brownie	7–11

Girl Guiding made its appearance in Austria before the First World War. In 1924 a National Organization was formed, but due to an increasingly difficult political situation, all Guiding had ceased by 1938. After the Second World War, Guide activities began again throughout the country. Following visits to Austria by the Director of the World Bureau in 1956, the Österreichischer Pfadfinderinnenverband St Georg was recognized as an Associate Member of the World Association at the 16th World Conference (Brazil, 1957). Its recognition as a Full Member at the 20th World Conference (Finland, 1969) gave new impetus to the Movement in Austria and membership figures immediately started to increase. The Association is now a merged one, having in October 1976 joined with the Pfadfinder Österreichs to become the Pfadfinder und Pfadfinderinnen Österreichs.

PROGRAMME AND TRAINING

Since 1970 much work and research has gone into the preparation of a new programme which was finally adopted in September 1975. A 'contact committee' and a working group set up to study possible means of co-operation with Boy Scouts have seen their efforts well rewarded. There has been a marked increase in membership figures, and better training facilities are now available for Leaders through the improved economic situation afforded by the joint Association. A new handbook for both Boy Scout and Girl Guide Leaders has been published, and a huge jamboree '1977 – One Jamboree all over Austria' was held in the summer of 1977.

CAMPING

Guide and Ranger camps are held throughout the year and the Association also welcomes Guides and Girl Scouts from other countries who come to camp or for 'walking weeks' in Austria. Since 1966 the Association has also organized camps for handicapped Guides.

SERVICE

Service is an important part of the programme in Austria. Rangers help underprivileged families to cope with housework, etc. while Guides collect and repair clothing and toys. They also do much valuable work with refugees.

Bahamas

The Bahamas Girl Guides Association

GUIDE

Promise

I promise that I will do my best:
To do my duty to God;
To serve the Queen, my Country
and help other people;
and
To keep the Guide Law.

Law

1 A Guide is loyal and can be trusted.
2 A Guide is helpful.
3 A Guide is polite and considerate.
4 A Guide is friendly and a sister to all Guides.
5 A Guide is kind to animals and respects all living things.
6 A Guide is obedient.
7 A Guide has courage and is cheerful in all difficulties.
8 A Guide makes good use of her time.
9 A Guide takes care of her own possessions and those of other people.
10 A Guide is self-controlled in all she thinks, says and does.

BROWNIE

Brownie Guide Promise

I promise that I will do my best:
To do my duty to God;
To serve the Queen, my Country
and help other people;
and
To keep the Brownie Guide Law.

Brownie Guide Law

A Brownie Guide thinks of others
before herself and does a good
turn every day.

Girl Guiding was started in the Bahamas in 1915 by the then Governor's wife, Mrs. Allandyce. It was decided to form two or three companies in Nassau, with Mrs. Allandyce as the first President. The first Guide companies were attached to schools, and the first coloured Brownie Pack was started in 1926.

DEVELOPMENT OF GUIDING

Girl Guide activities continued from 1915 to 1935, but were then suspended for a time due to lack of leaders. In January 1946, Guiding was restarted and the Units were opened to all races. In the same year the Association was visited by Olave, Lady Baden-Powell, World Chief Guide, which helped to inspire the girls and their leaders. Many new companies were opened in Nassau, and membership soon increased, with several trainers from the United Kingdom visiting the National Organization, giving assistance where needed and helping the leaders to start new companies and packs. In 1946, a Guide shop was opened at the Guide Headquarters and a hospital Ranger company was formed in 1947 for the purpose of training nurses in methods of public services and self-reliance. The Island Commissioner, realizing the importance to Guiding of having adequate trainers and leaders, sent senior Guides to a Training Camp in New York in 1947. The experience which they gained there contributed to the development of Guiding in the Bahamas.

TRAINING

Weekly trainings for Guiders are held throughout the summer and are very well attended. A residential Training for Leaders was held for the first time at the Association's new campsite in October 1975.

PARTICIPATION IN INTERNATIONAL EVENTS

In 1952, for the first time in the history of Guiding in the Bahamas, two Guides represented the islands at an International Camp in England; the Bahamas have since participated in many international events and welcomed visitors to the islands.

In October 1968, the National Organization held a 'Guide Week' in order to make the activities of the Association better known and to promote Guiding.

The Bahamas applied for membership of the Caribbean Link and their application was accepted in 1972. In 1975 the Bahamas Girl Guides Association was recognized as an Associate Member of WAGGGS at the 22nd World Conference, held in the U.K. The Association is now a member of the Western Hemisphere Region of WAGGGS.

SERVICE

Service is a very important part of the programme in the Bahamas, in both the Guide and Ranger age-groups. Guides and Rangers have helped in projects in hospitals, centres for the Deaf and work closely with both the Red Cross and the Salvation Army. They have collected for the needy and visited the elderly and disabled in their homes. Even the Brownies help with parties for underprivileged children.

Great interest is shown in the Duke of Edinburgh Award Scheme, and a number of Rangers are working towards their silver and gold medals. As this scheme includes adventure, expeditions, service and other activities encouraging initiative and endurance, it is satisfactorily incorporated into the Guide programme.

The members of this Association come from all social, economic and cultural groups. The majority of units are attached to schools, and the leaders are mainly teachers. Efforts are being made to encourage more teachers to join the Movement.

Bangladesh

Bangladesh Girl Guides Association

Promise

On my honour, I promise that I will do my best:

1 To do my duty to God, and my country.
2 To help other people at all times.
3 To obey the Guide Laws.

GUIDE

Law

1 A Guide's honour is to be trusted.
2 A Guide is loyal.
3 A Guide's duty is to be useful and to help others.
4 A Guide is a friend to all, and a sister to every other Guide, no matter to what creed, country or class the other belongs.

5 A Guide is courteous.
6 A Guide is a friend to animals.
7 A Guide obeys orders.
8 A Guide smiles and sings under all difficulties.
9 A Guide is thrifty.
10 A Guide is pure in thought, word and deed.

YELLOWBIRD

Yellowbird Promise

I promise to do my best:
1 To do my duty to God and my country.
2 To help other people every day.
Especially those at home.

Yellowbird Law

1 The Yellowbird gives in to the older folk.
2 The Yellowbird does not give in to herself.

Girl Guides have been active in the area which is now Bangladesh since 1928, when this area along with that of present-day India and Pakistan became a Founder Member of the World Association under the name of India. In 1973 Bangladesh was welcomed as a separate Member of the World Association. In Bangladesh the Girl Guide Association has become synonymous with youth welfare work and is the largest national organization giving leadership training to young girls.

EDUCATION AND TRAINING

The Association runs two centres for children, teaching primary education, cleanliness, drill, gardening, handicrafts; and two centres for adults, holding courses in adult education, handicrafts, knitting, sewing and hygiene. Training courses are given in machine knitting. In preparation for their proficiency badges, the girls attend courses in cooking, nutrition, food preservation, home skills and child care.

WORK WITH THE UNDERPRIVILEGED

Rangers have worked in isolated villages, in a remand home for socially maladjusted women, in a women's prison and in homes for orphans. A Residential Camp was held for 20 orphan girls.

ENVIRONMENT AND CONSERVATION

The Association observes Tree-Plantation Fortnight every year, planting various bushes, trees and shrubs, and looking after them during the following years. The Guides have helped the Government Forestry Department plant a picnic area and part of a national park in the suburbs of Dacca.

SERVICE

Rangers receive training in First Aid and organize Relief Centres for victims of natural calamities. In addition, they run Adult Education Centres in rural areas; they are also responsible for vaccination campaigns and run day-care centres in cities.

Guiders in Bangladesh are involved in W.H.O. activities and Guides and Yellowbirds work among destitute children in conjunction with the Red Cross.

CAMPING AND OUTDOOR ACTIVITIES

Many Regional Camps are held throughout the country every year where campcraft and other handicrafts are taught. Social education, map-reading and nature observation courses are among their other wide-ranging activities.

Barbados

The Girl Guides Association of Barbados

GUIDE

Promise

I promise that I will do my best:
To do my duty to God;
To serve the Queen and my Country
and help other people; and
To keep the Guide Law.

Law

1 A Guide is loyal and can be trusted.
2 A Guide is helpful.
3 A Guide is polite and considerate.
4 A Guide is friendly and a sister to all Guides.
5 A Guide is kind to animals and respects all living things.
6 A Guide is obedient.
7 A Guide has courage and is cheerful in all difficulties.
8 A Guide makes good use of her time.
9 A Guide takes care of her own possessions and those of other people.
10 A Guide is self-controlled in all she thinks, says and does.

Motto

Be Prepared

BROWNIE

Brownie Guide Promise

I promise I will do my best:
To do my duty to God;
To serve the Queen and my Country
and help other people;
To keep the Brownie Guide Law.

Brownie Guide Law

A Brownie Guide thinks of others
before herself and does a good turn
every day.

Brownie Guide Motto

Lend a Hand

Age Groups

Ranger	16–21
Guide	10½–16
Brownie Guide	7–10½ or 11

IMPORTANT DATES

1918 – beginning of Girl Guiding in Barbados
1919 – first rally
1930 – visit by Lord and Lady Baden-Powell
1947 – membership exceeds 1,000 girls
1959 – West Indies Guide Conference
1964 – opening of Pax Hill, the new headquarters
1968 – the Association celebrates its Golden Jubilee
1969 – introduction of a new Constitution and adoption of a new eight-point programme
– 20th World Conference of WAGGGS accepts Barbados as an Associate Member (Finland, 1969)
1972 – Barbados receives Full Membership of WAGGGS at 21st World Conference (Canada, 1972)

TRAINING AND SEMINARS

Emphasis is placed on training for Patrol Leaders, Guiders and potential Leaders. Active interest in regional training is maintained by representation on the Caribbean Link Training Committee.

Senior Guides, Rangers and young Leaders regularly attend seminars at the World Centres. In 1974 two delegates from Barbados took part in a conference on 'Working with the Handicapped' held at the University of Pittsburg, U.S.A.

COMMUNITY SERVICE

Programmes put a stress on community service, which is being carried out in many ways. Some of the projects include: looking after the grounds and gardens of a Child Care Centre, entertaining war veterans at Christmas time, visits to the Homes for the Elderly, Mental Institutions and Hospitals and work at day-nurseries throughout the island.

Following the discussions at the Western Hemisphere Conference in Peru in 1974 Guides organized a summer camp for underprivileged children aged 5–16, as part of their project 'Towards a Better Barbados' and similar camps are now held annually in various parts of the island. Other service projects include raising money for the 'Meals on Wheels' programme and setting up an Emergency Corps to help victims of natural disasters. In the case of an emergency, Pax Hill headquarters building will be used as a First Aid Post and a centre for distribution of clothing.

In 1970 two units for mentally retarded children were registered, but the Association encourages companies to include mentally handicapped Guides in their numbers and many of them have taken up this challenge.

COMBINED EVENTS

In February 1970 the first combined National Girl Guide and Boy Scout Service to celebrate Thinking Day took place, and this has been an annual event ever since. There is also co-operation between Rangers and Venture Scouts, and there is a Ranger/Venture Scout Council. Guides take part in most National Youth events and Independence Day celebrations.

PRESENT-DAY GUIDING IN BARBADOS

The year 1974 saw several changes in the structural set-up of Guiding in Barbados. The Queen's Guide Certificate with the Barbados Coat of Arms and the same syllabus as that used by the United Kingdom was approved, and two new badges were instituted – the Civics and the Barbados. Also a Barbados Friendship Pin was introduced, and a new Promise Pin has now been adopted. Girl Guides take part in the Duke of Edinburgh Award Scheme.

Provision has been made in the Council for Honorary Life Members.

In line with a WAGGGS' World Committee statement, the Guides in Barbados gave active support to International Women's Year, 1975, holding inter-district challenge competitions in three categories: arts, crafts and home skills.

Belgium

Comité National de Liaison du Guidisme en Belgique

Fédération des Eclaireurs et Eclaireuses
Federatie voor Open Scoutisme
Guides Catholiques de Belgique
Vlaams Verbond van der Katholieke Meisjesgidsen

FEDERATION DES ECLAIREURS ET ECLAIREUSES

Promesse	**Promise**
Je promets sur mon honneur de m'efforcer:	I promise on my honour to endeavour:
de servir Dieu, mon pays et l'amitié entre les hommes,	to serve God, my country and friendship between people,
d'aider mon prochain en toute occasion,	to help other people at all times,
de vivre la loi de l'éclaireuse.	to live according to the Girl Scout Law.
ou	*or*
Je promets sur mon honneur de m'efforcer:	I promise on my honour to endeavour:
de servir un idéal élevé,	to serve a high ideal,

GUIDE

mon pays et l'amitié entre les hommes,	my country and friendship between people,
d'aider mon prochain en toute occasion,	to help other people at all times,
de vivre la loi de l'éclaireuse.	to live according to the Girl Scout Law.

Loi	**Law**
L'éclaireuse:	A Girl Scout:
1 dit la vérité et tient parole.	is loyal, and speaks the truth.
2 respecte les autres dans leurs convictions.	respects the opinions of others.
3 se rend utile.	makes herself useful.
4 travaille en équipe, offre son amitié.	is a good team member and is friendly to all.
5 fait preuve de courtoisie.	is courteous.
6 aime et protège la nature.	likes and protects nature.
7 sait obéir.	knows how to obey.
8 aime l'effort et ne fait rien à moitié.	likes to be active and does nothing by halves.
9 respecte le travail et le bien de tous.	is thoughtful of other people's work and property.
10 reste maître de ses paroles, de ses actes, de ses pensées.	controls her words, acts and thoughts.

Motto

Etre prête	Be Prepared

CUB

Cub Promise

Je promets, avec l'aide de Dieu, de faire de mon mieux pour observer la loi des louveteaux et faire un bon tour chaque jour.	I promise, with the help of God, to do my best to keep the Cub Law and to do a good turn every day.
ou	*or*
Je promets de faire de mon mieux pour observer la loi des louveteaux et faire un bon tour chaque jour.	I promise to do my best to keep the Cub Law and to do a good turn every day.

Cub Law

Un louveteau écoute les vieux loups.	A Cub listens to the old wolves.
Un louveteau ne s'écoute jamais.	A Cub does not think of herself.

Cub Motto

De notre mieux	To do our best

Age Groups

Aînée	Ranger	16–21
Eclaireuse	Guide	11–16
Louveteau	Cub	7–11

FEDERATIE VOOR OPEN SCOUTISME

GUIDE

Belofte	**Promise**
Ik beloof, op mijn eer, te trachten:	I promise on my honour, to try:
– trouw te zijn aan God, koning, land en troep;	– to be true to God, King, country and company/troop;
– de guides wet na te leven;	– to live up to the Guide Law;
– elke dag een goede daad te stellen.	– to do a good deed every day.
of	*or*
Ik beloof, op mijn eer, te trachten:	I promise on my honour, to try:
– trouw te zijn aan een hoger ideaal, koning, land en troep;	– to be true to a higher ideal, King, country and company/troop;
– de guides wet na te leven;	– to live up to the Guide Law;
– elke dag een goede daad te stellen.	– to do a good deed every day.

Wet	**Law**
1 Een Guide is oprecht en heeft maar één woord.	A Guide is loyal, and speaks the truth.
2 Een Guide eerbiedigt de overtuiging van de anderen.	A Guide respects the convictions of others.
3 Een Guide maakt zich nuttig.	A Guide is useful.
4 Een Guide is een vriend van allen.	A Guide is a friend to all.
5 Een Guide is hoffelijk.	A Guide is courteous.
6 Een Guide kan gehoorzamen.	A Guide knows how to obey.
7 Een Guide staat open voor de natuur.	A Guide appreciates nature.
8 Een Guide laat zich niet ontmoedigen.	A Guide does not become discouraged.
9 Een Guide is ijverig.	A Guide Is a good worker.
10 Een Guide heeft eerbied voor zichzelf en voor de anderen.	A Guide respects herself and others.

Motto

Steed bereid	Be Prepared

Cub Promise

CUB

Ik beloof mijn best te doen, trouw te zijn aan God, land en welpenwet, iedere dag iemand te helpen.	I promise to do my best, to be loyal to God, Country and to the Cub Law, to help somebody every day.
of	*or*
Ik beloof mijn best te doen, trouw te zijn aan een hoger ideaal, land en welpenwet, iedere dag iemand te helpen.	I promise to do my best, to serve a high ideal, Country and Cub Law, to help somebody every day.

Cub Law

Een welp luistert naar de Oude Wolven.	A Cub listens to the old wolves.
Een welp luistert nooit naar zichzelf.	A Cub does not think of (listen to) herself.

Cub Motto

Wij doen ons best	We do our best

Age Groups

Aînée	Ranger	16–21
Guide	Guide	11–16
Welp	Cub	7–11

GUIDES CATHOLIQUES DE BELGIQUE

GUIDE

Promesse	**Promise**
Sûre de votre amitié,	Sure of your friendship,
Je promets de vivre selon la loi des guides:	I promise to live according to the Guides' Law:
Pour aimer davantage les autres,	In order to love others more,
Etre active dans toutes les communautés,	To be active in all communities,
Et répondre ainsi à l'appel de Dieu.	And thus to answer the call of God.

Loi	**Law**
1 La guide est vraie, elle mérite confiance.	A Guide is truthful, she can be trusted.
2 La guide est fidèle, elle tient ses engagements.	A Guide is loyal, she keeps her promises.
3 La guide est faite pour servir.	A Guide's purpose is to serve.
4 La guide est la sœur de tous et l'amie de toute guide.	A Guide is a sister to all and a friend to every other Guide.
5 La guide est courtoise.	A Guide is courteous.
6 La guide aime la nature et respecte la vie.	A Guide loves nature and respects life.
7 La guide sait obéir, elle va jusqu'au bout.	A Guide knows how to obey, she carries things through to the end.
8 La guide partage sa joie de vivre.	A Guide shares her joy of living.
9 La guide respecte le bien commun et participe à l'effort de tous.	A Guide respects the common good and participates in the efforts of all.
10 La guide est simple, pure et joyeuse.	A Guide is straightforward, pure and joyful.

Motto

Toujours prête	Always prepared

BROWNIE

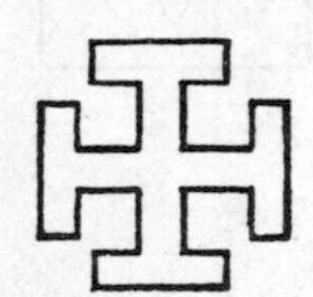

Brownie Promise

Avec l'aide du Seigneur Jésus, je promets de faire de mon mieux pour vivre selon la loi des lutins.	With the help of the Lord Jesus, I promise to do my best to live according to the Brownie Law.

Brownie Law

Le lutin pense d'abord aux autres.	The Brownie thinks first of others.
Le lutin apprend à faire plaisir.	The Brownie learns to give pleasure.
Le lutin est joyeux.	The Brownie is joyful.
Le lutin dit vrai.	The Brownie tells the truth.

Brownie Motto

De notre mieux	Of our best

Age Groups

Eclaireuse	Ranger	17+
Guide 'Horizon'	Guide	15–17
Guide 'Aventure'	Guide	11–14
Lutin	Brownie	7–11

VLAAMS VERBOND VAN DE KATHOLIEKE MEISJESGIDSEN

GUIDE

Beloftetekst	Promise
In oprechtheid en trouw begeleid door de Heer beloof ik mijn best te doen om meer gids te worden. Samen met mijn zus uit de gidsenkring 'n weg te gaan van dienst en groeiende inzet in een wereld, die door ons better kan worden.	Guided by the Lord I promise with sincerity and in truth to do my best to become a better Guide. Together with my sister Guides to tread the path of helpfulness and to give more and more to a world which can become better because of us.

Gidsenwet	Law
In het spoor van de Heer villen wij in vriendschap samen 'n weg zoeken in de grote stad der mensen.	Following in the path of the Lord we want, together in friendship, to find our way in the world.
Vol aandacht en bewondering willen wij stil worden bij de ontdekking der natuur en de ontmoeting van ieder mens.	We want to be thoughtful, attentive and full of admiration in the discovery of nature and in the meeting of people.
Zo willen wij ons bekwamen en inzetten om trouw, eerlijk, blij en handig mee te bouwen aan een nieuwe wereld waar het steeds beter wordt om samen te zijn.	Thus, we want to train ourselves to give truth, honesty, happiness and useful help in the building of a new world which will become a better place to live in together.

Motto

Wees Bereid	Be Prepared

BROWNIE

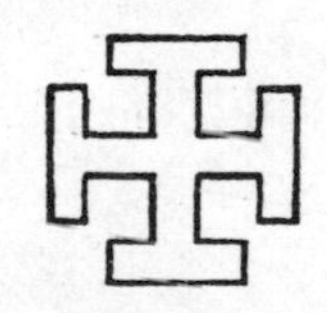

Brownie Promise

Ik wil graag bij de kabouters van het bloemenhuisje wonen en mijn best doen om een echte kabouter te zijn.	I would like to live with the Brownies of the flowerhouse and will do my best to be a good Brownie.

Brownie Law

Een kabouter kan luisteren.	A Brownie knows how to listen (obey).
Een kabouter is blij.	A Brownie is cheerful.
Een kabouter speelt mee.	A Brownie joins in the games.
Een kabouter doet graag pleziertjes.	A Brownie enjoys giving pleasure.

Brownie Motto

Op ons best	Do our best

Age Groups

Voortrekster	Ranger	16–17+
Gids	Guide	14–17
Jonggids	Junior Guide	11–14
Kabouter	Brownie	7–11

Belgian Guiding started in Brussels in 1915, and after the Armistice it continued to develop. In 1919 Belgium became a member of the International Council, and in 1928 the national organization joined the World Association as one of its Founder Members.

The Comité National de Liaison du Guidisme en Belgique links together:

1 Fédération des Eclaireurs et Eclaireuses (FEE)*
2 Federatie voor Open Scoutisme (FOS)*
3 Fédération des Guides Catholiques de Belgique (GCB)
4 Vlaams Verbond van der Katholieke Meisjesgidsen (VVKM)
(*In respect of their Girl Scout members)

The FEE and the FOS are undenominational while the GCB and VVKM are Catholic Associations. All four Associations aim to develop the character of the girls, giving them an all-round training with emphasis on service to the community.

When a girl joins a Guide company she does not make the Guide Promise for at least six months, during which time she is expected to show, by some personal effort, that she really understands the importance and meaning of the Promise and Law.

Outdoor life and camping are important aspects of Belgian Guiding and service camps take place regularly. International relations are encouraged by exchange visits with Guides of other countries. General and International Commissioners meet frequently to prepare for international meetings, regional and world conferences, participation of Girl Guides/Girl Scouts in international camps.

60TH ANNIVERSARY OF GUIDING IN BELGIUM

The 60th Anniversary of Guiding in Belgium was commemorated by an international camp in July 1975 in which 1,200 people from twenty-five countries took part. The Comité National de Liaison was responsible for the camp and preparations were made by the various Guide Federations.

FEDERATION DES ECLAIREURS ET ECLAIREUSES

The FEE is a co-educational Association whose aim is to encourage tolerance among young people and their personal involvement in matters of world concern.

GOLDEN JUBILEE

In 1969 the FEE (formerly with the FOS known as Girl Guides de Belgique) celebrated its Golden Jubilee in Brussels where the World Chief Guide attended the celebrations.

LEADERSHIP

Much work has gone into achieving a greater decentralization and special efforts have been made to meet the wishes of the adult leadership who want to give greater responsibility to young Leaders.

SERVICE

The FEE is active in various fields. They take part in 'Extra-job' campaigns to benefit the federation, are involved with conservation and have a special concern for the handicapped Guides in Extension Units, the 'Malgré Tout'.

FEDERATIE VOOR OPEN SCOUTISME

The FOS work along the same lines as the FEE while taking into account the needs of the Dutch-speaking part of the country.

GUIDES CATHOLIQUES DE BELGIQUE

The main objective of the GCB over the last few years has been a wish to find a new meaning for Guiding today. Under the heading 'Movement on the Move', as much information as possible was collected, and from this a dossier was compiled based on concrete facts classified in twelve sections. Following this the Regions and Districts set to work to investigate these various fields. Then, in April 1975, approximately 750 Guiders gathered together at a 'Festival' to consider the results of this research and to ascertain what it had achieved. This, however, is only the beginning of Guider participation in the planning of programmes and the running of the Movement. It is hoped to continue and increase this participation in the future.

SERVICE

In the field of service and development, the Association is determined to achieve its objectives by concrete action rather than working on theory. The following are examples of this. In 1973, following a year of preparation, thirteen Belgian leaders went to Mexico where, with financial assistance from UNESCO, they carried out a programme of community development work in a village near Puebla together with young Mexican girls. In 1975 eleven Mexican girls went to Belgium to learn about European social and political problems and, with the Belgian leaders they had met two years before, ran a camp for the children of migrant workers.

This ties in with the Association's concern about the role Guiding should play with regard to the children of foreign workers and people from other marginal groups. In an attempt to go some way towards finding an answer to this problem, holiday sessions for the children of migrant workers and those from the Third World have been held at the Domaine de Mozet GCB's centre for training and outdoor activities.

VLAAMS VERBOND VAN DE KATHOLIEKE MEISJESGIDSEN

As we go to press we notice that the VVKM has joined with the Scouts in the establishment of the Vlaams Verbond van Katholieke Meisjesgidsen en Scouts. A commission of the VVKM undertook a study some years ago on 'Attitude and Style – the Movement's way of being' in an overall effort to keep the Association in line with modern youth trends. The VVKM is divided into four branches as follows: The Pre-Clan Branch (16 years and over) the Guide Branch (14–16 years) the Young Guide Branch (11–14 years) and the Brownie Branch.

The Guide, Young Guide and Brownie branches publish a handbook for leaders, describing their methods and its application, and giving practical examples adapted to the different age groups.

Bénin

Guides du Bénin

GUIDE

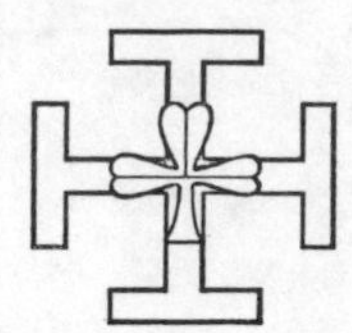

Promesse	**Promise**
Sur mon honneur je m'engage	On my honour, I promise
à servir Dieu et mon pays en toute circonstance	to do my duty to God and my country in all circumstances
à aider mon prochain	to help others
et à observer la loi des guides.	and to obey the Guide Law.
ou	or
Sur mon honneur je m'engage	On my honour, I promise
à servir mon pays en toute circonstance	to do my duty to my country in all circumstances
à aider mon prochain	to help others
et à observer la loi des guides.	and to obey the Guide Law.

Loi	**Law**
1 La guide: n'a qu'une parole	A Guide: is true to her word
2 est loyale	is loyal
3 est utile	is useful
4 est l'amie de tous	is a friend to all
5 est courtoise et sait obéir	is courteous and knows how to obey
6 découvre la nature et la protège	discovers Nature and protects it
7 est toujours de bonne humeur	is always in a good humour
8 est économe et travailleuse	is thrifty and a good worker
9 est propre dans ses pensées, ses paroles et ses actes	is pure in thought, word and deed
10 est civiquement consciente et sert les intérêts de son peuple.	has a civic awareness and serves the interest of her people.

Motto

Toujours prête	Always ready

BROWNIE

Brownie Promise

Je promets de faire de mon mieux: pour être fidèle à Dieu, à la Patrie, à mes parents, à la loi de la ronde, et pour faire chaque jour un plaisir à quelqu'un.	I promise to do my best: to be faithful to God, to my Country, to my parents and to the Law of the Pack, and to do a good turn to somebody every day.

Brownie Law

Une jeannette est toujours propre.	A Brownie is always neat.
Une jeannette est toujours active.	A Brownie is always active.
Une jeannette est toujours gaie.	A Brownie is always cheerful.
Une jeannette dit toujours vrai.	A Brownie always tells the truth.
Une jeannette pense d'abord aux autres.	A Brownie thinks first of others.

Brownie Motto

De notre mieux	Of our best

Age Groups

Guide aînée	Ranger	18 and over
Guide	Guide	12–17
Jeannette	Brownie	8–11

Girl Guiding was first started in a girls' secondary school in Porto Novo, Bénin (then Dahomey) in 1954. Two years later a Guide camp was held and in October 1956 the 1st Cotonou Girl Guide company was formed. During the following year several other companies were started up and both Brownie packs and Ranger companies had made their appearance by 1957. By 1958 Guides had begun to run their own camps. A few years later Guide companies started to 'adopt' villages where they carried out service projects with the villagers.

By the end of 1960 the Association was established on a sound basis and a constitution was drawn up. Les Guides du Bénin (then called Dahomey) was recognized as an Associate Member of WAGGGS at the 18th World Conference (Denmark, 1963). In 1974 the Girl Guides and Boy Scouts joined together to form Scoutisme du Bénin.

DEVELOPMENT OF GUIDING AND SERVICE

Guiding in Bénin has developed both in the main urban complexes and in the rural areas. Experienced leaders are working in the villages, and Rangers in turn are putting their training to practical use helping the women of these areas with classes in literacy, child care, sewing and hygiene. UNESCO has given valuable assistance towards this development.

Guides have built a well in one village, giving the villagers a pure water-supply for the first time.

Bolivia

Asociación Nacional de Guías-Scouts de Bolivia

GUIDE

Promesa	**Promise**
Yo prometo, por mi honor, hacer cuanto de mi dependa, para:	I promise, on my honour, to do my best:
Cumplir con mi deber hacia Dios y mi Patria;	To do my duty to God and my Country;
Ser útil al prójimo en todo momento y obedecer la Ley Guía-Scout	To help others at all times, and to obey the Guide-Scout Law.

Ley	**Law**
1 La Guía-Scout es persona en cuyo honor se puede confiar.	A Guide-Scout's honour is to be trusted.

2 La Guía-Scout es leal.	A Guide-Scout is loyal.
3 El deber de la Guía-Scout es ser útil y ayudar a otros.	A Guide-Scout's duty is to be useful and help others.
4 La Guía-Scout es amiga de todos y hermana de toda Guía-Scout.	A Guide-Scout is a friend to all and a sister to every other Guide/Girl Scout.
5 La Guía-Scout es cortés.	A Guide-Scout is courteous.
6 La Guía-Scout es buena con los animales.	A Guide-Scout is kind to animals.
7 La Guía-Scout obedece órdenes.	A Guide-Scout obeys orders.
8 La Guía-Scout sonrie y canta en todas las dificultades.	A Guide-Scout smiles and sings under all difficulties.
9 La Guía-Scout es económica.	A Guide-Scout is thrifty.
10 La Guía-Scout es pura de pensamiento, palabra y obra.	A Guide-Scout is pure in thought, word and deed.

Motto

Siempre Lista	Be Prepared

BROWNIE

Brownie Promise

Yo prometo hacer la mejor por amor a Dios y a mi Patria, ayudar a todos, y en especial a los de mi casa.	I promise to do my best to love God and my Country, to help other people, especially those at home.

Brownie Motto

Ayudar a todos	Help Others

Age Groups

Guía Mayor	Ranger	15–18
Guía	Guide	11–14
Alita	Brownie	7–10

Girl Guiding started in Bolivia in 1915 and gradually Girl Guide units began to appear in areas throughout the country. The first contact with the World Association of Girl Guides and Girl Scouts was made in 1954 when a Western Hemisphere Travelling Commissioner visited Bolivia. In 1958 the Asociación de Muchachas Guías de Bolivia was established and its Constitution set up. The Asociación Nacional de Guías-Scouts de Bolivia became an Associate Member of the World Association at the 19th World Conference (Japan, 1966).

MEMBERSHIP AND AIMS OF THE ASSOCIATION

Today the Association has about 100 groups and local councils all over the country. Its members constitute the largest and most organized girls' and women's organization in the country. The theme 'Let us know ourselves better in order to create a better Bolivia' is used to orientate the Movement's educational task, the main purpose of which is to provide the young girls with the means to participate more fully in the development of their country.

Through reading, games, service, handicrafts, trips abroad, etc., the Association teaches girls to voluntarily accept discipline and to aim for high ideals. They are also determined that Girl Guiding should be 'lived' rather than just practised, convinced of the importance of 'others' in all of our lives.

TRAINING

National Training Camps are held regularly in Bolivia, while members of the Association attend various international trainings and other gatherings throughout the Western Hemisphere and Europe.

SERVICE

The Association is also involved in working with the literacy programmes set up by the Ministry of Education, and collaborates with the Ministry of Health in a national vaccination campaign against smallpox.

CO-OPERATION WITH OTHER ORGANIZATIONS

The Asociación Nacional de Guías-Scouts de Bolivia is the sales representative for UNICEF cards and calendars and organizes their promotion and sale within the country. This scheme works both ways, since a percentage of sales benefits the Girl Guide Association.

Botswana

Botswana Girl Guides Association

Tsholofetso

Ke solofetsa gore ke tlaa dira bojotlhe jwa me:
Go direla Modimo tshwaneloya me,
Go direla lefatshe la gaetsho le go thusa batho ba bangwe, le
Go tshegetsa malao wa Bakaedi.

Promise

I promise that I will do my best:

To do my duty to God,
To serve my country and to help other people, and
To keep the Guide Law.

GUIDE

Melao ya Bakaedi

1 Mokaedi o boineelo, gape o ka ikanngwa.
2 Mokaedi o na le thuso.
3 Mokaedi o maitseo gape o na le kakanyetso.
4 Mokaedi o na le botsalano, ebile ke ngwana wa mma-Bakaedi ba bangwe.
5 Mokaedi o pelotlhomogi mo diphologolong gape o tlotla dilo tsotlhe tse di tshelang.
6 Mokaedi o na le kutlo.
7 Mokaedi o pelokgale ebile o nna pelotshweu mo gare ga mathata otlhe.
8 Mokaedi o sola dinako tsa gagwe tsotlhe molemo.

Guide Law

A Guide is loyal and can be trusted.
A Guide is helpful.
A Guide is polite and considerate.
A Guide is friendly and a sister to every other Guide.
A Guide is kind to animals and respects all living things.
A Guide is obedient.
A Guide has courage and is cheerful in all difficulties.
A Guide makes good use of her time.

9 Mokaedi o tlhokomela ditsagagwe le tsa batho be bangwe.	A Guide takes care of her own possessions and those of other people.
10 Mokaedi o ikefa mo go tsotlhe tse o di akanyang tse o di buang, le tse o di dirang.	A Guide is self-controlled in all she thinks, says and does.

Motto

Nna o ipaakantse	Be Prepared

SUNBEAM

Sunbeam Promise

Ke solofetsa gore ke tlaa dira bojotlhe jwa me:	I promise that I will do my best:
Go direla Modimo tshwanelo y me,	To do my duty to God,
Go direla lefatshe la gaetsho le go thusa batho ba bangwe le	To serve my country and to help other people and
Go tshegetsa molao wa Marang a Letsatsi.	To keep the Sunbeam Law.

Sunbeam Law

Lerang la Letsatsi le boammaaruri, le boikokobetso, le tletse boitumelo.	A Sunbeam is truthful, obedient and cheerful.
Lerang la Letsatsi le akanyetsa ba bangwe pele le ikgopola.	A sunbeam thinks of others before herself.

Sunbeam Motto

Kwa Godimo	Up and Upward

Age Groups

Ranger	Ranger	15–21
Mokaedi	Guide	11–16
Lerang la Letsatsi	Sunbeam	7–11

Girl Guiding began in Botswana (then called Bechuanaland) in 1924, with just one Guide patrol and six Brownies. After the establishment of a Girl Guide Company for African girls in 1928, numbers steadily increased and interest in the Movement spread throughout the country. (The girls were originally called 'Wayfarers', then 'Wayfarer Guides'; it was not until 1945 that they became known as Girl Guides.)

In 1966 the country became independent and began working towards Associate Membership of the World Association. Botswana was recognized as an Associate Member of WAGGGS at the 20th World Conference (Finland, 1969). In 1976 the Association hostessed a highly successful sub-regional gathering held in Botswana.

CAMPS AND TRAININGS

The first camp to be held in the country took place in 1932 and Guides have since attended many camps both in Botswana and in other African countries.

The first training for Guiders was held in 1951, and in 1956 a Trainer from Belgium visited the country bringing many new and useful ideas. Two agricultural trainings were held in 1971 with great success, as shown by the number of resultant service and food-growing projects undertaken by the

Guides. The present training programme has been adapted to suit the needs of the country and is constantly under review.

SERVICE

Guides give service to needy children, the aged and the sick. They have cleaned public buildings, raised money for village development projects and for the building of a headquarters, given assistance with the organization of and catering for conferences and state functions, and helped build clinics and classrooms.

The Botswana Girl Guides Association is doing much to preserve traditional arts and crafts and has inspired an interest in these in the country as a whole. It organizes projects for school-leavers where home-making skills, rug-making methods, etc., are taught by older women.

ENVIRONMENT

'Clean Your Village' and 'Keep Botswana Clean' campaigns have been in existence since 1972. Guides in various villages and towns have undertaken an anti-litter campaign, putting up posters, supplying bins and collecting litter. The campaign was followed by tree-planting and courses in agricultural training.

CO-OPERATION WITH OTHER ORGANIZATIONS

The Botswana Girl Guides Association co-operates with the Red Cross, YWCA, Botswana Christian Council and Botswana Council of Women.

PUBLIC RELATIONS AND PUBLICATIONS

Public Relations activities have included broadcasts and articles in the press.

A *Guiders' Training Newsletter* is published quarterly and the *Guide Builders' Handbook* was produced.

Brazil

Federação das Bandeirantes do Brasil

GUIDE AND BROWNIE

(*The text of the Promise and Law is not available at the time of going to press.*)

Guiding was started in Rio de Janeiro in 1919 since which time it has spread throughout Brazil. The Federação das Bandirantes do Brasil was recognized as a Full Member of the World Association in 1930 and was in fact the first association in South America to become a member of WAGGGS.

THE AIMS OF THE GUIDE MOVEMENT

The Federação das Bandirantes do Brasil adheres to the fundamental principles of the World Association of Girl Guides and Girl Scouts, and its members promise to uphold the ideals contained in the original Promise formulated by Lord Baden-Powell.

Guiding is an invitation to adventure, a shared adventure, an adventure which has as its main challenge the understanding of life in the world, and the challenge of building a better future.

DIRECTION

The highest directing body is the National Assembly, which has power to legislate and defines the general policy of the Movement in Brazil by evaluating yearly the projects which have been carried out. It is also a deliberating and electing body, comprising the National Collegiate and Co-ordinators and Presidents of the Regions. Meetings are held once a year.

The National Collegiate acts in the interval of the National Assemblies. It also has executive functions through its members.
It comprises:

- A National Board of Directors
- The National Co-ordinator
- The Substitute National Co-ordinator
- The Area Co-ordinators.

STRUCTURE

The Federação das Bandeirantes do Brasil, to accomplish its educational goals, divided Brazil into four geographical areas: North, North-East, Centre-East and South. These areas are under the supervision of a Co-ordinator who belongs to the National Directing Body, the Collegiate.

This geographical division was made for purposes of easier communication and more direct work at group level, and also to allow different regional characteristics of the various States (Bandeirante's Regions).

The Bandeirante Movement exists in 21 States, 1 Federal District (Brasilia) and 1 Territory of Brazil, with groups in 108 different cities. Most of the groups are located in the capital State cities.

The Movement is divided into four branches, which correspond to stages of development of children and young people, and offer opportunities for activities appropriate to these age groups.

They are:

– Cirandas	– aged from 6 to 9 years old.
– B1 Groups	– aged from 9 to 12 years old.
– B2 Groups	– aged from 12 to 15 years old.
– Ranger Groups	– aged from 15 to 18 years old.

FORM OF ACTION

The Federação das Bandeirantes do Brasil acts through its Areas, Regions, Districts and Groups, which develop a yearly Plan of Action including policies, objectives and programmes to be carried out at the different levels: National, Regional, District and Group.

The Assemblies, at each level, study and approve their own Plan of Action.

The Bandeirante Movement plans and develops its activities through different Projects. These Projects offer the girls the opportunities to participate in a series of camps, games, artistic and cultural activities and community action, which are fundamental for the development of the girl.

Projects are divided into Programmes that define the areas of action of the Bandeirante Movement.

PROGRAMMES

1 PLANNING AND SUPERVISION.

II STUDIES AND SURVEYS.
III TRAINING.
IV COMMUNICATION.
V INTERNAL ACTIVITIES.
VI PARTICIPATION IN COMMUNITIES.
VII INTEGRATION IN INTERNATIONAL GUIDING.
VIII ADMINISTRATIVE AND FINANCIAL RATIONALIZATION.

Burundi

Association des Guides du Burundi

GUIDE

Promesse

Sur mon honneur (et avec la grâce de Dieu)*
je m'engage à remplir de mon mieux mes devoirs envers (Dieu, l'Eglise et)* la Patrie;
à aider mon prochain en toutes circonstances,
et à observer la loi guide.

Promise

On my honour (and with God's grace)*
I promise to fulfil to the best of my power
my duties towards (God, the Church and)* my country;
to help other people at all times,
and to keep the Guide Law.

Loi

1 La Guide est vraie, elle mérite confiance.
2 La Guide est fidèle, elle tient ses engagements.
3 La Guide se rend utile et aide les autres.
4 La Guide est l'amie de tous et la sœur de toute autre Guide.
5 La Guide est courtoise.
6 La Guide aime et respecte la nature (œuvre de Dieu)*.
7 La Guide obéit joyeusement et ne fait rien à moitié.
8 La Guide est toujours de bonne humeur et courageuse dans les difficultés.
9 La Guide est économe et respecte le bien d'autrui.
10 La Guide est simple et pure.

* La mention entre parenthèses est facultative; elle peut être modifiée si nécessaire suivant les croyances.

Law

1 A Guide is true, she merits confidence.
2 A Guide is faithful, she is true to her word.
3 A Guide makes herself useful and helps others.
4 A Guide is the friend to all and a sister to all other Guides.
5 A Guide is courteous.
6 A Guide loves and respects nature (work of God)*.
7 A Guide obeys joyfully and does nothing by halves.
8 A Guide is always cheerful and is courageous in the face of difficulties.
9 A Guide is thrifty and respects the possessions of others.
10 A Guide's life is simple and pure.

* Words in brackets are optional; they can be modified if necessary according to creed.

Motto

Toujours prête	Always ready

Brownie Promise

Je promets d'être fidèle (à Jésus)*, à mes parents, à la loi de la ronde, et de faire chaque jour un plaisir à quelqu'un.	I promise to be faithful (to Jesus)*, to my parents, to the Brownie Law, and to do a good turn to somebody every day.

Brownie Law

La Bergeronnette écoute les Grands Oiseaux.	The Brownie listens to the fully fledged birds.
La Bergeronnette ne s'écoute pas elle-même.	The Brownie does not listen to herself.

Brownie Motto

De notre mieux	Of our best
* La mention entre parenthèses est facultative; elle peut être modifiée si nécessaire suivant les croyances.	* Words in brackets are optional; they can be modified if necessary according to creed.

Age Groups

Eclaireuse (Guide aînée)	Ranger	16+
Guide (Eclaireuse)	Guide (senior)	13–16
Guide (Eclaireuse)	Guide (junior)	10–13
Bergeronnette (Jeannette)	Brownie	7–10

Girl Guiding was started in Burundi in 1954/5 by Belgian social workers as part of the Catholic Guides of Belgian Congo, Rwanda-Urundi. After independence in 1962 an Association was formed and has grown steadily despite many difficulties. The Association des Guides du Burundi became an Associate Member of WAGGGS at the 21st World Conference (Canada, 1972).

STRUCTURE AND PROGRAMME

The National Team is composed of nine members and is responsible for all aspects of the Association's work.

Groups work on the patrol system. The programme has been drawn up for four age-levels and concentrates on the following points; general knowledge, self-expression, traditional arts of Burundi, service, health, home economics, faith, techniques and spirit of the Guide Movement, nature and camping.

Leaders in Burundi receive regular training; they also attend training events in other parts of Africa.

SERVICE

Great importance is given to service as a means of contributing to the development of Burundi. Senior Guides replace hospital staff, allowing them to take a holiday; they also give help to old people and together with Leaders organize literacy courses for Guides and non-Guides.

PUBLICATIONS AND PUBLIC RELATIONS

The programme and basic Guide handbooks are printed in French and Kirindi.

The Association endeavours to make itself known both to government bodies and to women's organizations in the country, and the Catholic Guide groups co-operate with the Catholic Youth Movements in Burundi.

Cameroon

Cameroon Girl Guides Association
Association des Guides du Cameroun

CAMEROON GIRL GUIDES ASSOCIATION

GUIDE

Promise

I promise on my honour and with the grace of God,
to do my best:
– to do my duty to God and my country,
– to help other people at all times,
– to obey the Guide law.

Law

1 A Guide's honour is to be trusted.
2 A Guide is loyal.
3 A Guide's duty is to be useful and to help others.
4 A Guide is a friend to all and a sister to every other Guide.
5 A Guide is polite.
6 A Guide explores nature in which she sees the work of God.
7 A Guide obeys orders.
8 A Guide smiles and sings in spite of difficulties
9 A Guide is thrifty.
10 A Guide practises self-control in all she thinks, says or does.

Motto

Be Prepared

ASSOCIATION DES GUIDES DU CAMEROUN

Promesse	**Promise**
Je promets sur mon honneur et avec la grâce de Dieu de faire tout mon possible pour:	I promise on my honour and with the grace of God to do my best to:
servir Dieu et ma patrie,	serve God and my country,
aider les autres en tout temps,	help others at all times,
obéir à la Loi des Guides.	obey the Guide Law.

Loi	**Law**
1 La Guide est sincère.	A Guide is sincere.
2 Elle est loyale.	She is loyal.
3 Elle est serviable.	She is helpful.
4 Elle est l'amie de tous et la sœur de toutes les autres Guides.	She is a friend to all and a sister to all other Guides.
5 Elle est polie.	She is polite.
6 Elle respecte la nature et y voit l'œuvre de Dieu.	She respects nature in which she sees the work of God.
7 Elle est obéissante.	She is obedient.

8 Elle sourit et chante malgré les difficultés.	She smiles and sings in spite of difficulties.
9 Elle est active et économe.	She is dynamic and thrifty.
10 Elle sait se dominer dans ses pensées, ses paroles et ses actes.	She practises self-control in all she thinks, says or does.

Motto

Sois Prête

Guiding began in 1943 with the formation of a Girl Guide company in Victoria, West Cameroon. During the years that followed Guiding spread to other areas of the country, and by 1947 its membership included Brownies.

The Girl Guide Movement was officially established in East Cameroon with the formation of Les Guides du Cameroun in 1963, but in some areas of the region Guide activities had been taking place since 1961.

In 1970 a Cameroon National Guide Council was formed and met for the first time in Yaoundé in the same year. This was followed by the federation in 1971 of the West Cameroon Girl Guides Association and Les Guides du Cameroun, and the National Organization thereby established, the Cameroon Union of Girl Guides and Girl Scouts, became an Associate Member of the World Association of Girl Guides and Girl Scouts at the 21st World Conference (Canada, 1972).

With the creation of the United Republic of Cameroon, which replaced the Federal Republic, and the overall development of Guiding in the country, it was decided in 1974 to dissolve the Cameroon Union of Girl Guides and Girl Scouts and in its place to establish one single Guide organization, the Cameroon Girl Guides Association (Association des Guides du Cameroun). This restructuring of the Movement in Cameroon has proved very successful and Guiding is progressing well.

INTERNATIONAL CONTACTS

Cameroon Girl Guides have been represented at international camps and conferences including World Conferences and ICCG meetings. They have also attended trainings abroad and exchanged visits with neighbouring African Girl Guide Associations.

SERVICE

Guides run different community service projects each year. They have launched a scheme, 'Better Nutrition for Villages', assisted patients in hospitals and have helped the Boy Scouts to construct a leper village. Their environmental interests concentrate on cleanliness, and Guide companies and Brownie packs take special care of fountains and parks, and keep tidy public places, especially in urban districts.

Canada

Girl Guides of Canada – Guides du Canada

GUIDE

Promise

I promise, on my honour, to do my best:
To do my duty to God, the Queen and my country;
To help other people at all times;
To obey the Guide Law.

Law

1 A Guide's honour is to be trusted.
2 A Guide is loyal.
3 A Guide is useful and helps others.
4 A Guide is a friend to all, and a sister to every Guide.
5 A Guide is courteous.
6 A Guide is kind to animals and enjoys the beauty in nature.
7 A Guide is obedient.
8 A Guide smiles and sings even under difficulty.
9 A Guide is thrifty.
10 A Guide is pure in thought, word and deed.

Motto

Be Prepared

BROWNIE

Brownie Promise

I promise to do my best:
To do my duty to God, the Queen and my country;
To help other people every day, especially those at home.

Brownie Law

A Brownie is cheerful and obedient.
A Brownie thinks of other people before herself.

Brownie Motto

Lend a Hand

Age Groups

Ranger	14–18+
Guide	10–13/14
Brownie	7–10

Guides Catholiques du Canada (secteur français)

GUIDE

Promesse	**Promise**
Avec vous toutes, Confiante dans le Seigneur Je m'engage à rendre les autres plus heureux à servir avec audace mon pays et à partager l'idéal de toutes les guides du monde	With all of you, Trusting in the Lord I undertake to make others happier to serve my country with boldness and to share the ideal of all the Guides of the world.

Loi	**Law**
1 La Guide est vraie et joyeuse.	A Guide is sincere and joyful.
2 La Guide est accueillante et fraternelle.	A Guide is welcoming and sisterly (a sister to all).
3 La Guide acquiert la maîtrise d'elle-même.	A Guide has self-control.
4 La Guide surmonte les difficultés.	A Guide overcomes difficulties.
5 La Guide aime la nature.	A Guide loves nature.
6 La Guide vit et fait vivre.	A Guide lives and makes live.
7 La Guide mérite et fait confiance.	A Guide deserves and gives her trust.
8 La Guide partage l'effort de tous.	A Guide shares in the efforts of all.
9 La Guide rend service.	A Guide renders service.
10 La Guide apprend à vivre avec le Seigneur.	A Guide learns to live with the Lord.

Motto

Sois prête	Be Prepared

BROWNIE

Brownie Promise

Je promets de faire de mon mieux, pour être fidèle à Dieu, à mes parents et à la loi de la Ronde; pour faire chaque jour un plaisir à quelqu'un.	I promise to do my best, to be faithful to God, to my parents and to the law of the pack; to do a good turn to somebody every day.

Brownie Law

Une jeannette est toujours propre.	A Brownie is always neat.
Une jeannette est toujours gaie.	A Brownie is always cheerful.
Une jeannette est toujours active.	A Brownie is always active.
Une jeannette dit toujours vrai.	A Brownie always tells the truth.
Une jeannette pense d'abord aux autres.	A Brownie thinks first of others.

Brownie Motto

De notre mieux	Of our best

Age Groups

Aînée	Ranger	18–21
Kamsok	Guide	15–17
Guide	Guide	12–14
Jeannette	Brownie	8–11

The first Canadian Guide company was established in St. Catharines, Ontario, in 1909 and by 1912 Guiding had swept right across Canada. Five years later the Dominion Government granted incorporation to the Canadian Girl Guides Association which in 1928 became a Founder Member of WAGGGS. In 1961 an amendment to the Act of Incorporation changed the name to Girl Guides of Canada–Guides du Canada. The headquarters of the overall national organization is in Toronto.

Guiding in Canada reflects the multinational origins of its people, and Guides of many national backgrounds contribute much of their culture. Their songs, dances and national costumes lend colour to rallies and pageants.

Guides Catholiques du Canada (secteur français) is open to French-speaking girls and women. It has representation on the National Council and its members participate in national and international events. The programme conforms to the policy of the national organization, Girl Guides of Canada–Guides du Canada.

PROGRAMME

The programme is constantly under review so that it can continue to be relevant for girls in a changing world. The Ranger programme focuses on service and the growth and development of the girl, not only as an individual, but also as a member of her group. There is now the same focus in the Discovery programme for the Guide.

Outdoor Guide and Brownie badges and Ranger challenges have been created, and since 1967 outdoor workshops have been held for campers and non-campers stressing leadership and personal challenge.

LONE AND EXTENSION GUIDES

Girls in sparsely populated regions may join Lone Companies and keep in touch with each other by means of a circular Company Letter; active companies invite Lone Guides to camp with them and take part in other activities whenever possible. Handicapped girls are encouraged to become members of regular groups to the benefit of both.

CAMPING

Camping, in both summer and winter, is one of the highlights of the Guide year. Canada offers fun and excitement for the pioneer camper. Many of the provincial and local Councils now own permanent Guiding campsites but Guides may also camp in the many provincial and national parks. Inter-provincial camps, which often include visitors from other countries, bring together Guides separated by thousands of miles but joined by their Promise and Law.

SERVICE TO THE COMMUNITY

In keeping with the Promise they make on enrolment, Canadian Guides help other people and serve their communities. They help in hospitals and at blood donor clinics, 'adopt' handicapped or elderly people by performing many useful services for them, and sometimes assume the financial responsibility of 'adopting' a child in another country through various organizations. The services performed by Canadian Guides depend on the needs in their own communities, e.g. Rangers organize classes for Eskimo women in isolated areas of Newfoundland, and the Northwest Territories.

In 1976, the year of the Habitat Conference in Vancouver, Habitat Challenges were introduced for every age-group of Canada's Guiding, where a study of their own environment encouraged girls to consider the natural and man-made environment throughout the world.

An International Camp with the theme 'Opportunities for Leisure-time and Service to Society Today and Tomorrow' was held in 1977 in Novia Scotia.

'Guiding On The Move – 1975' with an imaginative programme of travel and exchanges involved thousands of girls throughout Canada and sparked involvement in every community, with a special highlight being the ten-day National Capital Event in Ottawa.

TRAINING

Since training is considered to be of the utmost importance for the leaders of the girls, a five-day national event, Congress '76, was held for Trainers in Canada in conjunction with the young leaders in training.

The *Canadian Guider* is the national magazine sent to all Guiders and Commissioners. In addition, basic training material is published in English and French and many Canadian publications have been translated into Spanish to aid Latin American countries.

WORLD FRIENDSHIP FUND

The Canadian World Friendship Fund, to which packs and companies contribute, helps to bring Girl Guides/Girl Scouts from other countries to Canada and to send Canadian Guides to international events. Allocations are made to the World Thinking Day Fund, to the four World Centres, to Mutual Aid Projects and to help Guides when disaster strikes their countries.

PUBLICATIONS/UNIFORMS

Handbooks have recently been published for both girls and Leaders in all branches. Each Brownie pack now has its own booklet. All branches changed their uniforms in 1970.

The overall objective of the Guides du Canada (secteur français) is to give its young people the sort of training which will enable them to help build a better, more peaceful world, since they themselves will have a sense of responsibility towards other people and a desire for an effective participation in the work of development.

Central African Empire

Les Guides Centrafricaines

GUIDE

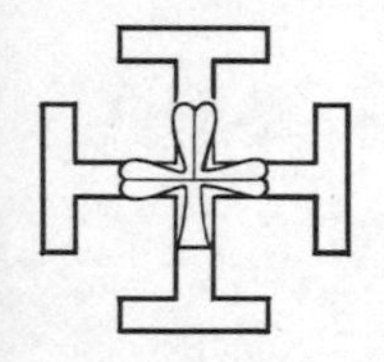

Promesse

Sur mon honneur, avec l'aide de Dieu, je promets de servir de mon mieux: Dieu (l'Eglise si la guide est catholique ou son église si elle est protestante); d'aider mon prochain en toutes circonstances, d'observer la loi des guides.

Promise

On my honour, with God's help, I promise to do my best to serve: God (the Church if the Guide is a Catholic or her church if she is a Protestant); and to help others at all times and to keep the Guide Law.

Loi	Law (translated literally)
1 La guide a un seul cœur et une parole.	A Guide is of one heart and one word.
2 La guide pense d'abord aux autres.	A Guide thinks first of others.
3 La guide met son cœur et ses mains au service des autres.	A Guide puts her heart and her hands at the service of others.
4 La guide est sœur des guides de toutes races, elle a l'esprit d'équipe.	A Guide is sister to Guides of all races, she has the spirit of the group.
5 La guide est accueillante, elle est là pour tous.	A Guide is friendly, she is there for all.
6 La guide respecte la nature, elle découvre l'œuvre de Dieu.	A Guide respects Nature, she discovers the work of God.
7 La guide sait obéir.	A Guide knows how to obey.
8 La guide sourit dans l'effort, elle ne fait rien à moitié.	A Guide smiles in her work, she does not do anything by halves.
9 La guide aime son travail et sait employer son argent.	A Guide loves her work and knows how to use her money.
10 La guide garde son corps, sa route est droite dans la joie de Dieu.	A Guide keeps her body, her way is straight in the joy of God.

BROWNIE

Brownie Promise

Je promets de faire de mon mieux pour être fidèle à Dieu, à mon pays, à mes parents, à la loi de la ronde; et pour faire chaque jour un plaisir à quelqu'un.	I promise to do my best to be faithful to God, to my Country, to my parents and the Law of the Pack; and to do a good turn to somebody every day.

Brownie Law

Une jeannette est toujours propre.	A Brownie is always neat.
Une jeannette est toujours active.	A Brownie is always active.
Une jeannette est toujours gaie.	A Brownie is always happy.
Une jeannette dit toujours vrai.	A Brownie is always true.
Une jeannette pense d'abord aux autres.	A Brownie thinks first of others.

Brownie Motto

De notre mieux	Of our best

Age Groups

Guide aînée	Ranger	16–21
Guide	Guide	12–16
Jeannette	Brownie	8–12

Girl Guiding began in the Central African Empire (known until 1976 as Central African Republic) in 1952, and by 1953 both Guide companies and Brownie packs had been established in the country.

In 1955 a combined camp was organized for Guides and Brownies, and during the next two years Guiding spread to many rural areas. In 1959 the Association was registered under the name 'Les Guides Centrafricaines'. By 1963 membership had risen to 1,600 and the first African National Commissioner was elected.

The 'Guides Centrafricaines' was recognized as an Associate Member of WAGGGS at the 18th World Conference (Denmark, 1963).

EXPANSION OF GUIDING

After this time, Guiding became established in 75 towns and villages throughout the Central African Empire. Guide methods, adapted for young girls in rural areas, enabled them to develop human and social contacts, thereby considerably improving their lifestyle.

TRAINING

Over the past 15 years Guiding has taken root firmly in rural areas. Village Guide groups have established contacts with girls in neighbouring rural areas where they organize three kinds of training sessions:

1 Three-day rallies which group girls from one 'sector', e.g. from seven or eight villages. These include technical training, discussions, programme planning, activities.
2 Annual camps (10–15 days) for patrol leaders and potential leaders.
3 Two-month courses. These are aimed at giving a basic training to village teams and include training in literacy, home economics, organization of a meeting, etc.

Each trainee is sponsored by her village, with the approval of the chief, so that the whole community is involved. The aim is to help girls raise the standard of living in their communities.

Guiding quickly took its place as a youth movement through the 'Conseil de la Jeunesse' and today plays an important part in the advancement of the status of women.

Chile

Asociación de Guías de Chile

GUIDE

Promesa	**Promise**
Yo prometo ante todos ustedes hacer cuanto de mí dependa para cumplir mi deber con Dios y mi Patria, ayudar al prójimo en todas las circunstancias y obedecer la Ley Guía.	I promise, before you all, to do my best to do my duty to God and my Country, to help my neighbour under all circumstances, and to obey the Guide Law.

Ley	**Law**
1 La Guía merece confianza porque es responsable.	A Guide merits trust because she is responsible.
2 La Guía es leal.	A Guide is loyal.
3 La Guía es servicial sin esperar recompensa.	A Guide serves without expecting reward.

4 La Guía es amiga y comparte con todos.	A Guide is a friend and shares with all.
5 La Guía es atenta y cordial.	A Guide is courteous and amiable.
6 La Guía ama la Naturaleza y en ella descubre la Obra de Dios.	A Guide loves nature and sees in it the work of God.
7 La Guía sabe obedecer y nada hace a medias.	A Guide knows how to obey and leaves nothing half done.
8 La Guía enfrenta las dificultades con optimismo.	A Guide faces difficulties with optimism.
9 La Guía cuida las cosas porque valora el trabajo.	A Guide takes care of things because she values them.
10 La Guía prepara su espíritu y su cuerpo para el verdadero amor.	A Guide cherishes her body, mind and spirit in order that she may give with true love.

Motto

Siempre lista	Always ready

Brownie Promise

Prometo hacer cuanto pueda para cumplir con Dios y mi Patria y ayudar a los demás especialmente en mi casa.	I promise to do as much as I can for my God and Country, and to help everybody, particularly at home.

BROWNIE

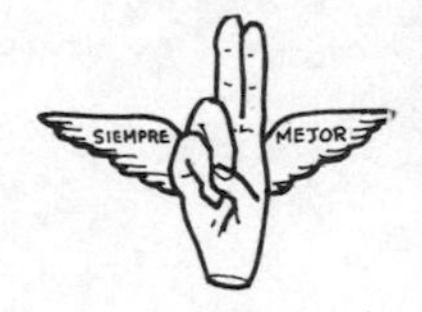

Brownie Law

La Alita está siempre alegre.	A Brownie must always be happy.
La Alita está siempre activa.	A Brownie must always be active.
La Alita dice siempre la verdad.	A Brownie must always tell the truth.
La Alita obedece a sus mayores.	A Brownie must always obey her elders.
La Alita piensa primero en los demás y después en si misma.	A Brownie thinks of her friends first and then of herself.

Brownie Motto

Dar y ayudar	To give and to help

Age Groups

Ranger	15–18
Guide	11–15
Brownie	7–11

Girl Guiding was started in Chile in 1913 under the auspices of the Boy Scouts. In June 1953 it was agreed that the Girl Guides should form a separate Association, and in 1957 the Asociación de Guías de Chile was recognized as an Associate Member of the World Association at the 16th World Conference held in Brazil.

DEVELOPMENT OF GUIDING

In 1959 the Association was honoured to receive the visit of Olave, Lady Baden-Powell, World Chief Guide. With the help of members of the Western Hemisphere Sub-committee the National Council was reconstituted in 1965 and from that time the Movement has made steady progress in Chile. The first National Convention for Commissioners and Trainers was held in Concepción in 1966.

ATTENDANCE AT NATIONAL AND INTERNATIONAL EVENTS

In the same year, two Chilean Rangers (on Juliette Low World Friendship Fund Scholarships) attended a Juliette Low Session at Our Cabaña, and two Chilean Trainers attended a Training for Trainers held in Oklahoma, U.S.A.

The Association was also represented at the Conference for Presidents and National Executive Secretaries in Venezuela in 1968. Delegates of the Asociación de Guias de Chile attended both the 21st World Conference in Canada in 1972 and the 22nd World Conference in the United Kingdom in 1975.

SERVICE

A major problem in Chile over the past years has been created by migration of people from rural areas to the cities. The Association has done much to extend Guiding to villages, strengthening community life and thereby helping to decrease migration to the towns.

Republic of China

The Girl Scouts Association of the Republic of China

GIRL SCOUT

Nuoh Yan	**Promise**
Pyng Woo de jen Cheing Woo Yuann duey Shang Tsang her Woo de Gwo jia Jinn Woo de been fenn Woo Yuann Swei Shyr bang juh ta ren Woo Yuann tzuen Shoou Neu torng jiun Guei liuh.	On my honour, I promise that I will do my best: To do my duty to God and my Country. To help other people at all times. To obey the Girl Scout Law.

	Neu torng jiun Guei liuh	**Law**
1	Neu torng jiun de rong Yuh Shyh Show ren Shinn Lay de.	A Girl Scout's honour is to be trusted.
2	Neu torng jiun Shyh jong Shin de.	A Girl Scout is loyal.
3	Neu torng jiun Shyh juh ren de.	A Girl Scout's duty is to be useful and to help others.
4	Neu torng jiun Shyh Yi Chieh ren de Perng Yeou Shyh Meei Wey Neu torn jiun de tzyy Mey.	A Girl Scout is a friend to all and a sister to every other Girl Scout.
5	Neu torng jiun Shyh Chian Gong de.	A Girl Scout is courteous.
6	Neu torng jiun Shyh Ay huh dong Wuhn de.	A Girl Scout is a friend to animals.
7	Neu torng jiun Shyh fwu tsorng de.	A Girl Scout obeys orders.
8	Neu torng jiun Shyh Kuay leh de.	A Girl Scout smiles and sings under all difficulties.

9 Neu torng jiun Shyh Chyn jean de.	A Girl Scout is thrifty.
10 Neu torng jiun de Sy Sheang Yan Yeu jui Shyng dong Shyh dong Shyh Chwen jye de.	A Girl Scout is pure in thought, in word and in deed.

Motto

Joen bey	Be Prepared.
ryh Shyng Yi Shann	Do a good turn daily.
ren Sheng Yii Fwu Wuh Wei Muh dih.	The greatest aim in life is to serve.

Brownie Scout Promise

I promise to do my best:
To do my duty to God and my Country;
To help other people every day,
especially those at home.

BROWNIE SCOUT

Brownie Scout Law

A Brownie gives in to the older folk.
A Brownie does not give in to herself.

Brownie Motto

Lend a Hand

Age Groups

Senior Girl Scout	16–20
Girl Scout	12–16
Brownie Scout	7–12

In 1953, women in the Republic of China interested in Girl Scouting made a concerted effort to assume responsibility for the planning, organization and training of the Chinese Girl Scouts, and in the same year succeeded in forming a Planning and Training Committee. The persistent efforts of the members of the Committee brought the Girl Scouts Association officially into being on 1 June 1958.

The Girl Scouts Association of the Republic of China, which comprises Taiwan and Fuken, was recognized as an Associate Member of WAGGGS at the 18th World Conference (Denmark, 1963), and became a Full Member at the 19th World Conference (Japan, 1966).

The Girl Scouts Association of the Republic of China has three levels: Senior Girl Scouts, Girl Scouts and Brownie Scouts. Activities such as camping, skill contests, pack holidays, etc. are arranged for Girl Scouts in twelve district sub-branches. Many Girl Scout projects involve keeping the environment clean and healthy.

TRAINING

Trainers for Brownie Leaders and Senior Leaders were sent to the Republic of China from the World Association, and a complete training system has now been set up with regular training given for voluntary Leaders at all levels. The National

Association has conducted Trainers' trainings and the province and city branches have arranged Girl Scout Leaders' and Troop Leaders' training courses. Publications are produced to promote training and Girl Scout skills.

INTERNATIONAL FRIENDSHIP

International friendship has been encouraged by the Association through exchanges between Girl Scouts in the Republic of China and those in other countries. Many activities, for example, are arranged between American and Chinese Girl Scouts. Members of the Association have taken part in international events in the U.S.A., Japan, Australia, Sweden, the Philippines, Belgium and at Our Cabaña.

Colombia

Asociación de Guías Scouts de Colombia

GUIDE

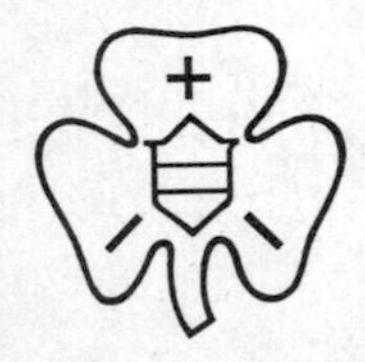

Promesa	**Promise**
Con la gracia de Dios yo . . . prometo por mi honor hacer cuanto de mi dependa para cumplir mis deberes para con Dios, mi Patria y mi familia; sur útil al prójimo en todas las circunstancias; y obedecer la Ley Guía.	With the grace of God, I . . . promise on my honour to do all that is expected of me, to fulfil my duties towards God, my country and my family, to be useful to others in all circumstances and to obey the Guide Law.

Ley	**Law**
1 La Guía es persona de honor.	A Guide's honour is to be trusted.
2 La Guía es leal.	A Guide is loyal.
3 La Guía tiene el deber de ser útil y ayudar al prójimo.	A Guide's duty is to be useful and help others.
4 La Guía es buena con todos y hermana de la demás Guías.	A Guide is a friend to all and a sister to every other Guide.
5 La Guía es cortés.	A Guide is courteous.
6 La Guía cuida a los animales y a las plantas y ve la obra de Dios en la naturaleza.	A Guide is a friend to animals and plants, and sees in nature the work of God.
7 La Guía es obediente, disciplinada y cumple a cabalidad con sus deberes.	A Guide is obedient and disciplined and fulfils her duties completely.
8 La Guía es alegre y sonrie en las dificultades.	A Guide is cheerful and smiles under all difficulties.
9 La Guía es económica.	A Guide is thrifty.
10 La Guía es pura en pensamiento, palabras y obras.	A Guide is pure in thoughts, words and deeds.

Motto

Siempre lista	Always ready

Brownie Promise

Prometo tratar siempre de cumplir con mis deberes para con Dios y mi Patria.	I promise to try to do my duty to God and my country.
Prometo tratar siempre de ayudar a los demás y especialmente a los míos.	I promise to try to help others, especially those at home.

Brownie Law

Una Hadita cede a las personas mayores.	A Brownie obeys her elders.
Una Hadita no cede a sus caprichos.	A Brownie must not give in to herself.

Brownie Motto

Ayudar a todos	Help everybody

Age Groups

Guía Mayor	Ranger	15 and over
Intermedia	Intermediate	13–15
Guía Menor	Guide	10–13
Hadita	Brownie	7–10

1936 – Beginning of Guiding in Colombia.
1953 – National Executive Council formed and Headquarters set up in Bogotá.
1954 – Colombia becomes an Associate Member of WAGGGS at the 15th World Conference (The Netherlands, 1954).
1957 – Full Membership status is given to Colombia at the 16th WAGGGS' World Conference (Brazil, 1957).

STRUCTURE

National Assemblies which are held regularly in Colombia are responsible for policy making and for ensuring that the Movement is kept in line with current needs and developments. The National Council is divided into two branches – Educational and Administrative – each with its own Vice-President. An Advisory Team composed of persons with wide experience in the Movement has been set up to advise the National Council on new methods and ways of responding best to the needs and interests of youth. With this in mind, work is being carried out at the national level to train the adult membership (Guiders, Committee and Council Members, etc.) and to enable them to project their work into the community in a more effective way.

The reorganization of the National Headquarters in 1970 to include professional staff was of great importance for the development of Guiding, as was the opening of National Headquarters in Bogotá in 1971.

PROGRAMME

National Camps have been a permanent feature of the programme since 1969. Their aim is the development in young girls of the sense of active citizenship; the theme of one of the camps was 'A new woman for a new Colombia'.

Patrol work has been emphasized and a system of Bars developed for Senior Guides who can qualify as Literacy Assistants, Recreational Assistants, Social Workers' Assistants and Assistants in Ecology and Environment.

TRAINING

To make the training programme more efficient, in view of the expansion of the Movement, the country has been divided into five zones. The training is carried out by teams of Regional Trainers under the supervision of the National Trainer and her Committee. Gatherings for Trainers are held at national level and international participation is welcomed.

PARTICIPATION IN NATIONAL AND INTERNATIONAL EVENTS

Attendance at National and International events has increased considerably thanks to financial assistance being provided by the Association. Girl Guides were represented at the second UNESCO/NGO Literacy Seminar in Colombia and organized an international gathering with the theme 'The young Girl and the Community' as their contribution to International Women's Year, 1975.

SERVICE AND CO-OPERATION WITH OTHER ORGANIZATIONS

Colombian Girl Guides do much to give service to the community through Literacy programmes and helping in underprivileged areas of their country. Groups of Girl Guides operate in slums, where the girls most need the Girl Guide programme.

The Asociación de Guías Scouts de Colombia is a member of the Colombian Association of Voluntary Service, ACOVOL, which enables the Movement to work on up-dating methods and other needs of formal and non-formal education in the country.

Costa Rica

Asociación de Guías y Scouts de Costa Rica

GUIDE AND BROWNIE

Promesa	**Promise**
Yo prometo por mi honor, hacer cuanto de mi dependa para cumplir con mi deber hacia Dios y mi Patria; Ser útil al prójimo en todas las circunstancias y obedecer la Ley Guía.	I promise on my honour to do my best to do my duty to God and my Country; To help my neighbours under all circumstances and to obey the Guide Law.
Ley	**Law**
La Guía es:	A Guide is:
HONORABLE: Integra ante sí misma y ante los demás en todos los actos de su vida.	HONOURABLE: she is honest to herself and to others in all she does.
LEAL: Para con Dios, su Patria, sus Padres, sus Dirigentes, subordinadas y compañeras.	LOYAL: she is loyal to God, her Country, her Parents, her subordinates and companions.
SERVICIAL: Ayuda a los demás sin esperar recompensa.	HELPFUL: she helps others without expecting a reward.

AMIGABLE: Es amiga de todas y hermana de toda Guía sin distinción de credo, raza, nacionalidad o clase social.	FRIENDLY: she is a friend to all and a sister to every Guide without distinction of creed, race, nationality or social class.
CORTES: Manifiesta su estima y consideración a los demás.	COURTEOUS: she shows appreciation and consideration of others.
BONDADOSA: Ve en la naturaleza la obra de Dios y la conserva.	KIND: she sees the work of God in nature and tries to conserve it.
OBEDIENTE: Acepta la legítima autoridad y obedece racionalmente.	OBEDIENT: she accepts legitimate authority and obeys in a rational way.
ALEGRE: Es optimista y jovial aún en sus dificultades.	CHEERFUL: she is optimistic and cheerful even in the face of difficulty.
TRABAJADORA: Hace buen uso del producto de su trabajo y es cuidadosa del bien ajeno. Hace las cosas en orden y completas.	HARDWORKING: she puts to good use the products of her own work and is careful with the possessions of others; she does things tidily and completely.
LIMPIA: Es limpia y sana en sus pensamientos, palabras y acciones.	PURE: she is pure in her thoughts, words and deeds.

Motto

Siempre Lista para Servir	Ever ready to serve

Brownie Promise

Yo prometo hacer cuanto de mi dependa para cumplir mis deberes hacia Dios y mi Patria; Obedecer la Ley de la Ronda y ayudar, todos los días a los demás, especialmente a los de mi casa.	I promise that I will do my best to do my duty to God and my Country; To obey the Brownie Law and to help other people every day, especially those at home.

Brownie Law

La Hadita escucha y obedece a ardillita.	A Brownie listens to and obeys her Leader.
La Hadita se vence a sí misma.	A Brownie is self-controlled.

Brownie Motto

Ayudar a todos.	Helps everyone

Age Groups

Guía Mayor	Ranger	15–18
Guía Intermedia	Guide	11–15
Hadita	Brownie	7–11

Guiding first started in Costa Rica in 1923 with a small number of isolated groups. By 1937, however, the Movement was well established. In 1942 the Asociación Guías de Costa Rica was formed and in 1946 was recognized as an Associate Member of the World Association at the 11th World Conference held in France.

Throughout the 1950s the Association underwent a period of reorganization and thanks to financial aid received from the government, Guiding was able to make good progress. In 1976 the Guías joined with the Boy Scouts in the establishment of the Asociación de Guías y Scouts de Costa Rica.

TRAINING

Most Guide companies in Costa Rica are attached to schools where Guiding is often an extra-curricular activity, and much stress is laid on the patrol system. Over the past ten years several trainings have been held, attended by Trainers from other countries, and Costa Rican Guides have attended trainings in Guatemala, Panama and Mexico. Recently, new handbooks and other training materials have been produced.

SERVICE

Guides in Costa Rica carry out a number of service activities including assistance in orphanages, helping in hospitals, organizing Christmas parties for underprivileged areas. They have also participated in the government's official 'Conservation of Natural Resources Week' and sent food and clothing to Guatemala after the earthquake there in 1976.

Cyprus

Girl Guides Association of Cyprus

GUIDE

Promise

I promise on my honour that I will
do my best:
To do my duty to God and Cyprus;
To help other people at all times;
To obey the Guide Law.

Law

1 The word of honour of a Guide is to be believed and respected.
2 A Guide is loyal and obedient to her parents and her elders.
3 A Guide is useful and always helps others.
4 A Guide is friendly to all.
5 A Guide is courteous and affable.
6 A Guide loves and protects animals and plants.
7 A Guide is reliable and punctual.
8 A Guide is calm, optimistic and joyful.
9 A Guide is conscientious, thrifty and tidy.
10 A Guide is pure in her thoughts, words and deeds.

Motto

Be Prepared

BUTTERFLY

Butterfly Promise

I promise to do my best:
To do my duty to God and Cyprus;
To help other people always
and bring happiness at home.

Butterfly Law

The Butterfly obeys her elders.
The Butterfly does not think only of herself but is a friend and sister to all other Butterflies.

Butterfly Motto

Help everywhere always

Age Groups

Senior Guide	15–18
Sea and Land (Forest) Guide	13–15
Guide	10–12
Butterfly	7–10

After a few attempts to form companies and setting up of the Council immediately after the Second World War, Guiding really established itself on the island in 1947; by 1954 there were companies in all towns and many villages.

There was a lull in Guiding between 1955 and 1959, but after Independence in 1960, interest was revived and a new Constitution drafted.

Representatives from the World Association of Girl Guides and Girl Scouts visited Cyprus to help and advise, and after long negotiations a National Council was formed composed of Greeks, Turks, and members of minority groups. By 1963 the numbers of registered Guides and Butterflies grew to 1,000 and many new Guiders were trained with the help of Swiss Trainers sent to Cyprus by the World Association.

Cyprus was recognized as an Associate Member of the World Association at the 17th World Conference of WAGGGS (Greece, 1960). In order to provide better programmes for all age groups, an additional branch was introduced in 1969.

DEVELOPMENTS AND EVENTS

All-island summer camps have become a regular feature of Guiding in Cyprus since the first all-island camp at Troods in 1966. All-Island seminars have been held every two years and district seminars every year.

The Association takes a lively interest in contacts with Girl Guides/Girl Scouts in other countries and many activities illustrate this interest: in 1971 the first international camp was held with participation from eight European and Middle Eastern countries; in 1972 a hospitality project for Girl Guides from other countries was launched in which twenty-five Guides from Australia, Greece, Egypt, Japan, the U.K., New Zealand and Sweden took part; in 1973 the International Guide hostel was opened in Famagusta thanks to the efforts of the local district.

SERVICE

Environmental service projects including tree-planting and forest cleaning have been carried out since 1971 when two districts joined in a one-month service project, cleaning and beautifying Yerani village in the Famagusta district.

During the war of 1974, Girl Guides met the challenge and mobilized all their resources, bringing help to the victims of the tragic events. All Guide camping equipment was made available for the accommodation of refugees, 300 tons of food, clothing, blankets and other materials were distributed to the needy people, and summer camps organized in 1975 for the refugee children. Girl Guides assisted in hospitals and worked with the Red Cross, Refugee Rehabilitation Service and other organizations dealing with displaced persons.

At WAGGGS' 22nd World Conference (U.K., 1975), the Girl Guides Association of Cyprus was awarded the Walter Donald Ross Certificate of Merit for excellent services rendered to the refugees of Cyprus.

Denmark

Pigespejdernes Faellesraad Danmark

DET DANSKE SPEJDERKORPS

GUIDE

VÆR BEREDT

Spejderløftet	**Promise**
Jeg lover at holde spejderloven.	I promise to keep the Guide Law.

Spejderloven	**Law**
Den, der er med i spejdernes faellesskab gør sit bedste for:	The Guide who is part of the Guide fellowship does her best:
at finde sin egen tro og have respekt for andre*	to find her own faith and respect the faith of others*
at vaere om naturen	to protect nature
at vaere en god kammerat, vaere hensynsfuld og hjaelpe andre	to be a good friend, considerate and helpful to others
at vaere til at stole på	to be trustworthy
at høre andres meninger og danne sine egne	to listen to the opinion of others and to form her own
at tage medansvar i familie og samfund.	to show responsibility in the family and in society (or, to take her share in responsibility for her family and her surroundings).

*Note: These words in Danish mean a spiritual faith, a belief in spiritual principles.

BROWNIE

Motto

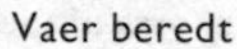

Vaer beredt	Be Prepared

Brownie Promise and Law

Brownies may use the same Promise and Law as the Guides, or the following:

Blåmejse	**Brownie Law**
Vær sand, lydig og god mod enhver.	Be honest, obedient, and a friend to all.

Brownie Motto

Vaer beredt	Be Prepared

KFUK-SPEJDERNE I DANMARK

GUIDE

Spejderløftet	**Promise**
Jeg lover at holde spejderloven.	I promise to keep the Guide Law.
Spejderloven	**Law**
Den, der er med i spejdernes faellesskab gør sit bedste for:	The Guide who is part of the Guide fellowship does her best:
at aere Gud og hans ord	to honour God and His word
at vaerne om naturen	to protect nature
at vaere en god kammerat, vaere hensynsfuld og hjaelpe andre	to be a good friend, considerate and helpful to others
at vaere til at stole på	to be trustworthy
at høre andres meninger og danne sine egne	to listen to the opinion of others and to form her own
at tage medansvar i familie og samfund	to show responsibility in the family and in society.

Motto

Vaern og tjen*	Protect and Serve*

*the international motto

Vaer beredt	Be Prepared

BROWNIE

Brownie Motto

Vi vil stå sammen	We will stick together
Vi vil gøre vort bedste	We will do our Best

DANSKE BAPTISTERS SPEJDERKORPS

GUIDE

Spejderløftet	**Promise**
Jeg lover at gøre mit bedste for at holde spejderloven	I promise to do my best to obey the Guide Law
Spejderloven	**Law**
Som spejder vil jeg lytte til Guds ord.	Being a Guide I will listen to the word of God.
Som spejder har jeg medansvar for det samfund, jeg lever i.	Being a Guide I have co-responsibility for the community in which I am living.
Som spejder vil jeg vaere hensynsfuld og hjaelpsom.	Being a Guide I will be considerate and ready to help.
Som spejder vil jeg vaere til at stole på.	Being a Guide I will be reliable.
Som spejder vil jeg lytte til andres mening og selv tage standpunkt.	Being a Guide I will listen to the opinion of others and make up my mind.
Som spejder vil jeg laere naturen at kende og vaerne om den.	Being a Guide I will be acquainted with nature and protect it.

Motto

Vaer beredt	Be Prepared
(Spejderflokken: Gør dit bedste)	(Guide-packs: Do your Best)

Age Groups

Det Danske Spejderkorps			*KFUK-Spejderne i Danmark*		
Seniorspejder	Ranger	15–20	Seniorspejder	Ranger	15+
Spejder	Guide	12–15	Spejder	Guide	13–15
Spire	Junior Guide	10–12	Juniorspejder	Junior Guide	10–13
Blåmejse	Brownie	8–10	Grønsmutte	Brownie	8–10

Danske Baptisters Spejderkorps

Pack work	7–10
Troop work	10–13
Group work	13–16
Rover/Ranger work	16+

HOW IT ALL BEGAN

A Founder Member of the World Association, Denmark started Guiding in 1910 when some girls joined a Boy Scout group. Within a few years the girls had their own organization, Det Danske Pigespejderkorps. In 1919 the YWCA Girl Guides (KFUK-Spejderne) in Denmark was formed. These two Associations comprised the National Organization – Pigespejdernes Faellesraad Danmark – until 1976 when the structure was changed to include the Danske Baptisters Spejderkorps (the Danish Baptist Guide and Scout Association) as a separate Association; previously they were members through the KFUK-Spejderne i Danmark.

The Metodist Kirkens Spejdere i Danmark (Guides and Scouts of the Methodist Church in Denmark) and the Frelsens Haers Pigespejdere (the Salvation Army Girl Guides) continue to be part of the National Organization through the KFUK-Spejderne i Danmark, whereas the Grønlands Spejderkorps (Greenland Scout and Guide Association) has international recognition through the National Organization.

H.M. the Queen Mother, Ingrid, is the Patron of both Det Danske Spejderkorps and the KFUK-Spejderne i Danmark, and H.R.H. Princess Benedikte is the very active president of the Joint Committee.

CHANGES IN THE ASSOCIATIONS

Det Danske Pigespejderkorps merged with Det Danske Spejderkorps on 1 January 1973 to form Det Danske Spejderkorps (the Danish Guide and Scout Association) which is open to girls and boys. The Danish Baptist Guide and Scout Associations, the Guides and Scouts of the Methodist Church and the Greenland Guide and Scout Associations are now also merged Associations.

The character of activities within the merged Associations varies: sometimes all activities for all age-groups are co-educational, sometimes only Ranger/ Rover sections carry out a joint programme.

PRINCIPLES

All the Associations base their work on the original principles as laid down more than sixty years ago, but the leaders in all the Associations feel the necessity of an annual critical review of methods, programmes, leader training, etc.

JOINT COMMITTEE

DET DANSKE SPEJDERKORPS (THE DANISH GUIDE AND SCOUT ASSOCIATION)

The DDS have been busy establishing their new Association and designing new programmes for all age levels which will be used by girls as well as boys. Provisions have been made to have equal representation of leaders of both sexes on the National Board, on all committees and on the staff at division and district levels.

The formation of the new Association was celebrated in 1974 at a big national camp in which about 17,000 girls and boys took part.

The Association publishes *Broen*, a magazine for Senior Girl Guides and Boy Scouts and Leaders, and *Spejd*, a magazine for children.

KFUK-SPEJDERNE I DANMARK (YWCA GIRL GUIDES IN DENMARK)

The YWCA Girl Guides have changed their programme after several years of studies and research which resulted in outlining a new, more relevant, up-to-date and flexible programme which gives a lot of freedom to girls and Leaders.

The YWCA Girl Guides and the YMCA Boy Scouts are free to co-operate in ways best suited to local needs and interests. At national level the Associations jointly publish two magazines, *Spejdertips* for the children and *Braendpunkt* for the Leaders.

DANSKE BAPTISTERS SPEJDERKORPS (DANISH BAPTIST GUIDE AND SCOUT ASSOCIATION)

The aims of the Association are to organize Boy Scout and Girl Guide activities within the Danish Baptist community, to help children and young people to develop as independent, responsible and democratic citizens with international understanding. All members of the DBS over 15 years of age may, if they wish, attend the Annual General Assembly. The Association is run by its members without the assistance of professional staff.

In the summer of 1976 a Scandinavian camp with 1,400 participants was held at the National Training Centre 'Oeksedal'.

The Association publishes two periodicals: *Spejdernyt* for the children and *Foerernyt* for the Leaders.

CO-OPERATION WITH OTHER YOUTH ORGANIZATIONS

Through the Dansk Ungdems Faellesraad (Danish Youth Council) the Girl Guide and Boy Scout Associations in Denmark maintain close links with various other youth organizations. The Associations are members of a special co-operation committee called 'Samraadet' which includes the Boys' and Girls' Brigade and the Falcon Movement.

Danish Girl Guides are active in the fields of literacy (teaching Danish to children of immigrant workers) and service to the community. They also organize conservation activities and anti-pollution campaigns and are concerned with problems of world population.

Dominican Republic

Asociación de Guías Scouts Dominicanas, Inc.

GUIDE

Promesa	Promise
Yo prometo por mi honor hacer cuanto de mi dependa para:	I promise, on my honour, to do my best:
Cumplir con mi deber hacia Dios y mi Patria,	To do my duty to God and my country;
Ser útil al prójimo en todo momento,	To help other people at all times;
Obedecer la Ley Guía.	To obey the Guide Law.

Ley	Law
1 La Guía es persona en cuyo honor se puede confiar.	A Guide's honour is to be trusted.
2 La Guía es leal.	A Guide is loyal.
3 El deber de la Guía es ser útil y ayudar a otros.	A Guide's duty is to be useful and to help others.
4 La Guía es amiga de todos y hermana de toda Guía.	A Guide is a friend to all and a sister to every other Guide.
5 La Guía es cortés.	A Guide is courteous.
6 La Guía es amiga de los animales.	A Guide is a friend to animals.
7 La Guía obedece órdenes.	A Guide is obedient.
8 La Guía sonríe y canta en todas las dificultades.	A Guide smiles and sings under any difficulty.
9 La Guía es económica.	A Guide is thrifty.
10 La Guía es pura de pensamiento, palabra, y obra.	A Guide is pure in thought, word and deed.

Motto

Siempre Lista	Be Prepared

BROWNIE

Brownie Promise

Prometo hacer todo lo que pueda para cumplir con mi deber hacia Dios y mi Patria y ayudar todos los días a los demás, especialmente a los de mi casa.	I promise to do my best: To do my duty to God and my country, and To help other people every day, especially those at home.

Brownie Law

La Alita accede a los deseos de sus mayores.	A Brownie gives in to the older folk.
La Alita nunca cede a sí misma.	A Brownie does not give in to herself.

Brownie Motto

Dar Ayuda	Lend a Hand

Age Groups

Guía Mayor	Senior Guide	15–18
Guía	Guide	10–15
Alita	Brownie	7–10

Guiding was first established on an organized basis in the Dominican Republic in 1961, when an Interim Committee was formed to draw up a constitution. By April of that year, girls from several schools had been enrolled as Guides.

In 1963 the National Commissioner attended an International Training in Puerto Rico. On her return to the Dominican Republic she endeavoured to extend Guiding throughout the country, and, with the formation of the first Ranger company in 1964, all three branches of the Movement were in existence.

At the 20th World Conference (Finland, 1969) the Asociación Nacional de Guías Scouts Dominicanas was recognized as an Associate Member of the World Association.

TRAINING

Much emphasis in the programme is laid on training, and members of the Association have travelled to other countries to study training methods. Three young Guiders from the Dominican Republic went to the Training for trainers at Our Cabaña in 1971 and have since been appointed as national trainers. Fifty Senior Guides attended a three-day meeting to discuss such subjects as the Promise and Law, preparation for marriage, and the young girl and her attitude to her community. A training course in Human Relations and Leadership for leaders and adult members was also held.

Close co-operation has been achieved between the National Council and the provinces. This contact is being strengthened by correspondence, and through the monthly bulletin on Information and Training as well as through visits to the provinces by the Executive Secretary.

FUND-RAISING

Fund-raising is always an important activity carried out by the Guides through raffles, charity sales and the annual 'Tell me with flowers' flower show in Santiago City.

Ecuador

Asociación Nacional de Guías Scout del Ecuador

GUIDE

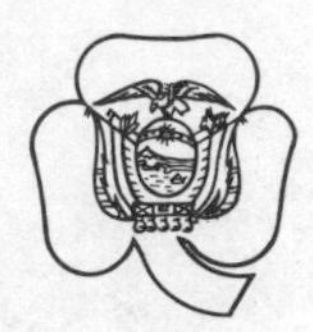

Promesa	**Promise**
Yo prometo, por mi honor, hacer todo cuanto de mi dependa: para cumplir mis deberes para con Dios y mi Patria; ser útil al prójimo en todo momento y obedecer la Ley Guía.	I promise, on my honour, to do my best: To do my duty to God and my Country; To help others at all times; and to obey the Guide Law.

Ley	**Law**
1 La Guía-Scout es persona en cuyo honor se puede confiar.	A Guide is a person whose honour is to be trusted.
2 La Guía-Scout es leal.	A Guide is loyal.
3 La Guía-Scout tiene el deber de ser útil y ayudar al prójimo.	A Guide's duty is to be useful and to help others.
4 La Guía-Scout es amiga de todas y hermana de las demás Guías.	A Guide is a friend to all and a sister to every other Guide.
5 La Guía-Scout es cortés.	A Guide is courteous.
6 La Guía-Scout ama a los animales y a las plantas y ve la obra de Dios en la naturaleza.	A Guide loves animals and plants and sees the work of God in nature.
7 La Guía-Scout es obediente y disciplinada.	A Guide is obedient and disciplined.
8 La Guía-Scout no desmaya ante las dificultades.	A Guide is not discouraged by difficulties.
9 La Guía-Scout es económica.	A Guide is thrifty.
10 La Guía-Scout es pura de pensamiento, palabra y obra.	A Guide is pure in thought, word and deed.

Motto

Siempre Lista	Be Prepared

BROWNIE

Age Groups

Guía Mayor	Ranger	15–18
Cadete	Cadette	13–15
Guía Intermedia	Guide	11–13
Alita	Brownie	7–10

The Girl Guide Movement began in Ecuador as early as 1916, but it was not until 1952 that it was firmly established and an Association formed with the assistance of the World Association Travelling Commissioner for the Western Hemisphere area. Girl Guiding gradually spread to all parts of the country, and Asociación Nacional de Guías Scout del Ecuador became an Associate Member of the World Association of Girl Guides and Girl Scouts at the 19th World Conference (Japan, 1966).

OFFICIAL SUPPORT

The government of Ecuador has recognized the importance of the Movement and has included its programme in the general plans of education. Educational authorities have officially encouraged the formation of troops in all public and private schools and credit has been given to those teachers who have received training in Girl Guiding. As further support, the Ministry of Education has paid the salary of highly qualified teachers to work full-time in the Girl Guides Association as staff. The appointment of the National Executive Co-ordinator has been supported by the Ministry of Education.

Support for the Association has come not only from the national government but municipal authorities as well. The Municipality of Quito donated a large piece of land to the Guides, within the urban limits of the capital city. This choice property has now been developed and the first building was constructed with funds donated by the Rotary Club of Quito; it is now fully furnished and this has been accomplished with private contributions as well as with a large grant from the Ministry of Social Welfare, which, in exchange for the grant, requested the Girl Guides Association to train youth workers in recreation and outdoor skills.

CAMP AND TRAINING CENTRES

The Girl Guides of Ecuador have named this camp/programme centre 'Juanita Baca de Dávila' to honour the President of the Association who through her efforts obtained the donation of the land and the support of the Rotary Club. This programme centre will be primarily used as a literacy centre and the Association has launched a Literacy Campaign which will include both training for teachers and courses for illiterates. This project has received financial assistance from UNESCO.

The Association owns and operates another camp in the coastal region, near Data, Province of Guayas. 'Doña Cary National Camp' has been operating for several years and it is a popular camping area for Girl Guides and their families, not only from the coastal provinces but from the provinces in the mountain region as well.

PROGRAMMES

The Association is particularly interested in the international aspect of Girl Guiding/Girl Scouting and participates regularly in international events, particularly at the regional level.

Much importance has been given to programme and training and the Association has been updating the programmes for all branches. Simple publications have been produced and it is hoped that handbooks for all branches can be published in the future.

Girl Guides of Ecuador are conscious of the needs of their communities and make efforts to improve the quality of life in their country. Service is an integral part of all programmes and there has been an increased involvement in various community development programmes. Their concern for the environment was evident when the Guides carried out a tree-planting project around villages in the mountain region, thereby preventing further erosion of the soil.

There has been some increase in membership and the Movement has spread to most provinces. Because of the lack of leadership and personnel to give full-time support to new groups the growth of the Movement is limited; however, its image is a positive one and the community as a whole recognizes the importance of Guiding as a valuable contribution to the education and promotion of women.

Egypt, Arab Republic of

Gamiet Morshidat Gomhoriet Misr El Arabieh

GUIDE

Methāk	Promise
Aedou Besharafi an assaa gohdi lean akoom belwagib alei nahow Allah walwatan, waan Osaed El Nass fi gamie elzoroof, waan otie Kanoon al morshidat.	I promise on my honour to do my best to do my duty to God and my country, to help other people at all times, and to obey the Guide Law.

	Kanoon	Law
1	Sharaf Almorshida iman wathik.	A Guide's honour is to be trusted.
2	Almorshida mokhlisa Lillah walwatan.	A Guide is loyal to God and her country.
3	Wagib Almorshida an takoon nafia waan toeen ghairaha.	A Guide's duty is to be useful and to help others.
4	Almorshida sadikat elgamie wa okht lekol morshida okhra.	A Guide is a friend to all and a sister to every other Guide.
5	Almorshida hamidat elsagaya.	A Guide is courteous.
6	Almorshida rafika belhayawan.	A Guide is kind to animals.
7	Totei Almorshida awamer walediha wa kaedat ferkatiha wa raissat kesmah taa khalissa.	A Guide obeys the orders of her parents and her Patrol Leader and Captain.
8	Tabtasim Almorshida lilshadaid watoka belha besabrin wa thabat.	A Guide smiles and meets all difficulties with patience and cheerfulness.
9	Almorshida moddakhira.	A Guide is thrifty.
10	Almorshida nakiat elsareera tabiyat elkaib wa kareemat elsagaya.	A Guide is pure in thought, word and deed.

Motto

Koony mostaeda	Be Prepared

BROWNIE

Brownie Promise

I promise to do my best:
To perform my duty towards God and my dear country;
To help people every day, especially my family.

Brownie Law

Brownies obey all people older than themselves.
Brownies do not give in to their own desires.

Brownie Motto

Helping people

Age Groups

Gawalat	Ranger	16+
Morshidat	Guide	11–16
Zahrat	Brownie	6–11

Guiding started in Egypt around 1913 and in 1925 it was introduced to schools; the Egyptian Girl Guides Association was formed in 1929 and was granted Full Membership of WAGGGS at the 6th World Conference (U.K., 1930). In recent years Egyptian Guiding has expanded and reached the factories and community clubs. Among its members are girls of many nationalities resident in Egypt, including Greeks, Italians and Americans. Activities are carried out in three main age groups – Brownies, Guides and Rangers – and the older girls have the choice between Land, Sea and Air Rangering.

PROGRAMMES

Programmes are given a new emphasis so as to meet best the needs of Egyptian youth and the country in general. Leadership training is given a special priority and Guides are encouraged to undertake greater responsibilities in planning and running of camps. Campaigns promoting cleanliness, literacy and family planning have been launched. Guides joined in the activities for International Women's Year, 1975, putting stress on literacy and family planning programmes in towns and villages. Rangers, as literacy teachers, who assisted in the government literacy campaign have been highly praised by the authorities for their work. The Association is very interested in providing vocational training for girls and it has established five vocational training centres where girls are taught knitting, embroidery, weaving and other traditional skills. Some of these centres have received financial support from UNESCO.

Camping and social service play a prominent part in Guide training. Frequent camps are organized for the Leaders. Seminars are held for commissioners and leaders of branches at headquarters. When regional camps are held, Guides from neighbouring Arab countries attend.

Apart from the usual training camps, a service camp was held in a slum area in co-operation with UNICEF and Giza Governorate. Another was held in the Canal Zone to join in reconstructing the destroyed towns; this project has received a partial grant from the World Association. There are also rural camps in the villages where the Guides co-operate with the villagers and learn the meaning of communal life and service to the community. They assist in the organization of various welfare projects such as the opening of nurseries and the care of families in need of help. Guides and Rangers are also involved in first aid and hygiene projects. In 1973, a time of emergency, Guides lived up to their motto 'Be Prepared', as groups were formed to do nearly any work needed in hospitals or making clothes for the soldiers and their families. Brownies also gave help by packing gifts.

Attempts are made to develop Guiding with the Handicapped. Service is given to the handicapped in co-operation with Faith and Hope Society, and a joint Girl Guide/UNICEF project is under way to set up children's clubs which would be attended by handicapped and healthy children alike.

El Salvador

Asociación de Muchachas Guías de El Salvador

GUIDE

Promesa	**Promise**
Yo prometo por mi honor hacer cuanto de mi dependa para: cumplir con mi deber hacia Dios y mi patria; ser útil al prójimo en toda circunstancia; obedecer la Ley Guía.	I promise on my honour to do all within my power: to do my duty to God and my country; to be helpful to my neighbour under all circumstances; to obey the Guide Law.

Ley	**Law**
1 La Muchacha Guía es persona en cuyo honor se puede confiar.	A Girl Guide is a person whose honour can be trusted.
2 La Muchacha Guía es leal.	A Girl Guide is loyal.
3 La Muchacha Guía debe ser útil y ayudar al prójimo.	A Girl Guide must be useful and help her neighbours.
4 La Muchacha Guía es amiga de todos y hermana de toda Guía.	A Girl Guide is a friend to all and sister to all Guides.
5 La Muchacha Guía es bien educada y cortés.	A Girl Guide is polite and courteous.
6 La Muchacha Guía admira a Dios en la Naturaleza.	A Girl Guide admires God in Nature.
7 La Muchacha Guía acepta y cumple órdenes.	A Girl Guide accepts and obeys orders.
8 La Muchacha Guía afronta animosamente las dificultades.	A Girl Guide faces all difficulties with courage.
9 La Muchacha Guía es económica.	A Girl Guide is thrifty.
10 La Muchacha Guía es pura de pensamiento, palabra y obra.	A Girl Guide is pure in thought, word and deed.

Motto

Siempre Lista	Always ready

BROWNIE

Brownie Promise

Prometo hacer todo lo que me sea posible, para cumplir con mi deber hacia Dios y mi Patria, ayudar todos los días a los demás, especialmente a los de mi casa.	I promise to do everything possible to do my duty to God and my country, help others every day, especially those at home.

Brownie Law

La Alita accede a los deseos de sus mayores.	A Brownie always obeys her elders.
La Alita nunca cede a sí misma.	A Brownie never gives in to herself.

Brownie Motto

Dar Ayuda	Give help

Age Groups

Guía Mayor	Ranger	15–18
Guía Intermedia	Guide	11–15
Alita	Brownie	7–11

Asociación de Muchachas Guías de El Salvador was founded in 1944, when a small group of Guides was set up at the Bethany Institute of Santa Tecla. The Association was officially recognized in 1949. After a period of decline, a fresh impetus was given to the Movement by the World Association's Western Hemisphere Travelling Commissioner who formed an executive committee, and Guiding was reborn with a dozen girls who had remained with the original organization. The Association, which in 1955 had fifteen members, now numbers almost a thousand.

Asociación de Muchachas Guías de El Salvador became an Associate Member of the World Association of Girl Guides and Girl Scouts at WAGGGS' 17th World Conference (Greece, 1960) and a Full Member at WAGGGS' 22nd World Conference (U.K., 1975).

PUBLICATIONS

El Salvador's publications include a magazine *Tahuil* ('Light'), a Guiders' manual in Spanish, programmes for the three branches, and a booklet of the bye-laws of the Association.

TRAINING

Attendance of Trainers from El Salvador at regional Training Seminars at Our Cabaña and national Training events in neighbouring countries have been helpful to the Association and there has been an improvement in the standard of training of Guiders. The National Training Committee (CODECAP) is extremely active and during the last few years it has aimed not only at working with Guiders and Committee Members but also at giving general informative talks on the Movement to university students, parents and the community in general.

SERVICE

Recognizing the potential contribution of Guiding as an educational movement to the development in Latin America, an emphasis has been placed on forming Guide Companies in slum areas. A national seminar on 'Guiding and the Process of Development in El Salvador' was held in 1974. Population was one of the topics discussed at this seminar, and a delegate from El Salvador represented the World Association at the International Youth Population Conference and the World Population Conference in Bucharest in 1974.

In 1974 the Association launched a literacy programme in the public markets in the capital city and Rangers and Guiders have had a very successful result. The number of Rangers who serve as Teachers has increased and there has been a marked interest in the women who receive classes right at the market place, in special areas secured for this purpose.

In 1976 UNESCO gave the Association a grant towards this literacy programme.

Salvadorean Guiders have also carried out a recreation project for handicapped children, and furthermore, the Association operates regular troops in the School for the Blind.

The Association has also been involved in programmes of environmental protection and conservation.

Guías de El Salvador support the UNICEF Children's Drawing Competition and promote the sale of UNICEF greeting cards annually.

Ethiopia

Girl Scout Section of the Scouts Association of Ethiopia

GIRL SCOUT

Promise

On investiture, a Girl Scout shall make the following Promise:
On my honour I promise that I will do my best,
To do my duty to God and my Country,
To help other people at all times,
To obey the Girl Scout Law.

Law

1. A Girl Scout's honour is to be trusted.
2. A Girl Scout is loyal to her country, her Scouters, her parents, her employers and those under her.
3. A Girl Scout's duty is to be useful and to help others.
4. A Girl Scout is a friend to all and a sister to every other Girl Scout no matter to what country, community or religion the other may belong.
5. A Girl Scout is courteous.
6. A Girl Scout is friendly to animals.
7. A Girl Scout obeys orders of her parents, patrol leader or her Scouter without question.
8. A Girl Scout is cheerful and courageous in all difficulties.
9. A Girl Scout is thrifty.
10. A Girl Scout is clean in thought, word and deed.

Brownie Promise

On investiture, a Brownie shall make the following Promise:
I promise to do my best,
To do my duty to God and my Country,
To help other people every day,
especially those at home.

Girl Scouting started in Ethiopia in 1946 in the schools as part of the activities of the Scouts Association of Ethiopia. In 1966 a World Association Adviser went to Ethiopia to help form the Girl Scout Section of the Scouts Association of Ethiopia, and in the same year the Girl Scout section was recognized as an Associate Member of WAGGGS at the 19th World Conference (Japan, 1966).

STRUCTURE

There is a National Committee for Girl Scouts which is responsible for the programme and activities of the Girls' Section. The Scout Association as a whole is governed by a National Council and managed by a National Executive Board which is representative of both the Girls' and the Boys' Sections.

DEVELOPMENT OF THE MOVEMENT

Between 1968 and 1971 Ethiopia was regularly visited by a World Association Trainer who trained 136 Leaders and prepared ten of them for trainers' courses. Since then Leaders from Ethiopia have also visited Greece for further training.

The Association, which has its Headquarters in Addis Ababa, also has a permanent campsite where camps and trainings are held. Companies in remote parts of the country are reached by a mobile training unit. Numbers in the Association are steadily increasing and there are now more than 500 Girl Scout Leaders in Ethiopia.

The Association undertakes various community service projects, including nutrition and child care, hygiene and first-aid courses, home economics training in rural areas and literacy courses for out-of-school children. The Girl Scout Section of the Association has been involved in emergency relief action, e.g. in drought-stricken areas in 1973–4 and has participated in activities for International Women's Year, 1975.

Finland

Suomen Partiotyttöjärjestö – Finlands Flickscoutunion r.y.

GUIDE

Partiolupaus *Finnish*

Tahdon rakastaa jumalaani ja lähimmäistäni,
isänmaatani ja ihmiskuntaa
toteuttaen elämässäni
partioihanteita.

Promise

I will love my God and my neighbour,
my native country and mankind
by fulfilling the Girl Guide ideals in my life.

Scoutlöftet *Swedish*

Jag vill älska min Gud och min nästa,
mitt land och mänskligheten,
i det jag söker förverkliga
scoutidealen i mitt liv.

Partioihanteet *Finnish*	Ideals
Partiolaisen ihanteena on	The ideal of a Girl Guide is . . .
– kehittää itseään ihmisenä	– to develop herself as a human being
– kunnioittaa toista ihmistä	– to respect other human beings
– auttaa ja palvella muita	– to help and serve others
– tuntea vastuunsa ja velvollisuutensa	– to recognize her responsibility and duties
– rakastaa ja suojella luontoa	– to love and protect nature
– olla uskollinen ja luotettava	– to be faithful and reliable
– rakentaa ystävyyttä yli rajojen	– to build friendships across borders
– etsiä elämän totuutta.	– to seek for the truth in life.

Scoutidealen *Swedish*

En scouts ideal är . . .
– att utveckla sig själv som människa,
– att känna aktning för andra,
– att hjälpa och tjäna sin nästa,
– att inse sitt ansvar och sina plikter,
– att älska och skydda naturen,
– att vara trofast och pålitlig,
– att främja vänskap över gränserna,
– att söka sanningen i tillvaron.

Motto

Finnish	*Swedish*
Ole valmis	Var redo

Be Prepared

BROWNIE

Brownie Promise

Finnish	*Swedish*
Lupaan koettaa rakastaa Jumalaa ja Suomi-kotia sekä auttaa muita ihmisiä, varsinkin kotiväkeäni, joka päivä.	Jag vill älska Gud och mitt fosterland, jag vill vara hjälpsam mot andra.

I promise to do my best to love God and my country, and to help other people every day, especially those at home.

Brownie Law

Finnish	*Swedish*
Tonttu puhuu totta ja tottelee, on hyödyski ja iloksi muille.	En tomte är lydig och sann, och till nytta och glädje för andra.

A Brownie speaks the truth and is obedient, is useful and a joy to others.

Brownie Motto

Finnish	*Swedish*
Tahdon tehdä parhaani	Jag vill göra mitt bästa

I will do my best

Age Groups

Name	Section		Age
Tarpoja (*Finnish*) Seniorscout (*Swedish*)	Ranger	Senior groups 17–21 Junior groups 15–17	15–21
Partiolainen (*Finnish*) Flickscout (*Swedish*)	Guide		10/11–15
Tonttu (*Finnish*) Tomte (*Swedish*)	Brownie		7–10

Finland's first Girl Guide company was formed in 1910, but the years that followed saw great political upheaval eventually resulting in a ban on Guiding. The Movement was officially revived in 1917, and from that time onwards went from strength to strength. Brownie packs were started in 1925 and the Association was recognized as a Founder Member of the World Association in 1928. The first Ranger company was formed in 1930 and Guiding for the handicapped was introduced in 1934.

The fast-growing interest in the Movement meant that before long there were five active Guide Associations in Finland. The Second World War created the need for closer co-operation and in 1943 a single Association, the Union of Finnish Girl Guides, was established.

Today the Union of Finnish Girl Guides works in very close co-operation with the Finnish Scout Union. In 1972 the two Unions concluded a formal Agreement of Co-operation. As a result most of the administration, for national events and trainings, is a combined undertaking, and many of the Girl Guide and Boy Scout districts also work together or in close co-operation. At the local level most companies are still working separately. After a careful study carried out in 1973 on the development of Girl Guiding and Boy Scouting in Finland, a long-term planning system for activities and finance was established, the Agreement of Co-operation was extended, the two Unions were reorganized and new plans were made for strengthening fund raising and public relations. Since the autumn of 1974 Girl Guides and Boy Scouts have had the same programme.

PROGRAMME

The programme, which stresses the development of the total personality, forms a whole, from the Cub/Brownie stage to the Ranger/Rover stage, with seven sections within each stage. These comprise: 1 outdoor activities and sports; 2 Girl Guiding/Boy Scouting in relation to society as a whole; 3 service; 4 principles and ideals of Girl Guiding/Boy Scouting; 5 knowledge of nature and conservation; 6 creativity and self-expression; 7 resourcefulness.

TRAINING

Trainings are held on all levels, arranged by the districts or by the Union. Special trainings for patrol leaders and Guiders include various Guide skills, outdoor life, administration, psychology of leadership, citizenship and cultural education.

There are gatherings on the national level for Guides, patrol leaders, Rangers and Guiders; nowadays many of the gatherings are joint.

CAMPING AND OUTDOOR ACTIVITIES

Camping, including pioneering, games and cross-country competitions, has always been considered the highlight of Girl Guiding/Boy Scouting activities in Finland.

A 7–10 days' camp under canvas is usually on the annual schedule of each company. The camps are held in the woods near a lake or the sea. Companies, patrols and Rangers also go for Sunday outings during terms and for overnight hikes during holidays. With regular intervals there are district camps, training camps for leaders and the international 'Camp of the Four Winds'. Ranger trainings are also held in Lapland during the skiing season.

PUBLIC RELATIONS

Very conscious of the importance of presenting a positive image, the new Association is endeavouring to use all available channels to promote the image of Girl Guiding and Boy Scouting and to secure the finance necessary for the organization of their various activities.

CO-OPERATION WITH OTHER ORGANIZATIONS

The Finnish Girl Guides and Boy Scouts co-operate closely with UNICEF and publicize UNICEF's work through the Girl Guide/Boy Scout magazine *Partio* and their other publications.

SERVICE

In line with its emphasis on service, the Association has helped establish workshops for the mentally handicapped. Guide units now exist in schools for the handicapped and in 1974 handicapped Guides attended a national camp for the first time.

Early in 1975 the Girl Guides and Boy Scouts participated in a fund-raising campaign for disabled war-veterans.

France

Scoutisme Féminin Français

L'ASSOCIATION DES ECLAIREUSES ET ECLAIREURS DE FRANCE

GUIDE

Promesse	**Promise**
L'une des deux formules est à choisir selon les convictions personnelles:	*One of these two versions is to be chosen, according to personal convictions:*
Je promets sur mon honneur de faire tous mes efforts pour: servir mon pays et l'amitié entre les hommes, rendre service en toute occasion, vivre notre Loi.	I promise on my honour to do my best to: serve my country and promote friendship among men, help others at all times and to live our Law.
ou	*or*
Je promets sur mon honneur, avec l'aide de Dieu, de faire tous mes efforts pour:	With God's help, I promise on my honour to do my best to:

servir mon pays et l'amitié entre les hommes, rendre service en tout occasion, vivre notre Loi.	serve my country and promote friendship among men, help others at all times and to live our Law.
Loi	**Law**
L'Eclaireuse	A Girl Scout
1 est loyale.	is sincere.
2 est propre, maîtrise ses paroles et ses actes.	is neat, controls her words and deeds.
3 sourit, même dans les difficultés.	smiles even under difficulties.
4 aime le travail et l'effort, ne fait rien à moitié.	likes to work and does not fear endeavour, does nothing by halves.
5 se rend utile.	makes herself useful.
6 sait obéir, et agit en équipe.	knows how to obey and has the team spirit.
7 respecte le travail et le bien de tous.	is considerate of other people's work and property.
8 écoute les autres et respecte leurs convictions.	listens to others and respects their convictions.
9 pratique la fraternité scoute.	practices Guide friendship.
10 aime et protège la nature et la vie.	loves nature and life and protects them.

Motto

Toujours prête	Always ready
à rendre joyeusement le service qui t'est demandé,	to render service willingly,
à prendre une décision,	to make a decision,
à decouvrir et à agir.	to discover and to act.

BROWNIE

Brownie Promise

Selon ses croyances et le désir de ses parents, le louveteau choisit l'une des deux formules suivantes:	*According to her own convictions and her parents' wishes, the Brownie chooses one of the two Promises:*
Je promets de faire de mon mieux pour obéir à la Loi des Louveteaux	I promise to do my best to obey the Brownie's Law.
ou	*or*
Je promets, avec l'aide de Dieu, de faire de mon mieux pour obéir à la Loi des Louveteaux.	With God's help, I promise to do my best to obey the Brownie's Law.

Brownie Law

Un louveteau dit vrai.	A Brownie speaks the truth.
Un louveteau obéit aux maîtres-mots de l'unité.	A Brownie obeys the 'pass word' of the pack.
Un louveteau cherche à faire plaisir aux autres.	A Brownie seeks to please others.

Brownie Motto

De notre mieux	Of our best

Age Groups

Branche aînée	Ranger	15/16–21
Branche moyenne (éclaireuse)	Guide	11–15/16
Branche cadette (louveteau)	Brownie	8–11

L'ASSOCIATION DES ECLAIREUSES ET ECLAIREURS ISRAELITES DE FRANCE

GUIDE

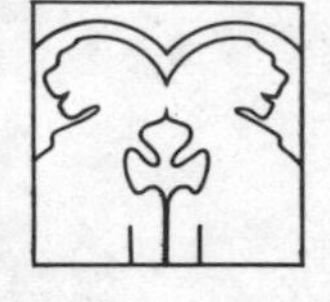

Promesse

Je m'engage à vivre la Loi des EEIF.

Promise

I take upon myself to live the Law of the EEIF.

Loi

L'E.I. participe à le vie de son groupe, des Communautés dans lesquelles (il, elle) vit en assumant sa part de responsabilités.
L'E.I. apprend à comprendre son prochain et le respecte.
L'E.I. fait face aux difficultés.
L'E.I. développe ses qualités morales et physiques.
L'E.I. découvre, aime et protège la nature.
L'E.I. s'efforce d'acquérir des connaissances nouvelles, d'étudier la Tora.

Law

The E.I. joins in the life of her group, in the Communities in which (he, she) lives by sharing in its responsibilities.
The E.I. learns to understand others and to respect them.
The E.I. faces up to difficulties.
The E.I. develops her moral and physical qualities.
The E.I. discovers, loves and protects nature.
The E.I. tries to acquire new knowledge and to study the Tora.

CUB

Cub Promise

Une louvette persévère dans ses efforts et progresse dans sa vie juive.

A Cub perseveres in her efforts and enters ever more deeply into the Jewish way of life.

Cub Law

Une louvette prend conseil auprès de ses aînées et participe à la vie de la Meute.

A Cub seeks advice from her seniors and enters into the life of the Pack.

Age Groups

Branche aînée	Ranger	17+
Branche perspective	'Perspective'	15–17
Branche moyenne (éclaireuse)	Intermediate (Girl Scout)	11–15
Branche cadette (louvette)	Junior (Cub)	8–11

GUIDE AND BROWNIE

ECLAIREUSES ET ECLAIREURS UNIONISTES DE FRANCE

Promesse

Je promets de faire tout mon possible pour écouter la parole de Dieu.
Pour me mettre au service des autres.

Promise

I promise to do my best to listen to the word of God.
To devote myself to the service of others.

Loi

Une Eclaireuse essaie de comprendre les autres pour les aimer et les aider.

Elle essaie de connaître le monde dans lequel elle vit pour y prendre ses responsabilités.
Elle est exigeante avec elle-même.
Elle s'efforce de vivre sa loi jusqu'au bout.

Law

A Girl Scout tries to understand others in order to be able to love and help them.
She tries to get to know the world in which she is living in order to take her share of its responsibilities.
She is exacting with herself.
She endeavours to live the Law fully.

Motto

Sois prête

Be Prepared

Brownie Promise

Avec les autres louvettes, petites ailes, louveteaux de . . . (nom de l'unité).
je promets de faire de mon mieux pour vivre la Loi de notre unité.

With all the other Cubs/Brownies of . . . (name of unit).

I promise to do my best to live the Law of our unit.

Brownie Law

Une petite aile, une louvette fait de son mieux pour . . .
(Elaborée par les enfants et les cheftaines au cours du Conseil de l'Unité, cette Loi est l'émanation du groupe, c'est la règle du jeu que se donne l'unité.)

A Brownie/Cub does her best to . . .

(Formulated by the children and leaders during a meeting of the Unit's Council, this Law expresses the feeling of the group, it is the rule of the game which the Unit sets up for its own guidance.)

Brownie Motto

Prêter la main

Lend a hand

Age Groups

Branche aînée	Ranger	15–18
Branche moyenne (éclaireuse)	Intermediate (Girl Scout)	12–15
Branche cadette (petite aile ou louvette)	Junior (Brownie or Cub)	8–11

LES GUIDES DE FRANCE

Promesse

Avec vous,
Confiante en Dieu qui m'aime,
Je promets de faire tout mon possible pour rendre les autres heureux,
Pour être utile à mon pays et vivre selon la Loi de toutes les guides du monde.

Promise

With you,
Trusting in God who loves me,
I promise to do my best to make others happy,
serve my country and to live in accordance with the Law of all Guides throughout the world.

GUIDE

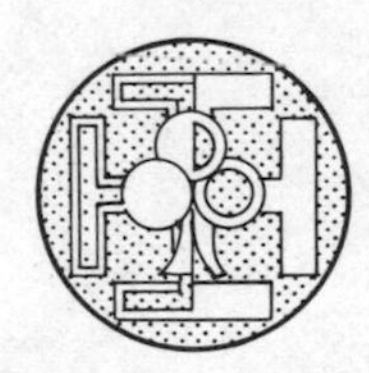

Loi	Law
1 La guide est loyale.	A Guide is loyal.
2 La guide pense d'abord aux autres.	A Guide thinks first of others.
3 La guide est généreuse; elle est prête à servir.	A Guide is generous; she is prepared to help.
4 La guide est accueillante; elle a l'esprit d'équipe.	A Guide is friendly; she has the team spirit.
5 La guide, sœur de toute autre guide, est présente à tous.	A Guide, sister to every other Guide, is available to all.
6 La guide découvre la nature; elle y voit l'œuvre de Dieu.	A Guide explores nature in which she sees the work of God.
7 La guide sait obéir.	A Guide knows how to obey.
8 La guide ne craint pas l'effort; elle ne fait rien à moitié.	A Guide does not fear endeavour; she does nothing by halves.
9 La guide aime son travail et respecte celui des autres.	A Guide likes her work and respects that of others.
10 La guide est maîtresse de soi; elle est pure et joyeuse.	A Guide practises self-control; she is pure and cheerful.

Motto

Toujours prête	Always ready

BROWNIE

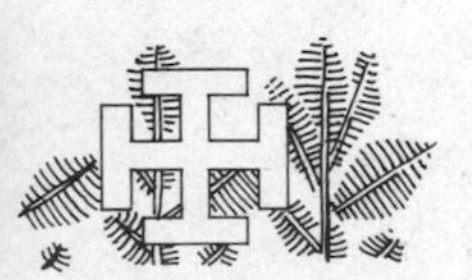

Brownie Promise

Je promets de faire de mon mieux	I promise to do my best,
Pour aimer Dieu,	To love God,
Connaître mon pays,	Know my country,
Dire oui à la loi de la Ronde,	Accept the law of the Pack,
Pour faire chaque jour un plaisir à quelqu'un,	To do a good turn to someone every day,
Et apporter la joie à la maison.	And bring joy into my home.

Brownie Law

Une jeannette est toujours propre.	A Brownie is always neat.
Une jeannette est toujours active.	A Brownie is always active.
Une jeannette est toujours gaie.	A Brownie is always cheerful.
Une jeannette dit toujours vrai.	A Brownie always tells the truth.
Une jeannette pense d'abord aux autres.	A Brownie thinks first of others.

Brownie Motto

De notre mieux	Of our best

Age Groups

Jeunes en marche	'Youth on the Move'	17+
Branche caravelle	'Caravelle'	15–16
Branche guide	Guide	12–14
Branche jeannette	Brownie	8–11

When the World Association of Girl Guides and Girl Scouts was established in 1928, France was recognized as one of its Founder Members.

Today Scoutisme Féminin Français is made up of four component associations: Les Guides de France; the female members of Les Eclaireuses et Eclaireurs de France; les Eclaireuses et Eclaireurs Unionistes de France; and les Eclaireuses et Eclaireurs Israélites de France. Each association strives to meet the needs of young people whatever their origin, class or religion. Each tries constantly to improve its methods, adapting them to keep in line with the current educational needs of its members.

Over the past ten years much work has gone into experiments and surveys in an effort to find the future direction of the Movement in France. Members are informed of progress made and conclusions arrived at through the various publications of the associations in France.

All four associations are actively involved in service to the community. Their service projects include literacy classes, work with the handicapped (France has numerous extension units) and with migrant families. They are also involved in projects to safeguard the environment. The Scoutisme Féminin Français also encourages international understanding and promotes international training at all levels. An example of this was the seminar on 'The Role of Girl Guiding/Girl Scouting in European Migration' held in Strasbourg and organized in co-operation with the European Youth Centre, Strasbourg.

L'ASSOCIATION DES ECLAIREUSES ET ECLAIREURS DE FRANCE

The Eclaireuses et Eclaireurs de France have been involved in studies on the aims of the Association, discussed by study groups at all levels, and on group leadership training, studies which have led to the drawing up and putting into operation of a new programme on sex education, moral training, the environment and creativity.

At the same time, true to its fundamental choices (democracy, openness to others, co-education) the Movement has continued to press:

- for greater participation of young people (Leaders and Rangers/Seniors) in the policy-making meetings of the Movement;
- for welcoming an increasing number of young non-Guides to camps;
- for the development of the branch for educationally subnormal children;
- for nature conservation, discussed at the national or local meetings;
- for a deepening of international relationships and an increase in projects to aid developing countries.

L'ASSOCIATION DES ECLAIREUSES ET ECLAIREURS ISRAELITES DE FRANCE

Several changes have been made over the past ten years.

1 New structures and age groups have been established
   - Cubs, Brownies (8–11 years) constituting the Junior branch (mixed)
   - Girl and Boy Scouts (12–15 years) representing the Intermediate branch (co-education)
   - The 'Perspectives' teams (15–17 years) teenager branch (mixed)
   - The Senior branch of the Movement (over 17) (mixed) which also includes the Leaders.

2 A reformulation of the Promise and Law for each branch, as well as a name which is more relevant to the Movement's methods of operation. Thus, the names 'Scouter' and 'Guider' have been replaced by those of 'organizer' and 'executive'.
3 Training: the Association's main aim in recent years has been leadership training. There have been more courses and the programmes have devoted a great deal of time to current psycho-educational methods, to the study of contemporary problems and to really living the Jewish way of life.

At present the tendency of the 'Perspective' and 'Senior' Teams is to play a much larger part in the community and to undertake service which will benefit the greater number of young non-Guides and non-Scouts.

ECLAIREUSES ET ECLAIREURS UNIONISTES DE FRANCE

In 1971 the Fédération Française des Eclaireuses Unionistes merged with the Eclaireurs Unionistes de France to become a federation called Eclaireuses et Eclaireurs Unionistes de France.

In 1972 the federation published training manuals for Leaders. In 1973 the National Council held a meeting for all Leaders in Grenoble, and in 1976 the federation organized 'Horizon '76', an interprovincial exchange programme.

LES GUIDES DE FRANCE

The Guides de France have recently carried out a survey in an effort to assess what progress has been made since their reorganization in 1966. By means of a questionnaire and interview they were able to get a clear picture of units, structure, leadership recruitment, motivation, needs in the training field, etc. This information it is hoped will enable them to achieve the progress suggested at each stage of Guide life.

GUIDES AND CARAVELLES

In 1974, 2,500 delegates of the Guide Branch worked for three days with representatives of fifteen other countries, while in eight towns throughout France the Caravelle Branch carried out service projects based on the needs of the community.

BROWNIES

The Guides de France organized a very successful Brownie Festival in eighty different regions of France in 1976. Thousands of Brownies took part in what was aptly named 'L'enfant aux mains de fête' (the child with joyful hands).

INTERNATIONAL CENTRE

Each summer the Mélan International Centre welcomes young people from all over the world offering them a choice of interesting programmes.

FUTURE PROJECTS

Future projects include a gathering of Young People on the Move planned for Easter 1978.

HANDICAPPED

The Guides de France section for the handicapped has extended its activities to work with the mentally handicapped. They now publish a special magazine *Pour Toi* which aims to help the mentally retarded adolescent through drawings.

INTERNATIONAL WOMEN'S YEAR

The Guides de France were active in promoting International Women's Year events, and a member of the association led WAGGGS' delegation at the East Berlin IWY World Congress.

PUBLICATIONS

Among the Association's interesting and informative publications are *Cap Levant* and *Guide de France*.

The Gambia

The Gambia Girl Guides Association

GUIDE

Promise

I promise on my honour that I will
do my best:
To do my duty to God, and my country;
To help other people at all times;
and
To obey the Guide Law.

Law

1 A Guide's honour is to be trusted.
2 A Guide is loyal.
3 A Guide's duty is to be useful and to help others.
4 A Guide is a friend to all and a sister to every other Guide.
5 A Guide is courteous.
6 A Guide is a friend to animals.
7 A Guide obeys orders.
8 A Guide smiles and sings under all difficulties.
9 A Guide is thrifty.
10 A Guide is pure in thought, word and deed.

Motto

Be Prepared

BROWNIE

Brownie Promise

I promise to do my best to do my duty to
God, and my country; to help other people
every day, especially those at home.

Brownie Law

A Brownie gives in to the older folk.
A Brownie does not give in to herself.

Brownie Motto

Lend a Hand

Age Groups

Guide	12–18
Brownie	7–11

There have been Girl Guides in Gambia since 1926, but it was not until 1957 that the Movement became firmly established. Guiding has expanded steadily ever since. In 1966 The Gambia Girl Guides Association joined the World Association of Girl Guides and Girl Scouts when the 19th World Conference in Japan welcomed Gambia as an Associate Member.

STRUCTURE AND PROGRAMME

The Association is administered by a National Council which meets every month, while a National Assembly meets annually.

Guide and Brownie programmes are based on those used in the U.K., but adapted to meet the interests of Gambian children. There is a real enthusiasm for Girl Guiding in Gambia among both the Council members and the girls, and new companies and packs are organized not only in urban areas but in settlements in the provinces as well.

SERVICE

The Association is a member of the National Youth Council, and alongside other voluntary organizations joins in service to the community. Girl Guides in Gambia are very much aware of the existing needs and try, whenever possible, to meet them by giving material assistance to the poor and the sick, and helping on various public occasions.

FUND-RAISING

An International Dinner is held annually for which residents from other countries contribute national dishes, tickets are sold to the public, and the proceeds go to Guide funds. Other methods of raising money include a sponsored walk and sales of food and vegetables. Plans are even being made to organize a 'midnight picnic' with music, dancing and a meal to which the public will be invited.

Germany

Ring Deutscher Pfadfinderinnenverbände

GUIDE

VERBAND CHRISTLICHER PFADFINDERINNEN UND PFADFINDER

Leitwort und Versprechen

Gott will, dass wir sein Eigentum werden zum Lobe seiner Herrlichkeit.

Principle and Promise

God wants us to become His in praise of His glory.

Im Vertrauen auf Gottes Hilfe bin ich bereit, mit meinen Gaben Gott zu dienen, meinem Nächsten zu helfen und meine Kräfte verantwortlich in Gesellschaft und Kirche einzusetzen.

Trusting in God's help I am prepared to serve God with my talents, to help my neighbour and to act responsibly in the service of society and the Church.

BROWNIE

Grundsatz der Ordnung

Die evangelische Pfadfinderin richtet ihr Leben aus an Jesus Christus, der allein das Wollen und Vollbringen schenkt.

Principles of Law

The Protestant Girl Guide models her life on Jesus Christ, who alone gives purpose and fulfilment.

Gemeinsam mit allen Pfadfinderinnen der Welt gilt für sie die Ordnung:

1 Wir wollen aufrichtig sein.
2 Wir wollen zuverlässig sein.
3 Wir wollen dankbar sein.
4 Wir wollen zuversichtlich und frölich sein.
5 Wir wollen Schwierigkeiten nicht ausweichen.
6 Wir wollen helfe, wo wir gebraucht werden.
7 Wir wollen mit dem, was uns anvertraut ist, verantwortlich umgehen.
8 Wir wollen die Natur kennenlernen und schützen.
9 Wir wollen den anderen achten.
10 Wir wollen in unserer Umgebung Frieden schaffen.

In common with all Girl Guides in the world, she obeys the Law:

We strive to be honest.
We strive to be trustworthy.
We strive to be grateful.
We strive to be confident and cheerful.
We strive not to evade difficulties.
We strive to help where we are needed.
We strive to treat responsibly what is entrusted to us.
We strive to know and protect nature.
We strive to respect others.
We strive to create peace around us.

Motto

Allzeit Bereit

Be Prepared

BUND DER PFADFINDERINNEN UND PFADFINDER, e.V.

GUIDE

Guide and Scout Promise

Ich will, im Vertrauen auf Gottes Hilfe, nach den Regeln der Pfadfinderinnen und Pfadfinder mit Euch leben.
(Das Versprechen kann auch ohne religiöse Formel abgelegt werden.)

With confidence in God's help, I promise to live with you in accordance with the Guide and Scout Law.
(The Promise can be given without the religious formulation.)

Guide and Scout Laws

Ich will hilfsbereit und rücksichtsvoll sein.
Ich will den anderen achten.
Ich will zur Freundschaft aller Pfadfinder und Pfadfinderinnen beitragen.
Ich will aufrichtig und zuverlässig sein.

I will be helpful and considerate.
I will be respectful.
I will be a friend to all Guides and Scouts.
I will be honest and trustworthy.

Ich will kritisch sein und Verantwortung übernehmen.
I will use my own judgement and assume responsibilities.

Ich will Schwiergkeiten nicht ausweichen.
I will not avoid difficulties.

Ich will die Natur kennenlernen und helfen, sie zu erhalten.
I will acquaint myself with nature and help to conserve it.

Ich will mich beherrschen.
I will become master of myself.

Ich will dem Frieden dienen und mich für die Gemeinschaft einsetzen, in der ich lebe.
I will serve peace and the community I live in.

BROWNIE

Brownie and Cub Promise

Ich will ein guter Freund sein und unsere Regeln achten.
I will be a good friend and respect our rules.

Brownie and Cub Rules

Ein Wichtel (Wölfling) nimmt Rücksicht auf andere.
A Brownie (Cub) is considerate.

Ein Wichtel (Wölfling) hilft wo es kann.
A Brownie (Cub) helps wherever she can.

PFADFINDERINNENSCHAFT ST. GEORG

GUIDE

Versprechen

Ich verspreche, mein Bestes zu tun, um Gott in meinem Leben zu erkennen, in der Gemeinschaft, in der ich lebe, mitverantwortlich zu handeln und die Spielregeln der Pfadfinderinnen zu beachten.

Promise

I promise to do my best, to recognize God in my life, to engage myself with responsibility in the community I live in, and to observe the rules of the Guides.

Gesetz

Die Pfadfinderin ist aufrichtig, man kann ihr vertrauen.
Die Pfadfinderin lernt, sich zu beherrschen.
Die Pfadfinderin bemüht sich, aus dem Glauben zu leben und übernimmt Verantwortung in Kirche und Gesellschaft.
Die Pfadfinderin versucht, den anderen zu verstehen.
Die Pfadfinderin kann sich in eine Gemeinschaft einordnen und ist zur Zusammenarbeit bereit.
Die Pfadfinderin weicht Schwierigkeiten nicht aus.
Die Pfadfinderin hilft, wo sie kann und tritt Unrecht entgegen.
Die Pfadfinderin lernt teilen und dankbar zu sein.
Die Pfadfinderin entdeckt die Natur und schützt das Leben.

Law

The Guide is sincere, she can be trusted.
The Guide learns to control herself.
The Guide strives to live by her faith and to accept responsibility within the Church and society.
The Guide tries to understand others.
The Guide is able to fit into a community and is prepared to co-operate.
The Guide does not avoid difficulties.
The Guide helps, where she can, and opposes injustice.
The Guide learns to share and to be grateful.
The Guide discovers nature and protects life.

BROWNIE

Brownie Promise

Ich will mein Bestes tun, um Gott und meine Eltern zu lieben und dem Wichtelgesetz zu gehorchen.	I will do my best to love God and my parents and to obey the Brownie Law.

Brownie Law

Das Wichtel denkt zuerst an andere.	The Brownie thinks first of others.
Das Wichtel öffnet Augen und Ohren.	The Brownie opens her eyes and ears.
Das Wichtel ist frölich.	The Brownie is joyful.
Das Wichtel ist sauber.	The Brownie is clean.
Das Wichtel geht mit gutem Beispiel voran.	The Brownie gives a good example.

Brownie Motto

Ich will mein Bestes tun	I will do my best

Age Groups

Ranger	Ranger	15+
Pfadfinderin	Guide	11–15
Wichtel	Brownie	7–11

Ring Deutscher Pfadfinderinnenverbände (the Union of German Girl Guide Associations) was recognized as an Associate Member of the World Association in 1950 at the 13th World Conference in Oxford in the United Kingdom following the federation in 1949 of three separate Girl Guides Associations. These Associations were: (i) the Bund Deutscher Pfadfinderinnen open to all girls, (ii) the Evangelischer Mädchenpfadfinderbund with the Bund Christlicher Pfadfinderinnen (only in Bavaria) which was open to all Protestant girls, and (iii) the Pfadfinderinnenschaft St. Georg open to all Roman Catholic girls.

The Union of German Girl Guide Associations became a Full Member of WAGGGS at the 15th World Conference held in the Netherlands in 1954.

In 1973 the Evangelischer Mädchenpfadfinderbund, the Bund Christlicher Pfadfinderinnen and the Christliche Pfadfinderschaft Deutschlands (Protestant Boy Scouts) amalgamated and are now a merged association known as Verband Christlicher Pfadfinderinnen und Pfadfinder (VCP). In 1976 the Bund Deutscher Pfadfinderinnen and the Bund der Pfadfinder merged and are known as Bund der Pfadfinderinnen und Pfadfinder e.V. (BdP), open to all girls and boys.

CAMPING AND TRAINING

Camping is very popular in Germany, and national and international camps are held every year in different parts of the country. A network of training centres and Guide homes provides excellent training facilities for members of all Associations.

SERVICE

The problems presented by the immigrant population in Germany are of special interest to the Union, and Leaders receive specific training to equip them for their work with this marginal group. The Union holds camps for migrant children and publicizes the problems of migrants in its magazines.

Guides and Rangers also help out in hospitals, visit the old and the sick in their homes and look after the welfare of girls and women in prisons.

VERBAND CHRISTLICHER PFADFINDERINNEN UND PFADFINDER

The VCP is a Protestant Merged Association for girls and boys of all denominations. Most of the groups are mixed at all age levels and all Leadership Training is carried out on a co-educational basis.

The question of faith plays an important part in the programme of the VCP and, apart from specific Guide and Scout activities, the Association lays particular emphasis on service to the community. There is a broad range of activities, mainly organized at regional level, such as working with marginal groups, campaigning for the rights of children in society, aiding community development, etc. Decisions are arrived at democratically through a system which offers members at all levels real opportunities to express their opinions. Through a special voting system, every member participates in the decision making at the Annual General Meeting of the VCP.

On the international level, the Association maintains close contacts with the other European Guide and Scout Associations.

BUND DER PFADFINDERINNEN UND PFADFINDER e.V.

The BdP is an interdenominational Merged Association founded on 1 January 1976, open to all girls and boys. This move was preceded by 3 years of intensive work on statutes, pedagogical concepts and the Training programme. There are now mixed leader teams at all levels, but local groups have the right to decide whether they wish to work in mixed or separate groupings. A national camp with participation of visitors from many other countries was the first large event organized by the merged Association and the highlight of 1977.

PFADFINDERINNENSCHAFT ST. GEORG

The most important event held in recent years has been the congress 'Spiral 1976', a meeting essentially geared towards the problems of adolescence, the opportunities open to young people and their potential contribution to a more just world.

The PSG's new section which co-operates with the Catholic Boy Scout Association (DPSG) in projects to help developing countries, has had much success and is an example of the new partnership-basis on which work is now conducted.

As a member of the Bund der Deutschen Katholischen Jugend (German Catholic Youth Movement), the PSG co-operates closely with other organizations working in the field of youth. It is also a member of various regional youth movements as well as the Union of German Youth Associations (Deutscher Bundes-Jugend-Ring DBJR) and the International Catholic Conference of Guiding (ICCG).

Ghana

The Ghana Girl Guides Association

GUIDE

Promise

I promise that I will do my best:
To do my duty to God;
To serve my country and help other people; and
To keep the Guide Law.

Law

1 A Guide is loyal and can be trusted.
2 A Guide is helpful.
3 A Guide is polite and considerate.
4 A Guide is friendly and a sister to all Guides.
5 A Guide is kind to animals and respects all living things.
6 A Guide is obedient.
7 A Guide has courage and is cheerful in all difficulties.
8 A Guide makes good use of her time.
9 A Guide takes care of her own possessions and those of other people.
10 A Guide is self-controlled in all she thinks, says and does.

Motto

Be Prepared

ANANSE GUIDE

Ananse Guide Promise

I promise that I will do my best:
To do my duty to God;
To serve my country and help other people; and
To keep the Ananse Guide Law.

Ananse Guide Law

An Ananse Guide is truthful, obedient and cheerful.
And thinks of others before herself.

Ananse Guide Motto

Always ready to help

Age Groups

Cadet	Girl in Training College
Ranger Guide	15–21
Girl Guide	10–15
Ananse Guide	8–10

Guiding was officially launched in 1921 in Accra where the Guide Headquarters was built in 1930. Over the twenty years that followed, Guiding spread to towns and villages all over the country. Since 1954 Cadet companies have been established in most of the women's training colleges. The Ghana Girl Guides Association was recognized as an Associate Member of the World Association in 1960 and as a Full Member at the 20th World Conference (Finland, 1969).

PROGRAMME AND TRAINING

Special emphasis is placed on teaching the girls to develop specific skills. Intensive orientation courses are held for adult leaders of the three branches, while opportunities for training are offered to adult leaders at regional and national levels.

CAMPING

Camping is popular in Ghana, and Guides camp both under canvas and in schools and colleges. Camps are also held at the Achimota training centre where there is a good campsite. Work camps are becoming increasingly popular with Guides helping with national projects, planting gardens and giving aid to children's homes.

GOLDEN JUBILEE CAMP

The Ghana Girl Guides Association was fifty years old in 1971 and a most successful Golden Jubilee Camp was held at its training centre, Achimota, from 13 to 25 August 1971. This was attended by over 400 Guides from all the nine regions in Ghana; about fifty Guides from other countries represented at the camp were from Upper Volta, Nigeria, the U.S.A., Israel, West Cameroon, Togo, Liberia and Ivory Coast. During the camp the Guides took part in various self-help projects at six nearby villages and helped to put up a clinic, school building and toilet facilities.

CO-OPERATION WITH OTHER ORGANIZATIONS

The Association works in close co-operation with the Ministry of Social Welfare and the National Youth Council in Ghana and is represented at many international conferences.

SERVICE

In response to the government's appeal to 'feed ourselves', Guides throughout the country helped in harvesting. Guides in Sikondi/Takoradi were given a plot of land where they have planted various crops which they maintain.

LITERACY

The Association was briefed by a team of Social and Community Development Officers on how to organize literacy classes. Since then Guides in Kumasi have been holding evening classes for illiterates.

EDUCATION IN POPULATION AWARENESS

The Association organized a national competition on population awareness, and sent a delegate to the International Youth Population Conference in Bucharest.

Greece

Soma Hellinidon Odigon

GUIDE

I Ipóshessi	**Promise**
Ipóshome stin timí mou ná prospathísso:	I promise on my honour to try:
Ná káno to kathíkon mou prós tón Theó ké tín Patrída	To do my duty to God and to my Country.
Ná voïthó ólous pantoú ké pántote.	To help everybody always and everywhere.
Ná ipakoúo stón Nómo tís Odigoú.	To obey the Law of the Guides.

O Nomos	**Law**
1 I Odigós léi ké sévete tín alíthia.	A Guide is truthful. She respects Truth.
2 Tirí toós nómous ké xéri ná pitharchí.	She is law abiding and disciplined.
3 Íne ikani ké próthymi ná phani chríssimi.	She is able and willing to be useful.
4 Íne kali phíli ké íne evghenikí mé ólous.	She is a good friend and courteous to all.
5 Íne aessiódoxi ke próschari.	She is gay and optimistic.
6 Aghapá tí phýssi ké prostatévi tá zóa ké tá phytá.	She loves nature and protects animals and plants.
7 Ergházete efsynídita ké íne synepís.	She is conscientious in her work and reliable.
8 Échi thárros ké psychraemía.	She has courage and does not panic.
9 Íni kalí nicokyrá ké sévete tín idioktyssía tón állon.	She is a good housekeeper and respects the property of others.
10 Íne axioprepís ké elénchi tís sképsis, tá lóghia ké tís práxis tis.	She has dignity and controls her thoughts, words and deeds.

Motto

Ésso Étimi — Be Prepared

BROWNIE

Brownie Promise

Ipóskhome ná prospathísso m'óli mou tí dýnami:	I promise to try as best I can:
Ná íme pistó stó Theó ké stín Patrída.	To do my duty to God and my country.
Ná voithó toús álous pántote ké ná férno ti khará stó spíti mou.	To help other people every day and bring cheerfulness to my home.

Brownie Law

To Pouli ipakoúhi próthyma.	A Brownie: Obeys willingly.
Den Sképtete móno ton eaftó tou ké.	Does not think only of herself.
Aghapá tous álous.	Loves those around her.

Brownie Motto

Dosse kheri — Lend a Hand

Age Groups

Megali Odigos	Ranger	15–20
Odigos	Guide	11–15
Pouli	Brownie (Bird)	7–11

The Guide Movement started in Greece in 1932. After a period of inactivity during the war, it was revived in 1945 and since then has been growing and spreading throughout the country. Greece was recognized as a Full Member of the World Association at the 12th World Conference (U.S.A., 1948). The Guide Movement in Greece has always been encouraged and supported by the Government which values its contribution in the service of the country and the people.

CAMPING AND SERVICE CAMPS

Camping is extremely popular in Greece. Since 1972, 4,606 girls have taken part in more than 100 camps. Ranger Service Camps have been held regularly in underprivileged and isolated areas with the aim of promoting mutual understanding and respect between Guides and the local population. Joint activities organized at the camps include housekeeping, health-care, baby-care, sanitation, nutrition, handicrafts and sports. On occasion Rangers from other countries have joined their Greek counterparts for camps, and Greek Rangers have organized an International Service Camp with 18 representatives from 14 countries.

HANDICAPPED

The development of the extension branch is one of the top priorities of the Association. Handicapped Guides camp regularly every summer, and take part in every competition and activity of the Soma Hellinidon Odigon. A very successful exhibition of handicrafts by handicapped girls was held. The Association operates a lending library of taped books for the blind.

TRAINING

Training courses are held in the National Centre near Athens, as well as in various districts. They cover training for beginners, experienced Guiders, Commissioners and Trainers. Refresher courses and special camp trainings are held regularly. Greek trainers have often been requested to undertake training assignments for the World Association.

The increase in membership has put a heavy burden on national and local leadership. Therefore, top priority is given to training at all levels of responsibilities, experience and age. Mobile training units help to maintain a highly intensified rhythm, especially in rural areas. A total of 7,450 Guiders were trained between January 1972 and December 1974.

P.R. AND PUBLICATIONS

The Association publishes its own handbooks, a monthly bulletin for Guiders and Commissioners, and leaflets for Rangers and Brownies. The Brownie, Guide and Ranger handbooks have been completely revised. Every endeavour is made to keep the public informed on Guiding Activities through the radio, press, exhibitions, films, etc.

INTERNATIONAL RELATIONS

Good international relations are sponsored through participation in international events, organization of such events in Greece, exchange of personnel and the Post Box. Thinking Day is widely promoted and donations to the Thinking Day Fund are encouraged.

PARTICIPATION IN NATIONAL AND INTERNATIONAL EVENTS

The Association participates in world and international events and accepts invitations to international gatherings in Europe and beyond. Greece is regularly represented at World Conferences and took part in the First European Scout and Guide Conference in Iceland in 1974, in the Joint Seminar on Development of Methods in Greece in 1976 and in the Second European Scout and Guide Conference in Ireland in 1977.

OTHER DEVELOPMENTS

The Association has developed very close links with UNICEF and co-operates with the National Council of Youth Organizations.

Greek Guide Troops have been established in Germany and Belgium to cater for emigrants to those countries.

Guatemala

Asociación Nacional de Muchachas Guías de Guatemala

GUIDE

Promesa	**Promise**
Por mi honor, yo prometo hacer cuanto de mi dependa para cumplir mis deberes hacia Dios y mi país, ayudar a mis semejantes en cualquier momento y cumplir las leyes de las Muchachas Guias.	On my honour, I promise to do my best to fulfil my duties to God and my country, help others at all times and carry out the law of the Girl Guides.

Ley	**Law**
1 La guía tiene honor.	A Guide's honour is to be trusted.
2 La guía es leal.	A Guide is loyal.
3 La guía es útil y ayuda a los demás.	A Guide is useful and helps others.
4 La guía es amiga de todas y una hermana para las demás guías.	A Guide is a friend to all and a sister to the other Guides.
5 La guía es cortés.	A Guide is courteous.
6 La guía ama a los animales y plantas.	A Guide loves animals and plants.
7 La guía es obediente.	A Guide is obedient
8 La guía sonrie y canta ante las dificultades.	A Guide smiles and sings under adverse conditions.

9 La guía es económica.	A Guide is thrifty.
10 La guía es pura.	A Guide is pure.

Motto

Siempre lista	Always ready

BROWNIE

Brownie Promise

Yo prometo hacer todo la mejor que me sea posible para cumplir mis deberes hacia Dios y mi Patria, ayudar a todos, todos los días, especialmente a los de mi casa.	I promise to do the best I can to do my duty to God and my country and to help other people every day, especially those at home.

Brownie Law

Una caperucita se deja guiar de sus mayores.	A Brownie allows herself to be guided by older people.
Una caperucita no se guia a si misma	A Brownie does not guide herself.

Brownie Motto

Dar Ayuda	Always helps

Age Groups

Guíadora	Leader	18 and over
Guía Mayor	Ranger	16 and over
Guía Intermedia	Guide	11–15
Caperucita	Brownie	7–10

Girl Guiding started in Guatemala in 1934, and the Girl Guides Association was officially formed in the following year. It became an Associate Member of the World Association at the 16th World Conference (Brazil, 1957) and a Full Member at the 20th World Conference (Finland, 1969).

DEVELOPMENT OF THE MOVEMENT

Guiding exists both in the capital city and the provinces and efforts are being made to introduce the Movement to different social groups. The first Indian Guide company was formed on a coffee farm several years ago; its members receive not only Guide training but also instruction in Spanish. Girl Guide troops are active in a school for blind children which was originally founded by the Guide Association.

The National Assembly, National Council and local committees hold regular meetings and greater emphasis is being put in the programmes on ways of involving older Guides in the work of the Association to ensure the continuity of the Movement.

GUIDE HOUSE

In recognition of the service they gave their country during the revolution of 1944, the Association received a plot of land on which a Guide House and a swimming pool were constructed. Girl Scouts from the U.S.A. and Girl Guides from Central America often stop here on their way to Our Cabaña; the hospitality of the Guide House is also extended to Guatemalan Guides from the provinces visiting the capital, and to adult members of the Movement when they come to the Assemblies. The Guide House also has a shop which sells uniforms and equipment to Guides all over the country.

CAMPS, EXCURSIONS, ETC.

Camping is a popular activity during the school holidays in November and December. The girls also join annual excursions with other Central American Guides to visit Mexico and Our Cabaña. Members of the Movement participate in special conferences and Adventure Weeks and the Association sends delegates to regional and international Girl Guide/Girl Scout events.

In 1972 the Guides of Guatemala were the hostesses of the Pan-American camp attended by participants from six countries of the Western Hemisphere.

SERVICE TO THE COMMUNITY

Service has always been among the chief concerns of the Guide Movement in Guatemala, and the Guides have distinguished themselves in relief work. In the disruption which followed the earthquake of 1976, the Girl Guides of Guatemala provided all kinds of service in the city and outside. Using the funds sent by other Guide Associations around the world, they provided new zinc roofs for the houses of Indian families in some of the villages worst hit by the disaster.

Community projects often feature in the programmes and the Guides are active in work on health and recreation for disadvantaged children.

PUBLICATIONS

The Guides of Guatemala publish a twice-yearly booklet under the title *Faro Guía*. This publication contains information on Girl Guide activities, instruction, articles by the girls, etc. It is distributed free to all members of the Association, and is sent to other Girl Guide/Girl Scout Associations outside Guatemala. More recently, a monthly bulletin entitled *Friendship* has been published by the Association and distributed to all members.

Guyana

The Guyana Girl Guides Association

Promise

I promise that I will do my best:
To do my duty to God;
To servé my country and help other people; and
To keep the Guide Law.

GUIDE

Law

1 A Guide is loyal and can be trusted.
2 A Guide is helpful.
3 A Guide is polite and considerate.

4 A Guide is friendly and a sister to all Guides.
5 A Guide is kind to animals and respects all living things.
6 A Guide is obedient.
7 A Guide has courage and is cheerful in all difficulties.
8 A Guide makes good use of her time.
9 A Guide takes care of her own possessions and those of other people.
10 A Guide is self-controlled in all she thinks, says and does.

Motto

Be Prepared

BROWNIE

Brownie Guide Promise

I promise that I will do my best:
To do my duty to God;
To serve my country and help other people; and
To keep the Brownie Guide Law.

Brownie Guide Law

A Brownie Guide thinks of others before herself and does a good turn every day.

Brownie Guide Motto

Lend a Hand

Age Groups

Ranger Guide	14–18 or 20
Guide	10–16
Brownie Guide	7–11

Girl Guiding was started in Guyana in 1922 and in 1924 the Movement was officially registered. By 1927 the Association had its own headquarters (based in the same pavilion that is in use today), and two Ranger companies by 1932. In the years that followed, much intensive training was undertaken throughout Guyana with the help of trainers from other countries. Guyana became an Associate Member of WAGGGS at the 20th World Conference (Finland, 1969). The hard work of its members and the growth of the Movement were rewarded with the recognition of Guyana as a Full Member of WAGGGS at the 22nd World Conference (U.K., 1975).

Since 1970 Guyana has been a Republic within the Commonwealth, and the Girl Guide Movement has taken its place along with the Republic's other youth groups. The Association joins in the annual National Youth Week, and Guides and Rangers are prominent in competitions and events held for youth organizations in the country.

JUBILEE CELEBRATIONS

In 1970 the Association celebrated the Diamond Jubilee of the worldwide Guide Movement with parties, camp fires, and torchlight ceremonies in all parts of the country, and in 1974 it was Guyana's turn to celebrate the Association's own

Golden Jubilee. On this occasion Guyana Guides were hostesses to an international camp where 500 participants represented seventeen countries.

ATTENDANCE AT INTERNATIONAL AND WORLD EVENTS

Since 1965 Guyana has been a member of the Caribbean Link and regularly attends its meetings.

The government chose a Guider to be part of the Guyana delegation to the United Nations World Youth Assembly in New York, and the Girl Guides Association regularly sends delegates to WAGGGS' World Conferences. Leaders from Guyana also attend international and regional Girl Guide/Girl Scout events.

SERVICE

Apart from their involvement in the traditional forms of service such as assistance at public events, visits to old people's homes, orphanages and hospitals, the Girl Guides in Guyana have joined the government campaign 'Advance Guyana', concentrating on environmental and community service projects.

Another important service project has been the 'Grow More Food' campaign through which individuals and organizations are expected to contribute to national development. The Guides make the most of local resources with projects promoting fish-culture, bee-keeping, poultry-farming and food preservation. They have received a government prize for their garden plots.

Haiti

Association Nationale des Guides d'Haïti

GUIDE

Promesse	**Promise**
Sur mon honneur et avec la grâce de Dieu, je m'engage à servir de mon mieux, Dieu, l'Eglise, la Patrie, à aider mon prochain en toutes circonstances et à observer la Loi Guide.	On my honour and with the grace of God, I promise to serve to the best of my ability God, the Church, the Country, to help other people in every way and to observe the Guide Law.

Loi	**Law**
1 La guide est loyale.	A Guide is loyal.
2 La guide pense d'abord aux autres.	A Guide thinks first of others.
3 La guide est généreuse, elle est prête à servir.	A Guide is generous, she is ready to serve.
4 La guide est accueillante, elle a l'esprit d'équipe.	A Guide is welcoming; she has the team spirit.
5 La guide, sœur de toute autre guide, est présente à tous.	A Guide, sister to every other Guide, is available to all.

6 La guide découvre la nature, elle y voit l'œuvre de Dieu.	A Guide explores nature in which she sees the work of God.
7 La guide sait obéir.	A Guide understands obedience.
8 La guide ne craint pas l'effort, elle ne fait rien à moitié.	A Guide does not fear endeavour; she does nothing by halves.
9 La guide aime son travail et respecte celui des autres.	A Guide likes her work and respects that of others.
10 La guide est maîtresse de soi; elle est pure et joyeuse.	A Guide controls herself; she is pure and cheerful.

Motto

Etre prête	Be Prepared

BROWNIE

Brownie Promise

Je promets de faire de mon mieux pour être fidèle à Dieu, à mon Pays, à mes parents, à la loi de la ronde et pour faire chaque jour un plaisir à quelqu'un.	I promise to do my best to be faithful to God, to my country, to my parents, to the law of the pack and to do a good turn to somebody every day.

Brownie Law

Une jeannette est toujours propre.	A Brownie is always neat.
Une jeannette est toujours active.	A Brownie is always active.
Une jeannette est toujours gaie.	A Brownie is always cheerful.
Une jeannette dit toujours vrai.	A Brownie always tells the truth.
Une jeannette pense d'abord aux autres.	A Brownie thinks of others.

Brownie Motto

De notre mieux	Of our best

Age Groups

Guide Aînée	Ranger	16 and over
Guide	Guide	12 and over
Jeannette	Brownie	7–12

Guiding in Haiti started with a club in a girls' school which included in its programme music, drama, sport and Guiding. At the same time, in the Pensionnat Ste Rose de Lima, another group of girls belonged to a youth organization called 'Guides de Sainte Rose'. These two groups joined together to become the first Guides of Haiti, and the first company was formed in October 1942.

The Association Nationale des Guides d'Haïti was recognized as an Associate Member of the World Association at the 11th World Conference (France, 1946) and as a Full Member at the 13th World Conference (U.K., 1950).

DEVELOPMENT

Membership of the Movement is on the increase in Haiti; Guiding has spread throughout the country and now reaches young people in all the provincial areas.

The young members of the Movement are taking a greater part in planning and organization and are anxious to have new programmes and techniques adopted.

SERVICE AND TRAINING

The official training programme includes courses on family education, hygiene and social service.

Camping and service to others are important aspects of the Guide programme. Guides work in collaboration with the Red Cross, they help in a canteen, and in a clinic; care for children and help to educate girls and mothers in underprivileged areas, giving courses in embroidery, crochet and cookery. One company runs a literacy centre for underprivileged children. A Guide magazine, *Fusée*, helps to publicize the activities of the Association.

Iceland

Girl Guide Section of Bandalag Íslenzkra Skáta

GUIDE

Promise

Ég lofa aÐ gera paÐ, sem í mínu valdi stendur til pess:	I promise to do my best:
AÐ gera skyldu mína viÐ GuÐ og aettjörÐina.	To do my duty to God and my country.
AÐ hjálpa öÐrum.	To help other people all the time.
AÐ halda skátalögin.	To obey the Guide Law.

Law

1	Skáti segir ávalt satt og gengur aldrei á bak orÐa sinna.	A Guide's honour is to be trusted and a Guide always keeps her word.
2	Skáti er tryggur.	A Guide is loyal.
3	Skáti er haeverskur í hugsunum, orÐum og verkum.	A Guide is courteous, clean in thought, word and deed.
4	Skáti er hlýÐinn.	A Guide obeys orders.
5	Skáti er glaÐvær.	A Guide is cheerful.
6	Skáti ér parfur öllum og hjálpsamur.	A Guide's duty is to be useful and to help others.
7	Skáti ér drengilegur í allri háttsemi.	A Guide is high principled in her life.
8	Skáti er sparsamur.	A Guide is thrifty.
9	Skáti er dýravinur.	A Guide is a friend to animals.
10	Allir skátar eru góÐir lagsmenn.	All Guides are good friends.

Motto

Vertu viobúinn	Be Prepared

BROWNIE

Brownie Promise

Eglofa að reyna eftir megni að halda ljósálfalögin og gera á hverjum degi eitthvað öðrum til gleàl og hjálpar.	I promise to do my best to keep the Brownie promise and to do a good turn to somebody every day.

Brownie Law

Vertu hlýðin.	Be obedient.
Gefstu ekki upp.	Do not give in to yourself.

Brownie Motto

Gerum okkar bezta	Let us do our best

Age Groups

Svannar	Rangers	18 and over
Dróttskátar	Seniors	15–18
Kvenskátar	Guides	11–15
Ljósálfar	Brownies	9–11

The first Guide troop in Iceland was formed in 1922 in the capital, Reykjavik, under the direction of the YWCA and Guiding was soon taken up in most of the towns and villages throughout the country, later becoming a separate organization under the leadership of Jakobína Magnúsdóttir who represented her national organization when Iceland became a Founder Member of WAGGGS in Hungary, 1928.

In 1944 the Girl Guide and Boy Scout Associations became a joint national association, taking the name Bandalag Íslenzkra Skáta (BÍS).

During the Second World War contact with Iceland was lost, but renewed when peace returned. Iceland was present as a Full Member of WAGGGS at the 15th World Conference (The Netherlands, 1954).

TRAINING CENTRE

There is a training centre at Úlfljótsvatn, near Reykjavik, where regular training courses are held for Leaders at all stages from patrol leaders to advanced adult leaders.

CAMPS

Every fourth year a national camp is held at Ulfljótsvatn and district camps whether at the centre or in other parts of the country are regular events.

PUBLICATIONS

BÍS produce several books and booklets on Girl Guiding and Boy Scouting. They also publish two magazines, *Skótin*, for Leaders, and *Foringinn*, for all age-groups.

RESCUE SQUAD

Bandalag Íslenzkra Skáta have since 1934 had special units known as HSSR, or Rescue Squads. Comprising both girls and boys from the older age-group, there is now one such squad consisting of girls only. The special services given by the Rescue Squad include: locating and rescuing people from lost or wrecked aircraft and stranded ships, searching for people lost in wild and uninhabited areas, training and maintaining rescue dogs, organizing blood-donor sessions, providing first-aid facilities at large gatherings, and giving specialist training in first-aid and in camping preparations for difficult climatic and geographical conditions.

HANDICAPPED

Guiding among handicapped girls started in 1959 and has become an important part of the work of BÍS. There is a company of handicapped Guides in a hospital and local Guides assist at meetings and visit after school.

INTERNATIONAL CO-OPERATION

Bandalag Íslenzkra Skáta was represented at a European Young Leaders Gathering at Netherurd and at the Olympic Games in Munich 1972. In 1974 the Association was host to the first European Joint Girl Guide/Boy Scout Conference which had as its theme 'How can Guiding and Scouting respond to the most urgent needs of European Youth?'

India

The Bharat Scouts and Guides

GUIDE

Pratigya	**Promise**
Main maryada purvak pratigya karti hoon ki yathashakti Ishwar aur apne des ke prati apne kartavya kā pālan karungi.	On my honour I promise that I will do my best: To do my duty to God and my country;
Sada dusron ki sahayata karungi.	To help other people at all times;
Guide Niyamon kā pālan karungi.	To obey the Guide Law.

Note: For Buddhist and Jain Guides the word 'Dharma' may be substituted for 'God'.

	Niyam	**Law**
1	Guide kā wachan wishvasaneeya hotā hai.	A Guide's honour is to be trusted.
2	Guide vafādār hoti hai.	A Guide is loyal.
3	Guide kā kartavya hai ki wah Ishwar, kā samman, apne Desh ki sevā aur doosron ki sahāyatā kare.	A Guide's duty is to revere God, serve her country and help others.
4	Guide sab ki mitra hoti hai aur pratyek doosri Guide ki behan hoti hai chahe vah kisee bhee desh, Jāti aur Dharma ki ho.	A Guide is a friend to all and a sister to every other Guide no matter to what country, class or creed the other may belong.
5	Guide vinamra hoti hai.	A Guide is courteous.
6	Guide pashu pakshi ki mitra hoti hai.	A Guide is a friend to animals.

7 Guide anushasansheel aur agyakari hoti hai.	A Guide is disciplined and obeys orders.
8 Guide veer hoti hair aur appatti men prassannachitta rehti hai.	A Guide is brave and smiles under all difficulties.
9 Guide mitavyayi hoti hai.	A Guide is thrifty.
10 Guide man, vachan aur karma se shuddha hoti hai.	A Guide is pure in thought, word and deed.

Motto

Taiyyar	Be Prepared

BULBUL

Bulbul Promise

Main pratigya karti hun ki yathashakti Ishwar aur apne desh ke prati apne kartavya kā pālan karungi, Bulbul jhund ke niyamon ko manungi tatha pratidin ek bhalai ka karya karungi.	I promise to do my best: to do my duty to God and my country, to keep the Law of the Bulbul Flock and to do a good turn every day.

Bulbul Law

Bulbul baron ki agya manti hai.	The Bulbul gives in to her elders.
Bulbul swacha aur vinamra hoti hai.	The Bulbul is clean and courteous.

Bulbul Motto

Koshish karo	Do your best

Age Groups

Ranger	17 and over
Guide	11–17
Bulbul (Brownie)	7–11

Girl Guides have been active in the area which is now India since 1911. In 1928 this area along with that of present-day Pakistan and Bangladesh became a Founder Member of the World Association under the name of India.

THE BHARAT SCOUTS AND GUIDES

In 1951, a few years after India became a Republic, the Girl Guides Association (India) merged with the nationally recognized Joint Movement which became known as the Bharat Scouts and Guides (Bharat being an ancient name for India). Scouts and Guides enjoy Jamborees, camp fires and special events together, but their training and camping programmes are carried out separately.

TRAINING

Training Jamborees are held for Rangers. During a Jamboree to celebrate the twenty-five years of the Bharat Scouts and Guides, Rangers undertook village service projects, including conducting adult literacy classes.

The Association is always interested in improving leadership training programmes, and leadership training sessions are held regularly.

PROGRAMME

Guiding has been a unifying force within the forty state branches, bringing together the various faiths, languages and ethnic groups of India. The Association has progressed steadily in its efforts to bring Guiding to girls in rural areas and in poorer districts of the cities. Programme development has tried to reflect the needs and aspirations of today's young people.

Guiding has also had a great influence on the education and advancement of women. Special programmes have been developed for young village women and literacy classes organized by the Association.

The Association has held seminars with the theme 'Population Problems in Villages' as part of a programme of Population Awareness and Education.

HANDICAPPED

The Association runs day care centres providing education and recreation for mentally and physically handicapped children from low-income families in several states. The Guides also run a workshop for vocational training of handicapped women.

The Association produces a number of publications in Braille.

SERVICE

In 1975 and 1976, a series of regional camps were held for women in rural villages as part of a project for International Women's Year. Rangers were involved in teaching the women such subjects as nutrition, child care, poultry and vegetable farming, personal hygiene and home economics along with the principles of Guiding. The programme of the camps included discussions on the role of women in society.

The Bharat Scouts and Guides are involved in government pilot projects in rural development, introducing Guiding skills and activities to aid in rural economic development. Guides have also been involved in projects to rebuild homes for the elderly, provide clean water, and help in setting up mobile dispensaries in rural areas.

NATIONAL AND INTERNATIONAL EXCHANGES AND EVENTS

A series of state camps have been held in order to bring together girls from different areas of India.

Indian Girl Guides have attended international events in the U.S.A. and the U.S.S.R., and American Girl Scouts have visited Indian Girl Guides under a Cultural Exchange Project. International Commissioners attended a Commissioners Meeting in Ghana and the Girl Guides have helped in the programme of a 'Know India' session at Sangam in 1974.

Indonesia

Gerakan Pendidikan Kepanduan Pradja Muda Karana

GUIDE

Promise (Tri Satya)

On my honour I promise that I
will do my best:
To do my duty to God, and to the
Republic of Indonesia, and to
carry out Pantjasila.
To help all living beings and be
ready to join the Community for
development,
To obey the Law.

Law (Dasa Dharma)

1 A Pramuka is reverent toward God.
2 A Pramuka has the spirit of Pantjasila and is a faithful patriot of Indonesia.
3 A Pramuka does her utmost to carry out the mission of relieving the suffering of people.
4 A Pramuka is willing to make sacrifices for justice and the good of Indonesia.
5 A Pramuka co-operates with other people to build up a Pantjasila Community.
6 A Pramuka is trustworthy, morally straight, and generous.
7 A Pramuka is thrifty, accurate and simple.
8 A Pramuka never despairs in overcoming difficulties.
9 A Pramuka strives, with responsibility and gaiety, to be useful.
10 A Pramuka has a noble character and acts with discipline.

Brownie Promise (Dwi Satya)

On my honour I promise that I
will do my best:
To do my duty to God and to the
Republic of Indonesia,
and to obey the Dwi Dharma
(Brownie Law),
To do a good turn every day.

Brownie Law (Dwi Dharma)

The Brownie obeys her parents.
The Brownie is valiant and never
despairs.

Girl Guiding existed on the islands of Indonesia as far back as 1912. At that time there were no fewer than sixty Girl Guide Associations.

GERAKAN PRAMUKA

In 1960 all these Associations merged to form a new Association, a single national movement for girls and boys whose aim was to apply throughout the country the basic principles of Girl Guiding and Boy Scouting. On 14 August 1961, this was achieved and the Gerakan Pendidikan Kepanduan Pradja Muda Karama (The Scouting Education Movement to serve Young People), known as Gerakan Pramuka, was established. The Movement is based on the Pantjasila, the state philosophy as expressed in the constitution of the country. It is regarded as a vital means of character- and nation-building and meets with general public support. Thanks to efforts directed towards the organization of the Association and the development of membership, by 1967 the Gerakan Pramuka had spread to all parts of the islands, to cities and townships as well as remote villages. In 1968 the Gerakan Pramuka was recognized as the only Girl Guide and Boy Scout Movement in the country. From this time onwards, the National Organization concentrated on the development of its programme. Guiding in Indonesia is not confined to the schools, but extends to the communities and large industrial complexes.

PROGRAMME

The broad outline of the programme of the Gerakan Pramuka is drawn up at national level. It is essentially an educational programme developed to suit the country's needs, intended as a bridge between school and the educational opportunities outside school. The programme is detailed in the twenty-six different provinces to meet the particular circumstances, needs and pace of development in those areas. This approach towards a flexible programme started in 1961, has proved most successful in all areas of the country, and has attracted many young people to the Movement.

Eighty per cent of Indonesia's population lives in rural areas where unemployment is high and the young people in these areas are naturally badly affected by this state of affairs. The Gerakan Pramuka is now endeavouring to integrate the rural youth in the development of their communities. This has the two-fold purpose of developing the areas in question and of helping to make rural life more attractive.

Besides the traditional Guide programmes, the Gerakan Pramuka uses programmes geared to equip the girls for adulthood and a career. These programmes are carried out through 'doing-to-learn', 'learning-to-earn' and 'earning-to-live'. 'Learning-by-teaching' is also effectively carried out by the Rangers. This is a method of self-education which encourages the girls to acquire a knowledge of home economics, first-aid, dressmaking, etc.

CAMPING

Camping plays an important part in the programme of the Gerakan Pramuka and a camp at national level is organized every two years, while several other camps are run at provincial and regional level during the dry season.

INTERNATIONAL GUIDING

There is a lot of interest in World Guiding, and international community service camps for Rangers and Rovers are organized regularly by the National Organization. Neighbouring countries are often invited and visitors from other

National Organizations are welcome at all Guide events. The Gerakan Pramuka has actively participated in all events organized by the Asia/Pacific Region and has also been represented at many international events. A representative from the Gerakan Pramuka served on the planning committee of the WAGGGS Seminar 'Guiding for the whole country', held in Sri Lanka in 1974.

The Gerakan Pramuka was recognized as an Associate Member of WAGGGS at the 22nd World Conference (U.K., 1975).

Iran

Iranian Scouting, Girl Scout Section

GIRL SCOUT

Promise

On my honour, I promise to do my duty, as well as I can,
to God, the King and my country,
and to obey the Scout Laws and Rules.
To help and assist all people.
To keep myself physically strong, mentally awake and morally straight.

Law

1. A Girl Scout's honour is to be trusted.
2. A Girl Scout is loyal.
3. A Girl Scout's duty is to be useful and to help others.
4. A Girl Scout is a friend to all, and a sister to every other Girl Scout.
5. A Girl Scout is courteous.
6. A Girl Scout is a friend to animals.
7. A Girl Scout obeys orders.
8. A Girl Scout is cheerful.
9. A Girl Scout is thrifty.
10. A Girl Scout is pure in thought, word and deed.

Motto

Be Prepared

ANGEL (BROWNIE)

Angel (Brownie) Promise

I promise to believe in one supreme God,
to love my King and my country
and to follow the Angel's Laws.

Angel Laws

Cheerfulness: an Angel is cheerful and always smiling.
Helpfulness: an Angel is a sister to other Angels and helps at home.
Politeness: an Angel is polite.
Obedience: an Angel is obedient and obeys the orders of her parents, leaders and teachers.

Angel Motto

Be happy

Age Groups

Ranger	15–20
Scout	11–15
Angel (Brownie)	7–11

Girl Scouting began in Iran in 1925 as a part of the Boy Scout Movement. Although interest waned during the Second World War, by 1956 Girl Scouting had again become popular. In 1957, Girl Scouting was completely separated from Boy Scouting in Iran.

The Girl Scout section of Iranian Scouting was recognized as an Associate Member of WAGGGS at the 18th World Conference (Denmark, 1963) and as a Full Member at the 20th World Conference (Finland, 1969). Its patron, HIM Queen Farah Pahlavi, Shahbanou of Iran, follows its activities with great interest. The Girl Scouts section will act as hostess to the 23rd World Conference which will be held in Iran in 1978.

TRAINING

Training is given in all Girl Scout skills, and technical programmes are also organized with specialists provided in each field as required. These are volunteers who undertake to assist Girl Scouts with whatever project they choose. Courses for leaders are arranged by the training team in training centres throughout the country.

Intensive training is given in Sea- and Air-Scouting, and Sea-Scout training centres have been built on both the Caspian Sea and the Persian Gulf.

Owing to the fact that much of the land in Iran is agricultural, special training is provided for people living in rural areas to suit their needs and way of life. This has led to an innovation, 'rural Scouting' which concentrates on enabling a girl to become a helpful and co-operative citizen in the village in which she lives.

CAMPING

Camping is popular in Iran, and most districts and divisions have permanent campsites. Day camps, summer camps and provincial camps are held, as well as travelling camps which involve visits to other regions of the country.

SERVICE

Rangers have undertaken service projects in hospitals, orphanages and for refugees in the frontier localities. Girl Scouts also carry out many projects, particularly during three special weeks: Good Turn Week, Job Week and Evaluation Week. Projects undertaken for Good Turn Week include blood donation and conservation, with illustrated booklets and leaflets distributed by the Girl Scouts.

In 1975 Iranian Scouting acted as host organization for the 3rd Conference on Leisure, Sport and Culture for the Disabled with 228 participants from 22 countries. They attended to the needs of the handicapped and organized visits to places of historical interest.

INTERNATIONAL WOMEN'S YEAR 1975

An international camp held in July 1974 promoted the idea of IWY which was further promoted by a publicity campaign in the Girl Scout press.

Two hundred Rangers took part in the National Congress of Women's Organizations in Teheran, and a Commissioners' seminar to investigate the situation and rights of women in different regions of the country was organized as part of the activities for International Women's Year.

Ireland

The Irish Girl Guides

GUIDE

An Gealltanas

Geallaim faoi bhrí m'onóra, chomh fada agus is féidir liom, mo dhualgas do Dhia agus don tír a dhéanamh, teacht i gcabhair ar dhaoine eile i gcónaí, agus bheith umhal do dhlí na mBantreoruithe.

Promise

I promise on my honour to do my best to do my duty to God and my country, to help other people at all times, and to obey the Guide Law.

An Dlí	**Law**
1 Is iontaofa onóir an bhantreoraí.	A Guide's honour is to be trusted.
2 Tá an bantreoraí dílis.	A Guide is loyal.
3 Tá se de dhualgas ar an mbantreoraí teacht i gcabhair ar dhaoine eile.	A Guide's duty is to be useful and to help others.
4 Is cara do chach an bantreoraí agus is deirfíur do ghach bantreoraí eile í.	A Guide is a friend to all, and a sister to every other Guide.
5 Tá an bantreoraí béasach.	A Guide is courteous.
6 Tá an bantreoraí cineálta leis na hainmhithe.	A Guide is a friend to animals.
7 Tá an bantreoraí umhal dá cinnirí.	A Guide obeys orders.
8 Tá an bantreoraí gealgháireach i ngach cruachás.	A Guide smiles and sings under all difficulties.
9 Tá an bantreoraí barainneach.	A Guide is thrifty.

10 Tá an bantreoraí geanmnaí ina smaointe, ina briathar, agus ina gníomh.	A Guide is pure in thought, word and deed.

Senior Branch

In addition to making the Guide Promise and following the Guide Law, the Senior Branch member has the special responsibility – 'To render service by taking this Promise out into a wider world'.

Motto

Bí ullamh	Be Prepared

Brownie Promise

BROWNIE

Geallaim go ndéanfaidh mé mo dhícheall mo dhualgas do Dhia agus tír a dhéanamh, teacht i gcabhair ar dhaoine eile gach lá, go mór-mhór orthu-san sa bhaile.	I promise to do my best to do my duty to God and my country, to help other people every day, especially those at home.

Brownie Law

Géilleann an Suaircín do dhaoine fásta.	A Brownie gives in to the older folk.
Ni ghéilleann an Suaircín di féin.	A Brownie does not give in to herself.

Brownie Motto

Cuidign le daoine	Lend a Hand

Age Groups

Ranger	$14\frac{1}{2}$–21
Guide	$10\frac{1}{2}$–16
Brownie	6–11

Girl Guiding started in Ireland in 1910 and, in line with changes in the country's constitution, became a national Movement in the year 1930. In 1932 at the 7th World Conference in Poland, the Irish Girl Guides were recognized as a Full Member of the World Association of Girl Guides and Girl Scouts.

STRUCTURE

The overall policy and organization of the Irish Girl Guides is the responsibility of its General Council. For administrative purposes the country is divided into seven regions with a Regional Commissioner in charge of each. The headquarters of the Irish Girl Guides is based in Pembroke Park, Dublin.

PROGRAMME

Guide activities in Ireland are many and varied. A system of tests and badges challenges each girl to reach the highest development possible. There is a wide choice of skills, and some 90 proficiency badges to work for. The patrol system forms the basis of almost all activities.

Programmes have been modified in order to keep pace with changing school syllabi and continue to meet the needs of young girls in Ireland. Since subjects previously included in Girl Guide programmes, e.g. map-making and botany, are now taught in schools, a more sophisticated approach to programmes has been adopted. Camping, adventure and hiking always have a place in the programme, and special emphasis is laid on craft-work and traditional skills.

DEVELOPMENT OF THE MOVEMENT

The government of Ireland has become more than ever aware of the benefits of Girl Guiding, and has, since 1970, provided grants which, among other things, have enabled the Irish Girl Guides to update publications with special reference to badge-work and training. Part of the grant has been used for administration and for training Trainers.

Membership of the Movement has increased rapidly in recent years and this trend is continuing. Many women with no previous experience of Guiding are coming forward to be trained as Leaders. Trainers have added to their experience by taking part in government- and industry-sponsored courses.

HANDICAPPED

A campaign has been mounted to encourage units to include handicapped members and involve them actively in as much of the programme as possible. Also, there is a Guide unit for long-term patients in a children's hospital and a handbook has been compiled for Guiders with handicapped children in their units.

SERVICE

Service to others includes helping with meals-on-wheels, service in old people's Homes, and conservation. To celebrate their Diamond Jubilee Girl Guides made Ireland bloom by planting hundreds of rose bushes.

JOINT ACTIVITIES

Joint activities with members of the Federation of Irish Scout Associations are particularly popular with the Ranger age-group. In 1977 the Irish Girl Guides helped to organize the first international Girl Guide/Girl Scout and Boy Scout camp in Ireland, and in the same year they were host, with the Scout Federation, to the Second European Scout and Guide Conference.

CO-OPERATION WITH OTHER ORGANIZATIONS

The Irish Girl Guides is a Founder Member of the National Youth Council of Ireland and Girl Guide Leaders are encouraged to work on its many committees.

Israel

Girl Scout Section of the Israel Boy and Girl Scouts Federation

GIRL SCOUT

Havtacha

Hineni mavtiah havtaha shlema,
laasot kol ma shbicholti:
Lemale et hovotai lealohai velemdinati.
Laazor lezulati bechol et.
Lekaim et midot hatsofe. *Or*
Hineni mavtiah havtaha shlema,
laasot kol ma shbicholti:
Lemale et hovotai lemdinati.
Laazor lezulati bechol et.
Lekaim et midot hatsofe.

'Higid lecha adam ma tov uma elohim doresh mimcha ki im asot meshpat veahavat chesed uehatsnaa echet im elohecha.'

Mic. 6:8.

Promise

I promise faithfully to do my best:

To do my duty to God and the State of Israel.
To help others at all times.
To keep the Scout Law. *Or*
I promise faithfully to do my best:

To do my duty to the State of Israel.
To help others at all times.
To keep the Scout Law.

The Tribe Leader addresses the Scouts taking this Promise with the following words from the Bible.
'He hath showed thee, O man, what is good; and what doth the Lord require of thee?'
The Scouts reply:
'To do justly, to love mercy, and to walk humbly with God.'
Mic. 6:8.

Midot

1 Hatsofe devaro emeth.
2 Hatsofe neéman lemdinato.
3 Hatsofe Chaver moil bachevra, hohev avoda veozer lezolato.
4 Hatsofe reaa lechol adam veach lecol tsofe.
5 Hatsofe adeev.
6 Hatsofe chovev et hachaie vehazomech uemagen aleahem.
7 Hatsofe ish mishmaat.
8 Hatsofe aeno nofel berucho.
9 Hatsofe chaschan.
10 Hatsofe tahor bedibure ubamaasaw.

Law

A Girl Scout's word is to be trusted.
A Girl Scout is loyal to the State of Israel.
A Girl Scout is a useful member of society, loves work and helps others.
A Girl Scout is a friend to all and a sister to every other Girl Scout.
A Girl Scout is courteous.
A Girl Scout is a friend to animals and plants, and protects them.
A Girl Scout obeys orders.
A Girl Scout is always cheerful.
A Girl Scout is thrifty.
A Girl Scout is clean in word and deed.

Motto

Heye nachon

Be Prepared

BROWNIE

Brownie Promise

Hineni nachon lemaleh et hukat eidat haofarim, leasot maaseh tov bchol yom veyom, uloazor bemyuchad bevet chorai.	I am ready to keep the pack law, to do a good turn every day, and to help my parents especially at home.

Brownie Motto

Nishma venaaseh	We'll listen and obey

Pack Law

Haofer metsayet latzvi.	The 'ofer' (Brownie, Cub) obeys the 'big deer'.
Haofer kovesh yetsiro.	The 'ofer' does not give in to himself/herself.

Age Groups

Tsofe	Ranger	15–18
Nachshon	Guide	11–14
Ofer	Brownie	9–10

The Israel Boy and Girl Scouts Federation is composed of six Associations: the Hebrew Scout Association, the Arab Schools Boy and Girl Scouts, the Israel Arab Boy and Girl Scouts, the Israel Christian Orthodox Boy and Girl Scouts, the Israel Catholic Boy and Girl Scouts and the Israel Druze Scout Association. The first five Associations cater for girls as well as boys, whereas the Israel Druze Scout Association is open to boys only.

The Movement in Israel is much older than the State of Israel itself. It dates back to 1919 when men who happened to be Scouts went to Palestine and soon aroused the interest of others to form a Scout Association. Scouting plays a special role in the life of the country, and in the programme emphasis is put on training in the service of the state and its people.

The Girl Scout Section which brings together all Girl Scouts within the Federation was recognized as an Associate Member of the World Association in 1957 and as a Full Member at the 18th World Conference (Denmark, 1963).

Since 1972 the Association has worked at developing national and political awareness, fuller involvement in community life, closer co-operation with the minority groups in the different Scout Associations, more self-government and a wider age-range in the older age group. A great deal of emphasis has been placed recently on developing programmes for the Ranger/Rover age group, the result of which has been an increase in Ranger/Rover membership.

SERVICE TO THE COMMUNITY

Community activities for the Ranger/Rover age group included the establishment of small mixed groups that spend a year between leaving school and undertaking their national service in development towns helping in youth clubs, kindergartens, schools and Scouting. Ten of these 'friendship groups' are at present in existence. In addition in 1976 some twelve groups of about 70–80 Rangers and Rovers went to kibbutzim as part of their national service. Another venture which reflects new thinking in community service is a similar large group doing its national service in a development town for a period of three years.

Scouting among underprivileged children has increased, and today 30 per cent of the membership comes from the low-income communities. Scouting among handicapped children has also increased.

TRAINING AND JAMBOREES

Training has continued as well as the year-round cross-country hikes and the summer camps attended by both Arab and Jewish Girl Scouts. The 11th National Jamboree took place in August 1973 marking the 25th anniversary of the State of Israel. It was attended by 15,000 campers, including representatives from the U.S.A., U.K., France, Belgium, Mexico, Argentina, Denmark, Switzerland, Ghana and Sierra Leone. The 12th National Jamboree is planned for the summer of 1977.

International Women's Year (1975) was marked by special issues of Scout journals.

ATTENDANCE AT CONFERENCES

Apart from regular attendance at WAGGGS' World Conferences, Israeli delegates have taken part in the Asia Pacific Seminar and other events at Sangam. The Association has also been represented at the International Commissioners' Meeting in Ghana.

There have been exchanges of visits between Israeli Girl Scout Leaders and Leaders and Guides in other countries.

Italy

Federazione Italiana Guide Esploratrici

ASSOCIAZIONE GUIDE E SCOUTS CATTOLICI ITALIANI

GUIDE

Promessa	**Promise**
Con l'aiuto di Dio prometto sul mio onore di fare del mio meglio: per compiere il mio dovere verso Dio e verso il mio Paese; per aiutare gli altri in ogni circostanza; per osservare la Legge scout.	With God's help I promise on my honour that I will do my best: to do my duty to God and my country; to help other people at all times; to obey the Scout Law.

Legge	**Law**
La Guida e lo Scout:	A Guide and a Scout:
1 pongono il loro onore nel meritare fiducia;	consider their honour to be trusted;
2 sono leali;	are loyal;
3 si rendono utili ed aiutano gli altri;	want to be useful and help others;

4 sono amici di tutti e fratelli di ogni altra Guida e Scout;	are friends to all and brothers/sisters to every other Guide and Scout;
5 sono cortesi;	are courteous;
6 amano e rispettano la natura;	love and respect nature;
7 sanno obbedire;	know how to obey;
8 sorridono e cantano anche nelle difficoltà;	smile and sing under all difficulties;
9 sono laboriosi ed economi;	are hardworking and thrifty;
10 sono puri di pensieri, parole ed azioni.	are pure in thought, word and deed.

BROWNIE

Brownie Promise

Prometto con l'aiuto di Gesù, di fare del mio meglio: nell'aiutare gli altri; nell'osservare la Legge del Cerchio.	With Jesus's help I promise that I will do my best: to help other people; to obey the Round Law.

Brownie Law

La Coccinella pensa agli altri come a se stessa.	A Brownie takes care of the other people as of herself.
La Coccinella vive con gioia insieme al Cerchio.	A Brownie lives joyfully with the Round.

UNIONE NAZIONALE GIOVANI ESPLORATRICI ITALIANE

GUIDE

Promessa	**Promise**
Sul mio onore prometto di fare del mio meglio per:	On my honour I promise to do my best in order to:
Compiere il mio dovere verso Dio, la Patria e la Famiglia;	Do my duty towards God, my country and my family;
Aiutare il mio prossimo in ogni circostanza;	Help my neighbour in all circumstances;
Osservare fedelmente la Legge Scout.	Faithfully observe the Scout Law.

Legge	**Law**
1 La parola dell'Esploratrice è sacra.	A Girl Scout's word is sacred.
2 L'Esploratrice ama la Patria, ed osserva le sue leggi.	A Girl Scout loves her country and observes its laws.
3 L'Esploratrice ama il prossimo e protegge il debole.	A Girl Scout loves her neighbour and protects the weak.
4 L'Esploratrice è sorella di ogni altra Esploratrice, di qualsiasi condizione sociale, paese e fede.	A Girl Scout is a sister to all other Girl Scouts, of any social condition, country and religion.
5 L'Esploratrice è cortese, leale e coraggiosa.	A Girl Scout is kind, loyal and courageous.
6 L'Esploratrice rispetta e protegge i luoghi, gli animali, le piante.	A Girl Scout respects and protects places, animals and plants.
7 L'Esploratrice obbedisce ai genitori, ai maestri, ai capi, e sa quando occorre prendere una iniziativa.	A Girl Scout obeys her parents, teachers, leaders, and knows when it is necessary to take the initiative.

8 L'Esploratrice si mantiene serena nelle difficoltà.	A Girl Scout remains calm in all difficulties.
9 L'Esploratrice è industriosa, economa e temperante non fa mai le cose a metà.	A Girl Scout is industrious, economical and temperate, never does incomplete work.
10 L'Esploratrice è pura di pensiero, corretta nelle parole e negli atti.	A Girl Scout is pure in thought, and correct in word and deed.

Motto

Sii preparata	Be Prepared

Brownie Promise

Prometto di fare del mio meglio per: amare Dio, la Patria, la Famiglia, osservare la Legge della Primula e compiere ogni giorno una buona azione verso qualcuno, cominciando dalla mia famiglia.	I promise to do my best: to love God, the country and the family, obey the Brownie Law and to do a good turn to somebody every day starting with my family.

BROWNIE

Brownie Law

La Primula è-obbediente e rispettosa.	The Primula is obedient and respectful.
La Primula non cede mai ai suoi capricci.	The Primula does not follow her own desires.

Brownie Motto

Fa meglio	Do better

Age Groups

Scolta	Ranger	16–19
Esploratrice	Guide	12–15
Primula	Brownie	7–11

FEDERAZIONE ITALIANA GUIDE ESPLORATRICI

The Federazione Italiana Guide Esploratrici (FIGE) was started in 1945 to link together the two existing Italian Associations of Girl Guides and Girl Scouts, the Unione Nazionale Giovani Esploratrici Italiane (UNGEI) and the Associazione Guide Italiane (AGI), which in 1974 merged with the Catholic Boy Scout Association to form Associazione Guide e Scouts Cattolici Italiani (AGESCI).

FIGE was recognized as an Associate Member of the World Association at the 11th World Conference (France, 1946) and as a Full Member at the 12th World Conference (U.S.A., 1948).

ASSOCIAZIONE GUIDE E SCOUTS CATTOLICI ITALIANI

AGESCI is open to Roman Catholic boys and girls and aims at providing them with a continuous out-of-school education and a practical approach to life. Their problems are not treated in isolation but as the problems of mankind in general. Co-education is not necessarily achieved through mixed units but rather through following the same educational methods. Nearly all Ranger and Rover units are mixed, but in the other branches activities are carried out in parallel units whose Leaders work together and organize suitable joint activities from time to time.

GENERAL ACTIVITIES

PROGRAMME

The programme is based on the methods as laid down by Baden-Powell. The aim is to help young people to personal growth through experience of community life, involvement in social problems and through the promotion of peace and justice.

THINKING DAY/SERVICE

On 22 February Girl Guides/Girl Scouts in Italy think not only of Girl Guides and Girl Scouts around the world, but of fellow human beings – people suffering from poverty, illness, oppression, those hit by natural disasters such as hurricanes, earthquakes, floods – victims of war, refugees. Not only do they *think* of these people, but they also *act* to alleviate their suffering.

Both Associations of the FIGE, the Unione Nazionale Giovani Esploratrici Italiane (National Organization of Italian Girl Scouts), and the Associazione Guide e Scouts Cattolici Italiane (AGESCI) set up working camps in the area of the disastrous Friuli earthquakes in 1976. Rangers, Girl Guide and Boy Scout Leaders worked in close co-operation with the government and other relief agencies. In conjunction with the Education Authorities, they helped people whose houses had been destroyed by the tremors to find and rescue their belongings, acted as store keepers and cooks, helped local farmers with hay-making, harvesting, and grape picking, to salvage as many crops as possible. The responsibility for monitoring fieldwork, by co-ordinating groups of volunteers, maintaining contacts, and manning emergency field telephones, was taken on by the Girl Guides/Girl Scouts, while the Boy Scouts helped clear rubble and free roads.

INTERNATIONAL ACTIVITIES

Among the international activities in Italy in 1977 was WITAN '77, the international camp which was held near Lake Maggiore, north-west of Milan in July.

WITAN is a camp which has taken place every two years since 1959. Its purpose is to overcome frontiers and promote better understanding among young people. The 1977 camp theme was: 'The international dimension of Guiding and Scouting'.

Ivory Coast

Scoutisme Féminin de Côte d'Ivoire

GUIDES DE CÔTE D'IVOIRE

GUIDE

Promesse	Promise
Sur mon honneur, avec la grâce de Dieu, je m'engage:	On my honour and with the grace of God, I pledge myself:
A servir de mon mieux Dieu, l'Eglise et la Patrie;	To do my best to serve God, the Church and the Country;
A aider mon prochain en toutes circonstances;	To help others in all circumstances;
A observer la loi des guides.	To observe the Guide Law.

Loi	Law
1 La guide est loyale.	A Guide is loyal.
2 La guide pense d'abord aux autres.	A Guide thinks first of others.
3 La guide est généreuse: elle est prête à servir.	A Guide is generous: she is prepared to help.
4 La guide est accueillante; elle a l'esprit d'équipe.	A Guide is welcoming: she has the team spirit.
5 La guide, sœur de toute autre guide, est présente à tous.	A Guide, sister to every other guide, is prepared to help all.
6 La guide découvre la nature; elle y voit l'œuvre de Dieu.	A Guide explores nature, in which she sees the work of God.
7 La guide sait obéir.	A Guide understands obedience.
8 La guide ne craint pas l'effort; elle ne fait rien à moitié.	A Guide does not fear endeavour; she does nothing by halves.
9 La guide aime son travail et respecte celui des autres.	A Guide likes her work and respects that of others.
10 La guide est maîtresse de soi; elle est pure et joyeuse.	A Guide controls herself; she is pure and cheerful.

Motto

Toujours prête	Always ready

Brownie Promise

BROWNIE

Je promets de faire de mon mieux: pour être fidèle à Dieu, à la Patrie, à mes parents, à la loi de la Ronde, et pour faire chaque jour un plaisir à quelqu'un.	I promise to do my best: to be faithful to God, to my Country, to my parents and to the law of the pack, and to do a good turn to somebody every day.

Brownie Law

Une jeannette est toujours propre.	A Brownie is always neat.
Une jeannette est toujours active.	A Brownie is always active.

Une jeannette est toujours gaie.	A Brownie is always cheerful.
Une jeannette dit toujours vrai.	A Brownie always tells the truth.
Une jeannette pense d'abord aux autres.	A Brownie thinks first of others.

Brownie Motto

De notre mieux	To the best of our power

ECLAIREUSES UNIONISTES DE CÔTE D'IVOIRE

GUIDE

Promesse	**Promise**
Avec l'aide de Dieu	With the help of God
Je promets sur mon honneur	I promise on my honour
de faire tout mon possible pour	to do all my best to
SERVIR Dieu, ma Patrie, ma Famille	SERVE God, my Country, my family
AIDER les autres en tout temps	HELP others at all times
OBEIR à la Loi des éclaireuses.	OBEY the Law of the Girl Scouts.

Loi	**Law**
1 Une éclaireuse n'a qu'une parole.	A Girl Scout's honour is to be trusted.
2 Une éclaireuse sait obéir et se dominer.	A Girl Scout knows how to obey and how to control herself.
3 Une éclaireuse est énergique et prête à servir.	A Girl Scout is energetic and ready to serve.
4 Une éclaireuse est accueillante.	A Girl Scout is friendly.
5 Une éclaireuse est la sœur de tout le monde.	A Girl Scout is a sister to everybody.
6 Une éclaireuse respecte et protège la nature.	A Girl Scout respects and protects nature.
7 Une éclaireuse est économe.	A Girl Scout is thrifty.
8 Une éclaireuse est toujours de bonne humeur.	A Girl Scout is always cheerful.
9 Une éclaireuse ne fait rien à moitié.	A Girl Scout does nothing by halves.
10 Une éclaireuse est pure dans ses pensées, ses paroles et ses actes.	A Girl Scout is pure in her thoughts, words and deeds.

Motto

Sois prête	Be ready

BROWNIE

Brownie Promise

Je promets de faire de mon mieux pour	I promise to do my best
Servir Dieu, ma famille	To serve God, my family
Obéir à la loi des Alouettes	To obey the Lark Law
Et faire chaque jour un plaisir à quelqu'un.	And to do a good turn to someone each day.

Brownie Law

Alouette, écoute ta cheftaine.	Lark, listen to your leader.
Alouette, aide sans te fatiguer.	Lark, help others without over-tiring yourself.

Brownie Motto

Alouette, aide joyeusement	Lark, help cheerfully

Age Groups

Eclaireuse	Girl Scout	11–16
Alouette	Lark	7–10

LES ECLAIREURS ET ECLAIREUSES DE CÔTE D'IVOIRE

Newly formed association. No information at time of going to press.

Two Associations today form the Scoutisme Féminin de Côte d'Ivoire. The first, Guides de Côte d'Ivoire, was formed in 1955. The second, Eclaireuses Unionistes de Côte d'Ivoire in 1959. Both Associations have now spread their membership throughout all areas of the country. Scoutisme Féminin de Côte d'Ivoire was recognized as an Associate Member of the World Association at the 18th World Conference (Denmark, 1963).

GUIDES DE CÔTE D'IVOIRE

Over recent years, considerable progress has been made in training and in the expansion of the Movement.

TRAINING

The national team has the overall responsibility for training Leaders and organizing training camps. A progress chart has been produced for training, showing the different stages which must be covered by Guides passing the tests. Training camps and inter-company camps are held, as are national and international camps. Members of the Association also attend international training camps held in other countries.

CO-OPERATION WITH OTHER ORGANIZATIONS

The Guides de Côte d'Ivoire maintain very good relations with other youth organizations in their country and are members of the Youth Council and the Collège du Scoutisme Ivoirien. In recent years co-operation with the Boy Scouts has also increased.

SERVICE

The Guides de Côte d'Ivoire are constantly searching for greater involvement in the social problems of the community in which they live. Service projects are organized to meet the specific needs of the different regions. Money collected by the Guides is used to dig wells in villages, to give assistance to old people and to undertake sociological surveys in order to be better able to serve the community. Since Guiding strives to remain as closely linked as possible to the life of the country, the Guides de Côte d'Ivoire have chosen to wear the traditional everyday dress as their Guide uniform.

ECLAIREUSES UNIONISTES DE CÔTE D'IVOIRE

Training is an important part of the programme of the Eclaireuses Unionistes de Côte d'Ivoire with national and international leadership training camps taking place regularly. The Association publishes a book of technical notes dealing with leadership training, first-aid and hygiene, manual skills and handicrafts.

SERVICE

As in the Guides de Côte d'Ivoire, service is an integral part of the programme. Over the past ten years the Association in collaboration with the government has made great efforts to involve itself in the overall development of the country.

SUB-REGIONAL GATHERING

In 1976 Scoutisme Féminin de Côte d'Ivoire was hostess to one of four sub-regional gatherings held in Africa.

Jamaica

The Girl Guides Association of Jamaica

GUIDE

Promise

I promise that I will do my best:
To do my duty to God;
To serve the Queen and my country,
and help other people;
And to keep the Guide Law.

Law

1 A Guide is loyal and can be trusted.
2 A Guide is helpful.
3 A Guide is polite and considerate.
4 A Guide is friendly and a sister to all Guides.
5 A Guide is kind to animals and respects all living things.
6 A Guide is obedient.
7 A Guide has courage and is cheerful in all difficulties.
8 A Guide makes good use of her time.
9 A Guide takes care of her own possessions and those of other people.
10 A Guide is self-controlled in all she thinks, says and does.

Motto

Be Prepared

BROWNIE

Brownie Promise

I promise that I will do my best:
To do my duty to God,
To serve the Queen and my country,
and help other people,
And to keep the Brownie Guide Law.

Brownie Law

A Brownie thinks of others before herself, and does a good turn every day.

Brownie Motto

Lend a Hand

Age Groups

Senior Branch	15–21
Guide	11–16
Brownie	7½–11

Girl Guiding started in Jamaica in 1915, when the first company was formed in Spanish Town. The first Guide camp was held in 1916 and by 1919 there was already sufficient demand to introduce a Ranger programme. When the country became independent in 1962 Jamaica applied for and was granted Associate Membership of the World Association at the 18th World Conference (Denmark, 1963). The Association became a Full Member at the 19th World Conference (Japan, 1966).

International contacts have always been very important for Jamaica and members of the Association regularly attend overseas conferences and training courses and also visit Guide centres in other countries.

JUBILEE CELEBRATIONS

The Association celebrated its Golden Jubilee in 1961 and the Diamond Jubilee of World Guiding in 1970 when it was hostess to 13 countries at one of the international Gatherings for Young Adult Leaders.

TRAINING

A regular Training Programme is maintained by the Association with the help of a full-time travelling trainer and the valuable assistance given by trainers from overseas. This training knowledge has also been shared with other territories of the Caribbean, thereby helping to strengthen the 'Caribbean Link' of which Jamaica is a member. Great efforts are also being made to find potential Trainers for rural areas.

Between 1972 and 1975 the Association spearheaded the formation of the National Consultation on Leadership Recruitment and Training which has proved very successful.

Special attention has been given to Ranger Training, as Jamaica is trying to expand this particular section.

Together with other Caribbean countries, Jamaica has produced a training leaflet under the title *Guiding Lights*.

HANDICAPPED GUIDES

The Association tries, wherever possible, to integrate physically handicapped girls into regular companies and packs. However, special units for handicapped Guides and Brownies also exist.

SERVICE

Girl Guides and Rangers endeavour whenever possible to identify themselves with community projects, and Brownies, not to be left out, have made their own contribution to community well-being in the form of anti-litter campaigns.

A 'Holiday Fun Project' (summer holiday camp for young children) is organized annually by the Guides. Senior Guides involve themselves in community development by organizing work camps in co-operation with local citizens for the building of elementary schools, and have also participated in work-camps organized by the Jamaica Youth Council.

Literacy classes have gone from strength to strength in Jamaica, and Guides now conduct Adult Literacy Classes for the underprivileged, including migrants. Much effort and thought go into their work in the field of Family Education, and their Ranger Section participates in the National Family Planning Programme. In response to an appeal made to non-governmental organizations in Jamaica, Rangers and Senior Guides helped with a public opinion survey on population.

Jamaican Girl Guides conduct lively fund-raising campaigns which reach large numbers of the population. The appointment of a Public Relations Officer underlines the Association's concern with the need for the imaginative presentation of the Movement before the public.

Japan

Girl Scouts of Japan

GIRL SCOUT

Yakusoku	**Promise**
Watakushi wa meiyo ni kakete:	On my honour, I will try:
Kami to kuni to ni taisuru tsutome o okonai;	To do my duty to God and my country;
Itsumo tano hitobito o tasuke;	To help other people at all times;
Gaaru Sukauto no okite o mamoru yoni itashimasu.	To obey the Girl Scout Law.

Okite	**Law**
1 Gaaru Sukauto no meiyo wa shinrai sareru koto de arimasu.	A Girl Scout's honour is to be trusted.
2 Gaaru Sukauto wa chujitsu de arimasu.	A Girl Scout is loyal.
3 Gaaru Sukauto no tsutome wa, hito o tasuke hito ni yakudatsu koto de arimasu.	A Girl Scout's duty is to be useful and to help others.
4 Gaaru Sukauto wa subeteno hitobito no tomodachi de ari, tano Gaaru Sukauto towa tagaini shimai de arimasu.	A Girl Scout is a friend to all and a sister to every other Girl Scout.
5 Gaaru Sukauto wa reigi o tadashiku shimasu.	A Girl Scout is courteous.
6 Gaaru Sukauto wa ikimono o kawaigari masu.	A Girl Scout is a friend to animals.
7 Gaaru Sukauto wa kiritsu ni shitagai masu.	A Girl Scout obeys orders.
8 Gaaru Sukauto wa kaikatsu de arimasu.	A Girl Scout is cheerful.

9 Gaaru Sukauto wa kenyaku shimasu.	A Girl Scout is thrifty.
10 Gaaru Sukauto wa omoi nimo, kotoba nimo, okonai nimo junketsu de arimasu.	A Girl Scout is clean in thought, word and deed.

Motto

Sonaeyo tsune ni	Be Prepared

Brownie Promise

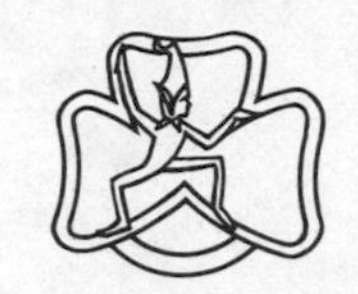

Watakushi wa kami to kuni o aishi, mainichi hitobito o tasuke tokuni uchino otetsudai o shimasu.	I promise to do my best to love God and my country; To help other people every day especially those at home.

Brownie Motto

Te o kase	Lend a Hand

	Age Group	Approx. Ages
Ranger	Grade 10–12 (Sr. high school)	15–17
Senior	Grade 7–9 (Jr. high school)	12–15
Junior	Grade 4–6	9–12
Brownie	Grade 1–3	6–9

Girl Guiding/Girl Scouting started in Japan in 1919 and in 1920 the Association took the name Nippon Joshi Hodadan (Girl Guides of Japan). Guiding gradually spread from Tokyo to other parts of the country, and Japan became a Founder Member of the World Association of Girl Guides and Girl Scouts in 1928. Although the Movement was banned in the 1930s and early 1940s, the spirit of Guiding remained, and in 1947 some former Guides and others interested in the welfare of young people got together to re-start Girl Guiding; in May 1948 the first three-day Leaders' training was held in Tokyo.

In 1948 and 1949 troops were formed in almost every part of Japan. The first national convention was held in Tokyo in 1949, and the Girl Scouts of Japan was formally established in that year.

At the 14th World Conference (Norway, 1952), the Girl Scouts of Japan was recognized as an Associate Member of the World Association, and at the 17th World Conference (Greece, 1960), Japan was recognized as a Full Member of WAGGGS.

CAMPING AND TRAINING SESSIONS

A national camp centre was established in 1960 in the Togakushi Highlands in Nagano Prefecture. Every summer several national camp sessions and training courses are held there for girls and Leaders from all over Japan, and often international visitors, too, have the chance to camp there in beautiful natural surroundings.

In autumn 1962 the Association was honoured by the visit of the World Chief Guide. In summer 1963 an Asian Camp was held at Camp Togakushi commemorating the 15th anniversary of the Girl Scouts of Japan. Four thousand girls from all over Asia and from North America participated.

WORLD CONFERENCE AND INTERNATIONAL GATHERINGS

In 1966 Japan hostessed the 19th World Conference of WAGGGS, the first World Conference ever held in Asia. At the 20th World Conference in Finland in 1969, Japan was chosen along with Canada, Great Britain and Jamaica to hostess one of WAGGGS's Diamond Jubilee Young Adult Gatherings in 1970. Girls from 17 countries gathered at Nosé, Osaka, for the gathering and for the international camp which celebrated the Diamond Jubilee of the Girl Guide Movement and the Golden Jubilee of the Girl Scouts of Japan.

An international rally with the theme 'A Diamond Shines; So Can Our Lives' was held at Expo '70 with over 12,000 Girl Scouts and Guides participating. Each year Young Adult Conferences are held in 8 regions of the country and then in the National Camp centre with representatives from the regions and many observers. The subject for discussion usually comes from the theme of the World Conference. In 1974 Japan hostessed the Asia Pacific Camp, the first organized for the members of the Region. This camp had the theme 'For a Greater Co-operation' and was attended by 4,000 participants.

PROGRAMME

In 1973 Japan put into practice the new programme which had been developed after a 5-year study by a special committee on the future needs of Girl Scouting. This programme focuses on three major points: 'Self Development', 'Human Relations' and 'Nature'. The age levels have been changed and in addition to Brownie, Junior, Senior and Ranger Scouts which cover girls from 6 to 17 years old, adult Girl Scouts (over 17) have been introduced. The programme is flexible, more appealing and designed to meet better the needs of contemporary girls. Activities based on the three points are developed and expanded according to each age level.

PUBLIC RELATIONS AND PUBLICATIONS

Leaders' magazine, newsletters, and international newsletters are issued every other month. The international newsletter reproduces articles from *Council Fire*, the *World Bureau Newsletter* and the *Regional Newsletter* translated into Japanese. It also publishes reports of international exchanges and events.

Many pamphlets have been produced to recruit Leaders and Girl Scouts and to publicize the Movement among the general public. Girl Scout activities and special events are often telecast, and several films have been made for public relations and educational purposes.

TRAINING AND SERVICE

Many Leaders join as advisers to the groups sent to foreign countries on goodwill missions sponsored by the government and by other youth organizations, and it is felt that the Girl Scouts are successfully promoting international understanding. Trainers are contributing by helping with leadership training for other youth organizations. More activities for the handicapped are being undertaken and Girl Scouts help with the national environmental campaign, planting trees to beautify the land and protect it from floods and air pollution.

Efforts are being made to create a 'Girl Scout Forest' on a long-term plan of 20–30 years.

Girl Scouts of Japan organized a workshop on the 'Role of Women in the Prevention of Juvenile Delinquency', and have a home-visiting project which enables them to get to know the U.S.A. Girl Scouts whose families live in Japan.

CO-OPERATION WITH OTHER ORGANIZATIONS

Japan co-operates with UNICEF and UNESCO, and one of the programme requirements is a knowledge of the workings of the United Nations and its Agencies.

Jordan

Girl Guides of Jordan

Promise

On my honour I will do my best;
To do my duty to God, my country,
and the King;
To help other people at all times;
And to obey the Guide's Law.

GUIDE

Law

1 A Guide is to be trusted.
2 A Guide is loyal to God, her country, the King, and her parents, employers, and employees.
3 A Guide is a friend to all and a sister to every other Guide.
4 A Guide is kind to animals.
5 A Guide is obedient to parents, and patrol leaders.
6 A Guide is helpful and useful to others.
7 A Guide is polite and courteous.
8 A Guide is cheerful, courageous and smiles in difficulties.
9 A Guide is thrifty.
10 A Guide is pure in thought, words and deeds.

Motto

Be Prepared

Brownie Promise

I promise to do my best:
To do my duty to God, my country,
and the King;
To obey the Brownie's Law, and to
carry out a good deed every day.

BROWNIE

Brownie Motto

Do my best

Age Groups

Ranger	18–23
Girl Guide	11–18
Brownie	7–11

Guiding started in Jordan in 1954 when the Ministry of Education began to recognize its usefulness. Girls in the schools were encouraged to become Guides, and courses were held for teachers wishing to become Guiders. Nowadays, most companies are attached to schools, but Guiding remains entirely voluntary. The Association works through a network of 12 districts, each with a regional committee.

In 1961 the Association was officially recognized and registered. Her Majesty the Queen Mother was the first Honorary President and in 1962 the first officers were elected. In 1963 H.M. King Hussein issued a decree placing the Association under royal protection and in the same year the Girl Guides Association of Jordan was recognized as an Associate Member of WAGGGS at the 18th World Conference (Denmark, 1963).

The predominant religion is Moslem, but the Association is open to girls of all creeds. Great emphasis is placed on the Promise and the Law, and Guiding as a whole receives the full support of those concerned with youth education and community development in the country.

TRAINING

Girl Guides of Jordan attach much importance to training at all levels. Summer training camps and short-term training and refresher courses are held throughout the year according to the needs of the districts. Between 1969 and 1975 a total of almost 800 Leaders attended training courses in Jordan as well as in Lebanon, Egypt and Syria.

JAMBOREES

These are popular events among Jordanian Guides who participate in their National Jamborees (500 Guides attended a Jamboree in Ajiloun, the National Camp Site). The Association usually sends large delegations to the Arab Jamborees for Girl Guides.

SERVICE

Guides in towns and villages throughout Jordan play their part in public and national services, helping others in their communities, planting trees to combat soil erosion, cleaning their countryside, etc. Most of the Guides and Leaders in the schools are trained in community service, life-saving and fire-fighting by specialized officers from the Jordanian Civil Defence Department. During the war the Guides gave assistance in hospitals and in the distribution of food, and set up refugee camps. They organize lectures on hygiene and sanitation and have also responded to an appeal for blood donors.

Guides and Brownies regularly visit hospitals, shelters, homes for the disabled and orphanages, bringing gifts and providing entertainment. Guides have also taken part in important national and religious ceremonies.

Kenya

Kenya Girl Guides Association

Promise

I promise on my honour that I will
do my best:
To do my duty to God and my
Country,
To help other people at all times,
and
To obey the Guide Law.

GUIDE

Law

1 A Guide's honour is to be trusted.
2 A Guide is loyal.
3 A Guide's duty is to be useful and to help others.
4 A Guide is a friend to all and a sister to every other Guide.
5 A Guide is courteous.
6 A Guide is a friend to animals.
7 A Guide obeys orders.
8 A Guide smiles and sings under all difficulties.
9 A Guide is thrifty.
10 A Guide is pure in thought, word and deed.

Motto

Be Prepared

Brownie Promise

I promise to do my best:
To do my duty to God and my
Country,
To help other people every day,
especially those at home.

BROWNIE

Brownie Law

A Brownie is truthful, obedient and
cheerful;
A Brownie thinks of others before
herself.

Brownie Motto

Lend a Hand

Age Groups

Ranger	15–21
Guide	11–16
Brownie	8–11

The first Kenyan Guide company was started in Nairobi in 1920. The earliest units were made up entirely of European girls, but by 1936 African and Asian units had been formed. The Guide Movement spread rapidly during the following years, its growth being halted only by the Second World War. By 1959 Cadet companies and Ranger units were in existence. The Kenya Girl Guides Association was recognized as an Associate Member of the World Association in 1963, and as a Full Member at the 22nd World Conference (United Kingdom, 1975).

The Association has its headquarters in Nairobi. It is also fortunate in having a residential training centre, Guide House, opened in 1963 by the World Chief Guide, and a good camping site.

TRAINING

The year 1949 saw the first residential training course and training camp for all communities in Kenya, and since then training has held a place of special importance in Kenyan Guiding. The Association regularly issues invitations to neighbouring countries to attend local trainings and camps, thereby developing closer ties with other African Guide Associations. WAGGGS Trainers have gone to Kenya to provide intense leadership training and, in line with a policy of decentralization, many Leaders are given training in their own regions.

SERVICE

The Association is actively involved in many areas of service. Handicapped children are encouraged to be part of the Movement. There are Guide and Brownie units in schools for the deaf and the blind and, wherever possible, handicapped children are integrated into non-handicapped units.

Dependent on its agriculture, water is of utmost importance in Kenya. A water pump was the welcome gift of the 'Freedom From Hunger' campaign in Kenya to the Kenya Girl Guides Association. Destined specifically for the Extension Project for Women and Young Girls in the Mitabeni in Machakos, the pump will provide the Guides with enough water to continue teaching health, hygiene, nutrition and child-care, and to continue growing their own vegetable garden.

Kenyan Guides are also taking part in the 'Water is Life' competition, run by the 'Freedom From Hunger' campaign, in co-operation with the Ministry of Agriculture and the Ministry of Water Development.

CO-OPERATION WITH OTHER ORGANIZATIONS

The Association works with the United Nations Environment Programme on world environment activities. Kenyan Guides represented WAGGGS at the NGO World Assembly on Environment and the Youth NGO Working Party on Environment held in Nairobi in March 1976.

SUB-REGIONAL GATHERINGS

In 1976 the Kenya Girl Guides Association was one of the four African associations to hostess a WAGGGS sub-regional gathering.

Korea

Girl Scouts of Korea

GIRL SCOUT

Sun-on	**Promise**
Na-neun na-e myung-ei-rul wi-ha-yo da-um-e jo-mo-geul gut-ge-ji-ki-get sum-ni-da:	On my honour, I will try:
1 Ha-na-nim-gwa na-ra-reul wi-ha-yo na-e him-eul da ha-get seum-ni-da.	To do my duty to God and my Country;
2 Hang-sang da-run sa-ram-ul do-wa joo-get sum-ni-da.	To help other people at all times;
3 Girl Scout-ui geu-eu-reul jal ji-ki get sum-ni-da.	To obey the Girl Scout Law.

Geu-eul	**Law**
1 Girl Scout-un jin-sil ha-da.	A Girl Scout's honour is to be trusted.
2 Girl Scout-un choong-sung han-da.	A Girl Scout is loyal.
3 Girl Scout-un na-mal dob-ko yu-ik-han i-rul han-da.	A Girl Scout's duty is to be useful and to help others.
4 Girl Scout-un u-ai hamyo da-run Girl Scout-ul hyung-je-ro yu-gi-go jun-se-gei sa-ram-ul dong-po-ro yo-gin-da.	A Girl Scout is a friend to all and a sister to every other Girl Scout.
5 Girl Scout-un yei-rul jon-joong han-da.	A Girl Scout is courteous.
6 Girl Scout-un dong-mu-rul ai-ho han-da.	A Girl Scout is a friend to animals.
7 Girl Scout-un soon-jong han-da.	A Girl Scout obeys orders.
8 Girl Scout-un kwe-hwal ha-da.	A Girl Scout is cheerful.
9 Girl Scout-un gum-yak han-da.	A Girl Scout is thrifty.
10 Girl Scout-un mom-gwama-um-ul get-geu-si ga-zin-da.	A Girl Scout is clean in thought, word and deed.

Motto

Joon-bi	Be Prepared

Brownie Scout Promise

Ha-na-nim-gwa na-ra-reul wi-ha-yo na-e him-eul da ha-get sum-ni-da. Hang-sang da-run sa-ram-ul dob-go teuk-hi jib-e-seu gae-jok-ul dob get sum-ni-da.	I promise to do my best, to love God and my country, to help other people every day, especially those at home.

BROWNIE SCOUT

Brownie Scout Law

Brownie Scout-un son-wit sa-ram-ei deut-ul bat-dum-ni-da.	A Brownie gives in to the older folk.
Brownie Scout-un Jei go-jib dai-ro ha-gi an-sum-ni-da.	A Brownie does not give in to herself.

Brownie Scout Motto

Do-ub-ja	Lend a Hand

Age Groups

Yun-jang dai-won	Senior Girl Scout	16–20
So-nyo dai-won	Intermediate Girl Scout	12–15
Yoo-nyo dai-won	Brownie Scout	8–11

The Girl Scout Movement in Korea began in the spring of 1946, but its expansion was halted by the war in 1950. The revival came in 1955 with a visit of the World Association Trainer. Korea was recognized as an Associate Member of WAGGGS at the 16th World Conference (Brazil, 1957) and as a Full Member at the 18th World Conference (Denmark, 1963). Until quite recently the Movement had been developing on a very limited scale, but it is gaining in popularity as a result of the continuous enthusiasm and persistence of its Leaders.

LEADERSHIP TRAINING

With continuous difficulties in recruiting sufficient numbers of Leaders, attempts are being made to involve university students. They are organized in special troops in which Leadership training is given. Every year Brownie, Junior and Senior Girl Scout Leaders meet for a three-day seminar and a training session at the Girl Scout Headquarters in Seoul to re-examine their programme and work out guidelines for the future.

SERVICE

In 1962 Girl Scouts of Korea were awarded the Walter Donald Ross Trophy for their work with literacy classes for village women over a period of two years. In 1973 they organized a 'Friends of Sangam' project to help the WAGGGS World Centre in India.

Korean Girl Scouts work in remote villages, instructing the population in hygiene and in ways to improve their daily life. In 1975 troops in the Pusan area welcomed Vietnamese refugees and taught reading and writing to hospital patients.

Also in 1975, as a celebration for International Women's Year, Girl Scouts made a special effort to promote the Movement in Korea.

CO-OPERATION WITH OTHER ORGANIZATIONS

Under the UNESCO Gift Coupon Programme the Association has received assistance to buy equipment for a new Leaders' training centre. They also work with the National Council of Youth Organizations.

1 ▶

▲4

2 ▶

1. The courtyard at Sangam.

2. Off for a day's ski-ing at Our Chalet!

3. A characteristic view of Our Cabaña.

4. The World Chief Guide with the Guider-in-Charge at Olave House.

3 ▶

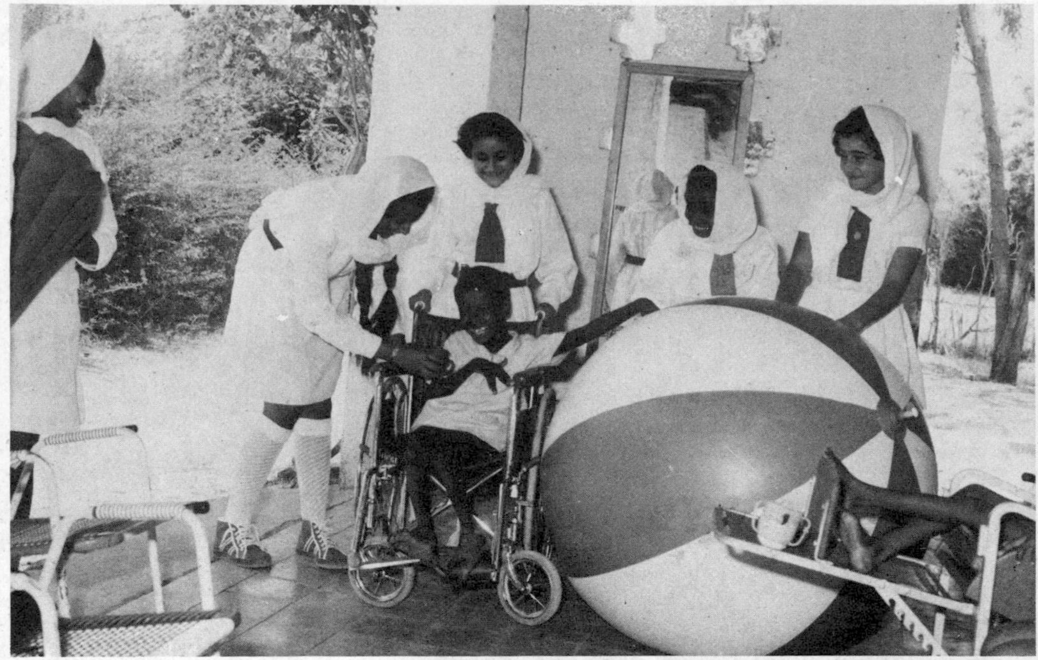

▲5

5. *Guides in Sudan help in a hospital for physically handicapped children.*

6. *South African Guides help the experts to clean oil from penguins caught on polluted beaches.*

7. *Brownies in the U.S.A. learn how to prepare a meal.*

8. *Iranian Girl Scouts clear up litter during Good Turn Week.*

9. *Greek Guides busy drawing posters for their 'protect nature' campaign.*

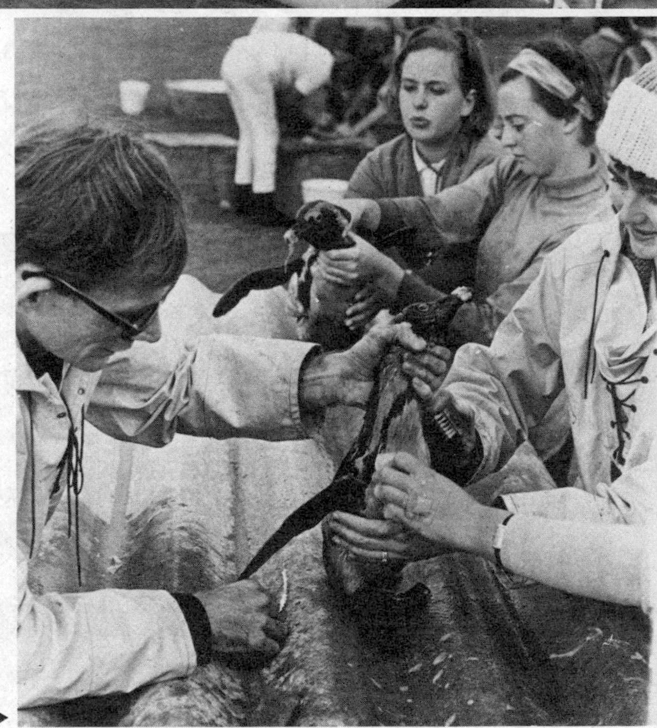

6 ▶

▼ 7

▼ 8

9

10 ▼

11 ▲

▼ 12

▼ 14

▲ 13

10. Kenyan Guides enthusiastically begin the daunting task of cleaning up the village.

11. Girl Scouts in the Philippines teach songs, games and handicrafts to children who do not attend school.

12. Brownies are always cheerful!

13. A Brazilian Guide totally involved in her handicraft.

14. A Mexican Brownie makes her Promise.

15. Israeli Girl and Boy Scouts gather together at the end of a day's hike.

16. Cave exploration is part of this Swedish Guide's programme.

17. Two Australian Guides on Thinking Day – their thoughts with Guides in other countries.

18. These Finnish Guides agree that cooking over an open fire is part of the fun of a camp.

19. Indian women are taught to read and write by Peruvian Guides as part of their Association's literacy programme.

20. French Brownies present a musical comedy.

15 ▶

▼ 16

▲ 17

▼ 18

▲ 19

▲ 20

▲ *21. Learning to sew could be the first step towards a future job for these Nigerian Guides.*

▼ *22. A Thinking Day ceremony in the U.K.*

Kuwait

Kuwait Girl Guides Association

GUIDE

Promise

I promise upon my honour to do my best,
in doing my duty towards God and my country;
in helping people under all circumstances;
in following the Law of the Girl Guides.

Law

1 The honour of the Girl Guides is faith and confidence.
2 The Girl Guide is sincere towards her country, her parents, her seniors and her juniors (sincere).
3 The Girl Guide should be useful to herself and to others (useful).
4 The Girl Guide is the friend to all and sister to every other Girl Guide (lovable).
5 The Girl Guide is of good character (polite).
6 The Girl Guide is kind to animals (kind).
7 The Girl Guide sincerely obeys her parents, the head of her division and the leaders of her group.
8 The Girl Guide smiles in the face of trouble and faces it with patience and steadfastness (smiling).
9 The Girl Guide is thrifty.
10 The Girl Guide is pure-hearted, decent in word and generous in deed (pure).

FLOWER

Flower Promise

I promise to do my best in carrying out my duty towards God and the Motherland, and in helping people under all circumstances, especially those at home.

Flower Law

The Flower must obey those who are older, must be resolute, must not yield to her whims, must take the Flower Promise.

Girl Guiding started in Kuwait on a very limited basis in 1957. By 1960, however, much improved programmes helped to put the Movement on a firmer footing, and Guiding then spread to most schools throughout the country. By 1965 the Association was established and licensed by the Ministry of Social Affairs and Labour, and the Kuwait Girl Guides Association became an Associate Member of the World Association at the 19th World Conference (Japan, 1966). Full

Membership was granted to the Association at the 21st World Conference (Canada, 1972). Guiding is now an active educational force in the country offering young girls and women the welcome opportunity for training in leadership.

PROGRAMME

Since the Association is a comparatively young one, the programme has been designed along modern lines and is well planned, based on the principles of educational psychology and sociology aiming to develop the girl's personality, making her self-sufficient, and encouraging her contribution to the community.

TRAINING

The Association is keenly aware of the need for Leaders, and trainings for all three branches (Flowers, Guides and Rangers) are held regularly. Guiders from Kuwait also attend trainings in other Arab countries.

SERVICE

Service includes participation in public services, cleaning the city, collecting clothes, food, etc., for the poor and generally helping in charity projects. Girl Guides also endeavour to give assistance to service projects in neighbouring countries.

PRESS AND PUBLIC RELATIONS

The Association has its own Information and Press Committees and publishes its own camp magazine. The various branches have publications relating to their programme and there is also a booklet, in Arabic and English, on the Girl Guides Association of Kuwait and several other pamphlets and leaflets on Guide activities.

The Association enjoys an excellent standing in the community, and Guiding has been acknowledged as the leading Movement for girls in the country.

Lebanon

Organisation Nationale Des Guides et des Eclaireuses du Liban

ASSOCIATION DES GUIDES DU LIBAN

Promesse

Avec vous toutes, confiante en Dieu qui m'aime, je promets de faire tout mon possible : pour rendre les autres heureux, pour être utile à mon pays, et vivre selon la loi de toutes les guides du monde.

Promise

With all of you, trusting God who loves me, I promise to do my best: to make others happy, to serve my country and to live in accordance with the Law of all Guides throughout the world.

GUIDE

Loi	Law
1 On peut compter sur une guide.	A Guide's honour is to be trusted.
2 La guide est loyale.	A Guide is truthful.
3 Le devoir d'une guide est d'être utile et de servir les autres.	A Guide's duty is to be useful and to help others.
4 La guide est l'amie de tous.	A Guide is a friend to all.
5 La guide est généreuse.	A Guide is generous.
6 La guide aime les plantes et les animaux.	A Guide likes plants and animals.
7 La guide sait obéir, elle a l'esprit d'équipe.	A Guide knows how to obey, she has the patrol spirit.
8 La guide est maîtresse de soi; elle réagit dans les difficultés.	A Guide masters herself and her difficulties.
9 La guide a le respect des autres et de leurs biens.	A Guide respects others and their belongings.
10 La guide est pure et joyeuse.	A Guide is pure and joyous.

Motto

Etre prête	Be prepared

Brownie Promise

Je promets de faire de mon mieux pour être fidèle à Dieu, au Liban, à la loi de la Ronde, à mes parents, et pour faire chaque jour un plaisir à quelqu'un.	I promise to do my best, to be faithful to God, to Lebanon, to the law of the Pack, and to my parents, and to do a good turn to somebody every day.

Brownie Law

Une jeannette est toujours propre.	A Brownie is always neat.
Une jeannette est toujours active.	A Brownie is always active.
Une jeannette est toujours gaie.	A Brownie is always cheerful.
Une jeannette dit toujours vrai.	A Brownie always tells the truth.
Une jeannette pense d'abord aux autres.	A Brownie thinks first of others.

BROWNIE

Brownie Motto

De notre mieux	Of our best power

Age Groups

Jeunes en marche	'Youth on the Move'	17–18
Caravelle	'Caravelle' Guide	15–17
Guide (Farandole)	'Farandole' Guide	12–15

ASSOCIATION DES ECLAIREUSES DU LIBAN

Promesse	Promise
Avec vous toutes, confiante en Dieu qui m'aime, je promets de faire tout mon possible: pour rendre les autres heureux, pour être utile à mon pays, et vivre selon la loi de toutes les éclaireuses du monde.	With all of you, trusting God who loves me, I promise to do my best: to make others happy, to serve my country and to live in accordance with the law of all Girl Scouts throughout the world.

GUIDE

Loi

L'éclaireuse envers elle-même
L'éclaireuse est courtoise et généreuse.
L'éclaireuse obéit sans réplique et ne fait rien à moitié.
L'éclaireuse est maîtresse d'elle-même, elle sourit et chante dans ses difficultés.
L'éclaireuse est économe et prend soin du bien d'autrui.
L'éclaireuse est pure dans ses pensées, ses actes et ses paroles.
L'éclaireuse envers la société
L'éclaireuse met son honneur à mériter confiance.
L'éclaireuse est faite pour servir et aider son prochain.
L'éclaireuse est amie de tous et sœur de toute éclaireuse.
L'éclaireuse envers son pays
L'éclaireuse est fidèle à son pays.
L'éclaireuse participe au développement du Liban.
L'éclaireuse et la nature
L'éclaireuse voit la beauté de la nature, elle aime les plantes et les animaux.

Law

The Girl Scout towards herself
A Girl Scout is courteous and generous.
A Girl Scout obeys without question and does nothing by halves.
A Girl Scout is self-controlled, she smiles and sings under difficulties.
A Girl Scout is thrifty and takes care of the belongings of others.
A Girl Scout is pure in her thoughts, deeds and words.
The Girl Scout towards society
A Girl Scout's honour is to be trusted.
A Girl Scout's duty is to serve and help others.
A Girl Scout is a friend to all and a sister to every Girl Scout.
The Girl Scout towards her country
A Girl Scout is loyal to her country.
A Girl Scout participates in the development of the Lebanon.
The Girl Scout and nature
A Girl Scout sees the beauty of nature, she loves plants and animals.

Motto

Etre prête

Be Prepared

BROWNIE

Brownie Promise

Je promets de faire de mon mieux pour obéir à Dieu, aimer mon pays, prêter la main chaque jour.

I promise to do my best to love God and my country and to lend a hand every day.

Brownie Law

La petite aile va à la découverte de son monde et propage l'amour et la gaieté.

The Brownie sets out to discover her world and radiates love and joy.

Brownie Motto

Fait de son mieux

Does her best

Age Groups

Eclaireuse aînée	Ranger	16–20
Eclaireuse	Girl Scout	13–16
Petite aile (Zahrat)	Brownie	7–12

Guiding started in the Lebanon in 1939 with the establishment of the Association des Guides du Liban. This Association, accepted then as the national organization in the Lebanon, became an Associate Member of WAGGGS at the 15th World Conference (The Netherlands, 1954).

In 1958 the Association des Eclaireuses du Liban was established.

In 1960 The Guides du Liban and the Eclaireuses du Liban joined together to form the Organisation Nationale des Guides et des Eclaireuses du Liban, and in 1963 at the 18th World Conference (Denmark) this organization, now recognized as the national organization in the Lebanon, became a Full Member of WAGGGS.

METHODS

In the years 1970–3 Commissioners and Leaders of the National Organization concentrated on rethinking the methods used in the Movement, with a view to reforming their own methods in order to make Guiding more effective and attractive to young people. The result of this study was that the Guide branch was divided into 'Farandole' and 'Caravelle' groups, with modified activities more suitable to their particular tastes and needs.

SERVICE

Guides in Lebanon have always been concerned with serving their country. They have held regular work camps in co-operation with the Office of Social Development, and have always worked with handicapped and underprivileged children.

During the civil war the Girl Guides and Boy Scouts worked with other voluntary organizations and with the government, bringing relief in the stricken areas and helping to maintain services in Beirut where the municipal authorities were unable to continue.

As well as helping Red Cross and other medical workers to provide emergency health services during the main troubles, some Leaders and Commissioners set up a centre for the handicapped where people severely injured in the fighting but needing no further medical treatment could be rehabilitated. They ran the centre, located at an old convent in the mountains, until a comprehensive centre was opened by a Beirut association for the handicapped.

Liberia

The Liberian Girl Guides Association

GUIDE

Promise

I promise on my honour that I will do my best:
To do my duty to God;
To serve my country and help other people;
And to keep the Guide Law.

Law

1 A Guide is loyal and can be trusted.
2 A Guide is helpful.
3 A Guide is polite and considerate.
4 A Guide is friendly to all and a sister to all Guides.
5 A Guide is kind to animals and respects all living things.
6 A Guide is obedient.
7 A Guide has courage and is cheerful in all difficulties.
8 A Guide makes good use of her time and talent.
9 A Guide takes care of her own possessions and those of other people.
10 A Guide controls herself and is clean in all she thinks, says and does.

Motto

Be Prepared

Brownie Guide Promise

I promise that I will do my best:
To do my duty to God;
To serve my country and help other people;
And to keep the Brownie Guide Law.

Brownie Guide Law

1 A Brownie Guide thinks of others before herself.
2 A Brownie Guide does a Good Turn every day.

Brownie Guide Motto

Be Helpful

Age Groups

Ranger	16–21
Guide	12–16
Brownie	7–11

Girl Guiding was started in Liberia in 1920 and when the World Association of Girl Guides and Girl Scouts was formed in 1928, Liberia became one of its Founder Members. However, by 1930 all contact between WAGGGS and the Liberian National Organization was lost, and its membership was cancelled in 1931. From 1953 to 1955 efforts were made to restart Guiding, and in 1955 a representative of the World Association visited Liberia and helped to bring together isolated groups of Guides and to form the nucleus of a National Organization. Over the next 10 years Girl Guiding spread to all areas of the country.

Liberia regained her membership of the World Association, becoming an Associate Member of WAGGGS at the 19th World Conference (Japan, 1966). The Liberian Girl Guides Association was recognized as a Full Member of WAGGGS at the 22nd World Conference (U.K., 1975).

STRUCTURE

The governing body of the Liberian Girl Guides Association is the National Council which meets once a year. The Executive body, which meets every month, is responsible for carrying out the decisions of the Council and for the administration of the Association.

PROGRAMME

Girl Guiding is mainly confined to the schools and is based on the U.K. Guide programme adapted to suit the needs of the Liberian girl.

Much is being done to stimulate interest and increase numbers in the Ranger Branch, the one most adversely affected by girls leaving the rural areas to study in towns.

The National Organization is also working on a literacy programme which it plans to introduce into the Guide programme in an effort to make it more suitable to the needs of the girl and her background.

The international aspect of Guiding is well emphasized in the programme. Guides and Rangers are encouraged to develop contacts with Girl Guides in other countries and the Liberian Girl Guides Association is regularly represented at international and world events.

TRAINING

Training in Liberia is the responsibility of a team composed of the Trainer/Adviser, the Chief Commissioner, Deputy Commissioner and two others.

A Leadership Training is held annually at national level. These Trainings cover all aspects of Guiding and are held in a different country each year. Emphasis is often placed on the training of Leaders from rural areas as part of the Association's policy of promoting Guiding in the less developed areas of the country.

PUBLICATIONS

The Association publishes a handbook which covers test-work as well as general information on Guiding, and plans to increase its publications. The Association also publishes an annual report of its activities.

PUBLIC RELATIONS/CO-OPERATION WITH OTHER ORGANIZATIONS

The National Organization maintains good contacts with the public through the press, radio and television. The Liberian Girl Guides Association is a member of Liberia's National Council of Youth and participates in its activities. It is a member of the National Federation of Liberian Women's Organizations and the Liberian National Council of Social Welfare. It also works closely with the Urban Youth Council through which it is a member of the World Assembly of Youth.

ATTENDANCE AT INTERNATIONAL EVENTS

The Association was represented at the International Youth Population Conference held in Bucharest in 1974. A delegation also represented Liberia at the Regional Seminar for Africa held in Sierra Leone in 1975, and the Association sent delegates to the 22nd World Conference of WAGGGS held in the U.K. in 1975.

SERVICE

The Association organizes an annual camp, at which subjects such as health, sanitation and child-care are taught. In this context agriculture, gardening, cooking and handicrafts are also sometimes included. Lectures are given by experts, and at camp the Guides run their own vegetable garden. Guides also visit the sick and house-bound, old people's homes and local hospitals, and are active in campaigns for the protection of the environment.

The Association is working on a project to help a school for handicapped children.

Libya

The Girl Guides of Libya

GUIDE

Al'Ahed

Owahido moksimatan be sharafi ala an akuma biwagibi:
Nahwa Allah walwatan wal Malik;

Limosaadati annas wa baki almakhlukat fi colli hin;
Li itaat Shariat Almorshidat.

Promise

On my honour I promise:
To do my best in carrying out my duty to God, the country and the King;
To help people and other creatures at all times;
To obey the Guide Law.

Asharia

1 Shafu Almorshida youtaku bihi wa youtamado alayhi.
2 Al'Morshida mpkhlisa lwaly amriha wa wataniha wa lkullin min roasaiha wa marushida.
3 Al'Morshida nafia wa tusaid al' akharin.
4 Al'Morshida sadikatan lilgamia wa okhton likolli Morshida.
5 Al'Morshida mohaddabah.
6 Al'Morshida mohibatan lilhayawan.
7 Al'Morshida motiatan li'awliyaaha wa roasaiha dona taradod.
8 Al'Morshida tabsam wa tahza bessiab.
9 Al'Morshida moktasida.
10 Al'Morshida tahirato alficri wal'couli wal'amal.

Law

A Guide's honour is to be trusted and relied upon.
A Guide is loyal to her guardian, her country and both her superiors and subordinates.
A Guide is useful and helps others at all times.
A Guide is friend to all and sister to every Guide.
A Guide is courteous.
A Guide is kind to all animals.
A Guide is obedient to her guardians and superiors without hesitation.
A Guide sings and smiles in times of difficulties.
A Guide is thrifty.
A Guide is virtuous in thought, word and deed.

Motto

Waidou

Stand ready

BROWNIE

Brownie Promise

Aedo bean abthola gohdi:
Le'an akuma biwagibi nahwa Allah walwatan walmalik;
Li an amal beshariat Azzaharat, wa amal khairan kulla yawm.

I promise on my honour that I will do my best:
To do my duty to God, country and the King;
To obey the Brownie Law.

Brownie Law

Azzahra tutia Alyamama.
Azzahra la tutia nafsaha.

A Brownie gives in to older folk.
A Brownie does not give in to herself.

Brownie Motto

Abdula johdi	I do my best

Girl Guiding was first established in Libya in 1958. Initially Guiding did not extend beyond a small number of women teachers and students, but gradually more and more people joined the Movement. Guiding in Libya strives to promote a continuous education in the spheres of social, religious and physical development. The principles of the Movement have won support and respect throughout the country. The Girl Guides of Libya was recognized as an Associate Member of the World Association at the 19th World Conference (Japan, 1966).

TRAINING

The importance of training is emphasized, and the Girl Guides headquarters has made great efforts to train leaders and qualify them to assume various leadership responsibilities. They have, from time to time, sent a number of Libyan leaders to London for training.

ARAB REGIONAL ACTIVITIES

The Girl Guides of Libya acted as hostess to various other Girl Guides Associations, participating in both the first Arab Girl Guides' Jamboree and the Arab Girl Guides' Conference which were held in Tripoli in 1966.

SERVICE

The Girl Guides of Libya endeavour to foster a spirit of service and carry out a wide range of activities among which are work in the field of literacy and assistance to the handicapped. They are also involved in aiding families in need, participating in world child and mother day celebrations and help during national traffic weeks.

Liechtenstein

Pfadfinderinnen des Fürstentums Liechtenstein

GUIDE

Versprechen	**Promise**
Ich bin bereit im Vertrauen auf Gott dem Frieden zu dienen, für Fürst und Vaterland einzustehen und nach dem Pfadfinderinnengesetze zu leben.	Trusting in God, I am prepared to serve the cause of peace, to support my Prince and my country and to live according to the Girl Guide Law.

Gesetz	**Law**
1 Ich will aufrichtig und zuverlässig sein.	I will be honest and reliable.
2 Ich will hilfsbereit und rücksichtsvoll sein.	I will be helpful and considerate.

3 Ich will den anderen achten.	I will respect other people.
4 Ich will die Verantwortung anderer anerkennen und selbst Verantwortung übernehmen.	I will accept the responsibility of others and am willing to take over responsibility myself.
5 Ich will das Leben achten.	I will respect and take care of life.
6 Ich will die Zeit und meine Fähigkeiten richtig nutzen.	I will make good use of time and of my gifts.
7 Ich will Schwierigkeiten nicht ausweichen.	I will not evade difficulties.
8 Ich will mich beherrschen.	I will practise self-discipline.
9 Ich will die Natur kennenlernen und helfen sie zu erhalten.	I will get to know the natural world and help to preserve it.
10 Ich will meinen Weg zu Gott suchen.	I will seek my way to God.

Motto

Allzeit bereit	Be Prepared

BROWNIE

Brownie Promise

Ich will mir Mühe geben, mein Bestes zu tun um Gott, meinen Eltern und dem Bienligesetz zu gehorchen.	I promise to do my best to do my duty to God, my parents and to obey the Brownie Law.

Brownie Law

Das Bienli gehorcht seinen Eltern, Erziehern und Führerinnen und hilft seinen Mitmenschen.	The Brownie obeys her parents, teachers and leaders and helps other people.

Brownie Motto

Freudig helfen	To help joyfully

Age Groups

Ranger	Ranger	19+
Jung-Ranger	Young Ranger	16–18
Pfadfinderin	Guide	11–16
Bienli	Brownie	8–11

The Girl Guide Movement started in Liechtenstein in 1938 with one small group of Guides. Ten years later Liechtenstein became an Associate Member of the World Association at the 12th World Conference (U.S.A., 1948), and was recognized as a Full Member at the 14th World Conference (Norway, 1952).

From such a small beginning the Movement has developed and spread throughout the principality, and its membership is now relatively high.

CONTACTS AT NATIONAL AND INTERNATIONAL LEVEL

Since 1973 Guides in Leichtenstein have been holding annual provincial meetings which take place during a week-end in autumn. Each meeting has a definite theme (1973 – the countries of Europe; 1974 – Energy sources throughout the centuries; 1975 – Girl Guides yesterday, today and tomorrow; 1976 – Girl Guides study the scope of leisure centres).

Liechtenstein recognizes the importance of contact with Girl Guides from other countries, and its Guides have attended camps in France, Switzerland, Luxembourg, Austria, Germany, Denmark, Norway and Belgium. Within Liechtenstein itself, the different Branches of the Movement hold Easter and summer camps. Young Leaders also attend educational courses and seminars in Switzerland and in Austria.

CO-OPERATION WITH OTHER YOUTH ORGANIZATIONS

In recent years efforts have been made in Liechtenstein to bring about better co-operation between the Girl Guide Movement and other youth organizations in the country; these efforts illustrate the Members' belief that the Guide Movement needs to be 'open' to all influences affecting the youth of the country.

Regular contacts are maintained with Boy Scouts and in 1975 the Guides of Liechtenstein worked alongside the Scouts in the organization of general educational courses.

SERVICE

Rangers have been active in promoting women's rights within their country, and the Guide programme includes lectures on the legal situation of women in Liechtenstein and on issues of interest to them.

The organization of day-care centres for children also comes within the gamut of Ranger service, as does assistance in a national home for handicapped children.

The Guides are concerned about the well-being of the aged, and hold an 'Alt-Leute Tag' (Old Folk's Day) as part of their project 'Contact between Young and Old'. This day is celebrated with a festive lunch and dances and plays performed by the Brownies.

On every first Saturday of Advent, Guides in all the districts hold a Christmas market. All profits go towards the Liechtenstein Missionary fund.

Luxembourg

Bureau de Liaison des Associations Guides de Luxembourg

Association des Girl Guides Luxembourgeoises

GUIDE

Promesse	**Promise**
Ech verspriechen op meng E'er, mei Bescht ze mân fir:	I promise on my honour to do my best:
Trei zu God an zum Land ze stoen;	To serve God and my country;
Allen de'an der No't sin ze hellefen;	To help all those in need;
d'Guidegesetz ze befolijen.	To obey the Guide Law.

Code	**Law**
1 Eng Guide – e Wuert.	A Guide – a word.
2 Eng Guide stét trei ze hirer Pflicht.	A Guide does her duty faithfully.

3 Eng Guide ass ömmer berét ânere beizestoen.	A Guide is always ready to help others.
4 All Guide si Schwesteren.	All Guides are sisters.
5 Eng Guide ass offen an he'ferlech ge'nt jidderén.	A Guide is sincere and polite to everyone.
6 Eng Guide ass gudd ge'nt De'eren.	A Guide is kind to animals.
7 Eng Guide huet Disciplin.	A Guide is disciplined.
8 Eng Guide ass ömmer fro'.	A Guide is always cheerful.
9 Eng Guide ass energesch, fleisseg a spuersam.	A Guide is energetic, industrious and thrifty.
10 Eng Guide ass proper u Kierper a Se'l; sie sét a mecht neischt Schlechtes.	A Guide remains clean in body and mind; she speaks and does no evil.

Motto

Solidarité	Solidarity

BROWNIE

Brownie Promise

Ech verspriechen mei Bescht ze man fir:	I promise to do my best:
Wichtelchesgesetz ze befollegen; All Dag eppes Gutts ze dun.	To obey the Law of the Brownies and to do a 'good thing' every day.

Brownie Law

Eng Wichtelchen ass fröndlech a frou.	A Brownie is friendly and happy at heart.
Eng Wichtelchen ass urdentlech a propper.	A Brownie is organized and cares for cleanliness.
Eng Wichtelchen sét t'Worecht a follegt gudd.	A Brownie speaks the truth and listens to advice.

Brownie Motto

Solidarité	Solidarity

Age Groups

Ranger	Ranger	16–18
Guide	Guide (Senior)	14–16
	Guide (Junior)	11–14
Wichtelchen	Brownie	7–11

Letzeburger Guiden

GUIDE

Promesse	**Promise**
Ech verspriéchen op meng Eer a mat der Höllef vum Herrgott, mei Bescht ze dun, fir dem Herrgott, der Kiréch an der Hémecht ze dengen,	I promise on my honour and with the help of God to do my best to serve God, the Church and my Country.
alle Leit ze höllefen wé a wo ech kann, an d'Guidegestez ze befollechen.	To help everybody where and how I can and to follow the Guide Law.

Loi	Law
1 Eng Guide ass zouverlässeg.	A Guide is reliable.
2 Eng Guide stét a fir hire Glaw.	A Guide is true to her Faith.
3 Eng Guide mécht sech nötzlech an helleft gär.	A Guide makes herself useful and likes to help.
4 Eng Guide ass gudd zu all Mönsch.	A Guide is good and kind to everybody.
5 Eng Guide ass fair an hölt Rücksicht.	A Guide is fair and not selfish.
6 Eng Guide hält d'Liéwen an Eiren.	A Guide respects Life.
7 Eng Guide huet Disziplin.	A Guide has discipline.
8 Eng Guide färt keng Ustrengung an ass gudd opgeluegt.	A Guide does not mind any hard work and is always good tempered.
9 Eng Guide beherrscht sech u Kierper a Géscht an ass e froue Mönsch.	A Guide controls her body and her mind and is a gay human being.

Motto

Ommer beret	Be Prepared

BROWNIE

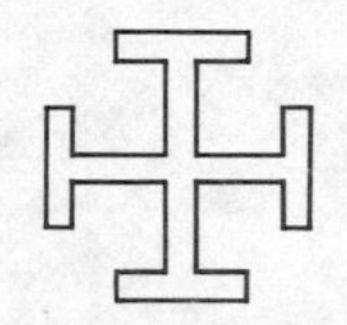

Brownie Promise

Ech verspriéche mei Bescht ze dun, fir dem Herrgott, mengen Eltern an dem Gesetz ze follechen, an all Dag engem eng Fréd ze machen.	I promise to do my best to be obedient to God, to my parents and to the Law and to give pleasure to somebody every day.

Brownie Law

De Wichtelchen denkt fir d'escht un dé aner.	A Brownie thinks first of other people.
Dem Wichtelchen entgét neischt.	A Brownie sees and hears everything.
De Wichtelchen ass ömmer propper.	A Brownie is always clean.
De Wichtelchen sét ömmer d'Worecht.	A Brownie always tells the truth.
De Wichtelchen ass ömmer fro'.	A Brownie is always full of joy.

Brownie Motto

Mir dun eist Bäscht	We do our best

Age Groups

Guide aînée	Ranger	over 16
Caravelle	Caravelle	14–16
Aventure	Adventure	11–13
Wichtelchen	Brownie	8–11

Guiding in Luxembourg started in 1915, and in 1916 an association called Association des Guides du Luxembourg was formed which united the many different troops in the country. In 1921 the AGGL (Association des Girl Guides Luxembourgeoises) was constituted; it became a Founder Member of the World Association in 1928.

The Letzeburger Guiden (Catholic Luxembourg Girl Guides) was founded in 1938 by the Director of the Action Catholique Féminine Luxembourgeoise.

The Bureau de Liaison des Associations Guides du Luxembourg was formed following the signing of an agreement, in October 1958, between the Association des Girl Guides Luxembourgeoises and the Letzeburger Guiden. In 1960, by decision of the 18th World Conference, the World Association of Girl Guides and Girl Scouts formally recognized the Bureau de Liaison as the national organization of Luxembourg. Thus membership of WAGGGS, which was granted to Luxembourg in 1928 in the name of the Association des Girl Guides Luxembourgeoises, was extended to include the Letzeburger Guiden.

Girl Guiding and Boy Scouting are recognized as public services in Luxembourg and Guides and Scouts are represented in the Conseil Supérieur National de l'Education Physique (National Council for Physical Education).

Association des Girl Guides Luxembourgeoises

PROGRAMME AND ACTIVITIES

A new Guide programme was adopted in 1970 and has since been modified to allow more flexibility and to enable girls to carry out the activities in their own way. Rangers especially have much freedom in the preparation of their programme.

Activities of the AGGL regularly feature tree-planting campaigns and fund-raising for an additional building to be constructed on the grounds of the training centre.

INTERNATIONAL GUIDING

International Guiding has always been the aim of AGGL and this is still one of the dominant characteristics of the Association which has now established 'Troop Twinning' with other countries. Many decisions taken over the years have reflected this interest, one example being the adoption of the World Flag as the flag of the AGGL in 1931.

Thinking Day is a truly international occasion with European Guides and U.S.A. Girl Scouts, who live in Luxembourg, working together to celebrate the day and promote the Thinking Day Fund.

Association des Girl Guides Luxembourgeoises has an International Guide Centre which since its opening in 1969 has been used by Girl Guides/Girl Scouts from many countries. Also, in 1966, the Association organized an international training for leaders from eight European countries.

CO-OPERATION WITH OTHER ORGANIZATIONS

The Association was active in the establishment of the General Conference of the Youth of Luxembourg and maintains good relations with other youth movements and with many women's organizations. It also gives assistance to a Children's Home run by the Red Cross.

Letzeburger Guiden (Catholic Luxembourg Girl Guides)

ACTIVITIES IN BRANCHES

The division into four new age groups some years ago has been successful and played a significant part in improving the standard of activities. Every year in May, the Wichtelcher (Brownies) hold a big rally for Wichtelcher from all over the country. Each rally has a theme such as that used in 1975 'The City – a Community'. Apart from this, they hold weekly meetings, outings and a camp which lasts for several days.

The Aventure branch (girls aged 11–13) organized a national camp in 1975.

Joint activities have been popular for some years at Ranger/Rover level; joint meetings are organized and joint trainings of Guiders and Scout Chiefs encouraged.

Handicapped Guides (called 'Gamma') are active members of the Movement; they have set up a recreation centre, hold bazaars and take part in camps.

LEADERSHIP TRAINING

Training weekends and teaching sessions for Leaders are organized, each Leader spending some time in a troop other than her own. Attendance at Training Camps for Leaders is an essential requirement for those wishing to obtain a Leader's certificate. Many Leaders' Days are held throughout the year.

SERVICE

Several troops have worked hard at a 'forest clearance' project which earned them the congratulations and thanks of the local authorities. Rangers, in co-operation with Rovers, have also been instrumental in beautifying the area surrounding an old pilgrims' church.

CO-OPERATION WITH OTHER ORGANIZATIONS

The Letzeburger Guiden regularly send delegates to meetings of other organizations in Luxembourg such as the Service National de la Jeunesse and the Association 'Natura' whose concern is Environment.

At the request of the Association Populaire et Familiale, the Letzeburger Guiden co-operated in a big exhibition held in 1975 on the following theme 'Nos femmes . . . nos enfants'. They set up displays and presented slides and photos in an effort to promote the Movement by explaining Guiding to parents.

IFOFSAG

The Luxembourg branch of IFOFSAG organizes a twice-yearly meeting during which former Guiders hold lectures on such themes as education, environment, youth employment, etc. They have also held some very successful Charity Bazaars for a project entitled 'S.O.S. Children's Village'.

In 1974 the Regional Gathering of IFOFSAG for the Benelux countries, Great Britain and Ireland was held in Luxembourg.

INTERNATIONAL CONTACTS

The Letzeburger Guiden are anxious to establish contacts with as many Guides from other countries as possible. They participate in Training Camps and

International Gatherings. Several troops have attended international camps in England, Finland, France and Norway, and have welcomed foreign Guide troops visiting Luxembourg.

Madagascar

Skotisma Zazavavy Eto Madagasikara

FANILON'I MADAGASIKARA

GUIDE

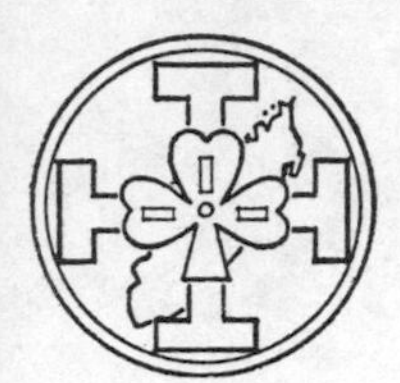

Promesse	Promise
Sur mon honneur et avec la grâce de Dieu, je m'engage à servir de mon mieux: Dieu, l'Eglise et la Patrie, à aider mon prochain en toutes circonstances, à observer la loi des guides.	On my honour and with the grace of God, I pledge myself to do my best to serve God, the Church and the Country; to help my neighbour in all circumstances and to observe the Guide Law.

Loi	Law
1 La guide est loyale.	A Guide is loyal.
2 La guide pense d'abord aux autres.	A Guide thinks first of others.
3 La guide est généreuse, elle est prête à servir.	A Guide is generous, she is ready to serve.
4 La guide est accueillante, elle a l'esprit d'équipe.	A Guide is welcoming, she has the team spirit.
5 La guide, sœur de toute autre guide, est présente à tous.	A Guide, sister to every other Guide, is available to all.
6 La guide découvre la nature, elle y voit l'œuvre de Dieu.	A Guide explores nature in which she sees the work of God.
7 La guide sait obéir.	A Guide understands obedience.
8 La guide ne craint pas l'effort; elle ne fait rien à moitié.	A Guide does not fear endeavour; she does nothing by halves.
9 La guide aime son travail et respecte celui des autres.	A Guide likes her work and respects that of others.
10 La guide est maîtresse de soi; elle est pure et joyeuse.	A Guide controls herself; she is pure and cheerful.

Motto

Toujours prête	Always ready

BROWNIE

Brownie Promise

Je promets de faire de mon mieux: pour être fidèle à Dieu, à mon pays, à mes parents, à la loi de la ronde, et pour faire chaque jour un plaisir à quelqu'un.	I promise to do my best: to be faithful to God, to my Country, to my parents and to the law of the Pack, and to do a good turn to somebody every day.

Brownie Law

Une jeannette est tourjours propre.	A Brownie is always neat.
Une jeannette est toujours active.	A Brownie is always active.
Une jeannette est toujours gaie.	A Brownie is always cheerful.
Une jeannette dit toujours vrai.	A Brownie always tells the truth.
Une jeannette pense d'abord aux autres.	A Brownie thinks first of others.

Brownie Motto

De notre mieux	Of our best

MPANAZAVA ETO MADAGASIKARA

GUIDE

Promesse	**Promise**
Je promets sur mon honneur de faire tout mon possible pour: servir Dieu, la Patrie, la famille; aider les autres chaque jour; obéir à la loi des Mpanazava. C'est avec l'aide de Dieu que je le promets.	On my honour I promise to do all I can: to serve God, the Country, the family; to help others every day; to obey the Girl Scout Law. By Almighty God, I so promise.

Loi	**Law**
1 Une Mpanazava est loyale; on peut compter sur elle, elle ne ment jamais.	A Girl Scout is loyal and can be depended upon, she never tells a lie.
2 Une Mpanazava est disciplinée, obéit avec joie, ponctuelle et ordonnée.	A Girl Scout is disciplined, obeys cheerfully, is punctual and tidy.
3 Une Mpanazava est calme, elle sait se maîtriser.	A Girl Scout is quiet, she has self-control.
4 Une Mpanazava est courageuse, travailleuse, elle ne craint point les difficultés.	A Girl Scout is brave, industrious and does not fear difficulties.
5 Une Mpanazava est bonne, polie, aide les autres.	A Girl Scout is good, polite and helpful to others.
6 Une Mpanazava est l'aime de tout le monde et la sœur des autres éclaireuses.	A Girl Scout is the friend of all the world and the sister of other Girl Scouts.
7 Une Mpanazava est simple, elle sait se modérer dans ses goûts et sa toilette.	A Girl Scout is unsophisticated, she is moderate in her tastes and her dress.
8 Une Mpanazava est l'aime des animaux et des plantes.	A Girl Scout is the friend of animals and plants.
9 Une Mpanazava est toujours de bonne humeur, elle fait tout son possible pour faire régner la paix autour d'elle.	A Girl Scout is always good-humoured, she does everything she can to create peace around her.
10 Une Mpanazava est pure dans sa pensée, sa parole et sa conduite.	A Girl Scout is pure in her thoughts, her word and her deeds.

Motto

Prête	Ready

BROWNIE

Brownie Promise

Je promets de faire de mieux en mieux pour servir Dieu, aimer ma patrie, aider chaque jour.	I promise to do my very best to serve God, love my Country, help someone every day.

Brownie Law

Les Petites Ailes écoutent la Cheftaine.	The Brownies listen to their Leader.
Les Petites Ailes s'aiment comme des sœurs.	The Brownies love each other like sisters.

Brownie Motto

Aider	To help

KIADIN'I MADAGASIKARA

GUIDE

Promesse	Promise
Je promets sur mon honneur et devant Dieu de faire tous mes efforts pour:	I promise on my honour and before God to do all I can:
ou (selon les convictions)	or (according to her convictions)
Je promets sur mon honneur de faire tous mes efforts pour:	I promise on my honour to do all I can:
Servir mon pays, rendre service en toute occasion, obéir à la loi de l'éclaireuse.	To serve my Country, to render service on every occasion, to obey the Girl Scout Law.

	Loi	Law
1	L'éclaireuse n'a qu'une parole.	A Girl Scout is true to her word.
2	L'éclaireuse est loyale et chevaleresque.	A Girl Scout is loyal and chivalrous.
3	L'éclaireuse se rend utile et fait chaque jour une bonne action.	A Girl Scout is useful and does a good turn every day.
4	L'éclaireuse est l'amie de tous et la sœur de toutes les éclaireuses.	A Girl Scout is the friend of all and the sister to all Girl Scouts.
5	L'éclaireuse est courtoise et respectueuse des convictions des autres.	A Girl Scout is courteous and respects the convictions of others.
6	L'éclaireuse est bonne pour les animaux.	A Girl Scout is kind to animals.
7	L'éclaireuse sait obéir.	A Girl Scout understands obedience.
8	L'éclaireuse est toujours de bonne humeur.	A Girl Scout is always cheerful.
9	L'éclaireuse est travailleuse, économe et respectueuse du bien d'autrui.	A Girl Scout is industrious, thrifty and respects the property of others.
10	L'éclaireuse est propre dans son corps, ses paroles, ses pensées et ses actes.	A Girl Scout is pure in her body, her words, her thoughts and her deeds.

Motto

Tout droit	Keep straight

Brownie Promise

Je promets de faire de mon mieux et avec l'aide de Dieu, pour être fidèle à la loi des louvettes;	I promise to do my best and with God's help, to be faithful to the law of the Brownies;
ou (selon ses croyances et le désir de ses parents)	or (according to her belief and the wish of her parents)
Je promets de faire de mon mieux pour être fidèle à la loi des louvettes.	I promise to do my best to be faithful to the law of the Brownies.

BROWNIE

Brownie Law

Une louvette dit toujours vrai.	A Brownie always speaks the truth.
Une louvette cherche à faire plaisir aux autres.	A Brownie seeks to please others.
Une louvette obéit aux maîtres mots de la Meute.	A Brownie obeys the 'password' of the Pack.

Brownie Motto

De notre mieux	Of our best

Age Groups

Eclaireuse aînée	Ranger	17–21
Mpanazava, Eclaireuse	Guide, Girl Scout	12–16
Jeannette, Petite Aile, Louvette	Brownie	7–11

The Skotisma Zazavavy eto Madagasikara is composed of three associations: the Fanilon'i Madagasikara (Guides de Madagascar), the Mpanazava eto Madagasikara (Eclaireuses Unionistes de Madagascar) and the Kiandin'i Madagasikara (female branch of the Eclaireuses et Eclaireurs de Madagascar).

Soon after the establishment of Guiding in Madagascar, the Skotisma Zazavavy eto Madagasikara decided to launch a project to take Guiding to rural areas thereby allowing girls in villages to benefit from the education provided through the Movement.

Skotisma Zazavavy eto Madagasikara was recognized as an Associate Member of the World Association at the 18th World Conference (Denmark, 1963).

FANILON'I MADAGASIKARA

This Association was started, although not under its present name, in Madagascar by a Commissioner of the Guides de France in 1941.

The following are some important dates in its development:

1942 – Formation of first Guide company and Brownie pack.
1946 – First Guide camp.
1951 – First rally.
1960 – Formation of first company for handicapped girls.
1961 – The Association took the name of Fanilon'i Madagasikara.

The Fanilon'i Madagasikara co-operates regularly with other youth movements in the country.

MPANAZAVA ETO MADAGASIKARA

Mpanazava eto Madagasikara is a Guide Association started by Missionary Sisters for Protestant girls. It organized its first training camp for Guides in May 1941 and, three months later, three Guide companies and a Brownie pack were in existence, and a Training Centre for Guiders had been opened. Before long the Association spread its membership to rural areas and by 1946 a Ranger branch had been formed.

KIADIN'I MADAGASIKARA

Kiadin'i Madagasikara (the female branch of the Eclaireuses et Eclaireurs de Madagascar), the youngest of the three component associations of the Skotisma Zazavavy eto Madagasikara is open to girls of all races and creeds.

The Association is conscious of its role, with the National Organization, as regards the promotion and advancement of women and the development of the country as a whole.

Malaysia

Persatuan Pandu Putri, Malaysia

GUIDE

Persetia'an	**Promise**
1 Bahawa dengan sa-sunggoh-nya saya berjanji dan bersetia dengan sadaya upaya menunaikan kewajipan saya kapada Tuhan, Raja dan Negara.	On my honour I promise that I will do my best; to do my duty to God, King and the country; to help other people at all times and to obey the Guide Law.
2 Menulong orang sa-tiap masa.	
3 Dan menurut Undang2 Pandu Putri.	

Undang2 Pandu Putri	**Law**
1 Ada-lah Pandu Putri itu saorang yang boleh di-perchayai.	A Guide's honour is to be trusted.
2 Ada-lah Pandu Putri itu saorang yang ta'at dan setia.	A Guide is loyal.
3 Ada-lah Pandu Putri itu saorang yang berguna dan yang menulong orang lain.	A Guide's duty is to be useful and to help others.
4 Ada-lah Pandu Putri itu saorang yang bersahabat dengan semua orang dan adek beradek dengan lain2 Pandu Putri.	A Guide is a friend to all, and a sister to every other Guide.
5 Ada-lah Pandu Putri itu saorang yang berbudi pekerti yang tinggi.	A Guide is courteous.
6 Ada-lah Pandu Putri itu saorang kawan kapada binatang.	A Guide is a friend to animals.

7 Ada-lah Pandu Putri itu saorang yang menurut perentah.	A Guide obeys orders.
8 Ada-lah Pandu Putri itu saorang yang selalu tersenyum dan menyanyi walaupun dimasa kesulitan.	A Guide smiles and sings under all difficulties.
9 Ada-lah Pandu Putri itu saorang yang berjimat chermat.	A Guide is thrifty.
10 Ada-lah Pandu Putri itu saorang yang suchi dalam fikiran dan perbuatan.	A Guide is pure in thought, word and deed.

Chogan	**Motto**
Selalu Sedia	Be Prepared

BROWNIE

Brownie Promise

Dengan sa-sunggoh-nya saya berjanji:	I promise to do my best:
1 Akan menjelankan kewajipan kapada Tuhan, Raja dan Negara.	To do my duty to God, King and the Country.
2 Menolong orang sa-tiap hari, terutama mereka yang dalam rumah.	To help other people every day, especially those at home.

Brownie Law

1 Brownie selalu menurut ajaran orang yang tertua daripada-nya.	A Brownie gives in to the older folk.
2 Brownie tidak turut kehendak hati-nya sahaja.	A Brownie does not give in to herself.

Brownie Motto

Tolong Orang Selalu	Lend a Hand

Age Groups

Ranger	Ranger	15–21
Pandu Putri	Girl Guide	10–15
Brownie	Brownie	7–10

Girl Guiding started in Malaya in 1916, and it has gathered momentum and strength ever since. It has become one of the leading movements in the country and has gained particular recognition for its contribution towards unifying the various racial groups in the multi-racial society of Malaysia.

The Girl Guide Association of Malaya was recognized as an Associate Member of WAGGGS at the 17th World Conference (Greece, 1960). In 1963 the new country of Malaysia was inaugurated and on 8 December 1964 the Girl Guides Associations of Sabah and Sarawak joined the eleven states of Malaya. The Girl Guides Association of Malaysia was recognized as a Full Member of WAGGGS at the 19th World Conference (Japan, 1966).

The Association has its National Headquarters in Kuala Lumpur in a new building which houses the administrative office and training facilities, as well as guest rooms and hostel accommodation open to Girl Guides/Girl Scouts from all over the world.

TRAINING

Training is an important part of the Association's programme. Emphasis is laid on stimulating interest, promoting efficiency, ascertaining needs and ways in which to meet them, and methods of work. The national language is being used increasingly and the Association has produced a bilingual handbook to enable the Movement to reach the rural areas. Two more states have now acquired their own headquarters and training halls, but in spite of progress made, there is still a great shortage of young Leaders.

VOCATIONAL TRAINING

With the programme work being orientated towards national development and especially towards serving the needs of women, the Movement attaches considerable importance to vocational training for girls. The Association develops activities that provide training in vocational skills and offer employment opportunities; it also promotes career guidance schemes.

SERVICE

The Senior branch has shown a definite expansion and is directing all efforts to bringing Guiding to the rural areas by giving assistance in rural health clinics and kindergartens. They visit resettled areas to educate the mothers in hygiene and health. Guiding has been introduced into a reformatory rehabilitation home where the training has enabled many girls to learn new skills and earn their own living. Guides give regular service to the aged; visit the local hospital; have helped in building toilets for district schools; and collected clothes for the needy.

Brownies, Guides and Rangers in Johore have helped to sell foodstuffs to collect money for handicapped children in the area. Guides have also participated in service projects of national interest organized by the Ministry of Culture, Youth and Sports during Youth Week which generally take the form of opening up land for recreation, and 'cleaning-up campaigns' in underprivileged areas.

INTERNATIONAL WOMEN'S YEAR

In 1975, members of the Girl Guides Association participated in International Women's Year in co-operation with the National Council of Women's Organizations. For example, the Selangor Girl Guides organized a series of exhibitions, pageants and service projects, culminating in a programme called 'Women on the March' at which about 5,800 women marched in the final rally to show the progress of Malaysian women through the years.

Malta

Malta Girl Guides Association

GUIDE

Weghada

Inwieghed li naghmel mill-ahjar li naghmel id-dmir tieghi lejn Alla
Inservi lill Pajjizi, u nghin lill-proxmu tieghi
Li nzomm il-Ligi tal-Girl Guides.

Promise

I promise that I will do my best:
To do my duty to God;
To serve my country and help other people;
And to keep the Guide Law.

Il-Ligi

1 Il-Girl Guide hija lejali u ta' min jafda fiha.
2 Il-Girl Guide tghin lil kulhadd.
3 Il-Girl Guide taf iggib ruhha u tquis kulma taghmel.
4 Il-Girl Guide hija habiba u l-oht ta'Kulhadd.
5 Il-Girl Guide hija hanina ma' L-annimali u tirrispetta l-hlejjaq kollha.
6 Il-Girl Guide tobdi.
7 Il-Girl Guide hija kuragguza u tibqa ferhana f'kull saram.
8 Il-Girl Guide thaddem sewwa l-hin taghha.
9 Il-Girl Guide tiehu hsieb l-affarijiet taghha u ta haddiehor.
10 Il-Girl Guide taf tikkontrolla ruhha f'kulma tahseb, tghid u taghmel.

Law

A Guide is loyal and can be trusted.
A Guide is helpful.
A Guide is polite and considerate.
A Guide is friendly and sister to all Guides.
A Guide is kind to animals and respects all living things.
A Guide is obedient.
A Guide has courage and is cheerful in all difficulties.
A Guide makes good use of her time.
A Guide takes care of her possessions and those of other people.
A Guide is self-controlled in all she thinks, says or does.

Motto

Be Prepared

BROWNIE

Brownie Promise

Inwieghed li naghmel mill-ahjar li naghmel id-dmir tieghi lejn Alla.
Inservi lir-Regina, lill Pajjizi, u nghin lill-proxmu tieghi.
Li nzomm il-Ligi tal-Brownie Guides.

I promise that I will do my best
To do my duty to God.
To serve the Queen and my country and help other people.
And to keep the Brownie Law.

Brownie Motto

Lend a Hand

Age Groups

Ranger	15–21
Guide	11–15
Brownie	7–11

There were English Guide companies in Malta from 1918, and in 1923 some Maltese girls became Guides. To begin with there were two divisions, one for the Maltese and one for the English. In 1938 these divisions amalgamated and became the Malta Girl Guides Association.

Malta gained independence in 1964 and at the 19th World Conference (Tokyo, 1966) the Malta Girl Guides Association was recognized as an Associate Member of the World Association. It became a Full Member at the 21st World Conference (Canada, 1972).

CURRENT TRENDS

The trends of Guiding at present are towards the increased participation by young people in their communities, more mixed activities with other organizations, and a drive towards greater involvement in planning their own activities. The international aspect of Guiding is encouraged and exchange visits are on the increase.

SERVICE

Service to others plays an important part in the programme. For example, Rangers give service in orphanages and old people's homes. An annual competition is held to judge the service projects undertaken during the year and a cup is awarded to the winners. A unit for deaf Guides has recently been started, and fund-raising is undertaken to help Guides in other countries.

OUTDOOR ACTIVITIES

Guides from different parts of the island are able to meet each other at island rallies, for camping at the open-air campsite where Trainings are also arranged, for sports and pack holidays.

District outdoor events are also arranged as well as organized joint Girl Guide/Boy Scout activities. Emphasis at camps is frequently placed on the study of nature, making the young people aware of their environment.

Mauritius

The Girl Guides Association of Mauritius

GUIDE

Promise

I promise that I will do my best:
To do my duty to God,
To serve the Queen, my Country
and help other people
and
To keep the Guide Law.

Law

1 A Guide is loyal and can be trusted.
2 A Guide is helpful.
3 A Guide is polite and considerate.
4 A Guide is friendly and a sister to all Guides.
5 A Guide is kind to animals and respects all living things.
6 A Guide is obedient.
7 A Guide has courage and is cheerful in all difficulties.
8 A Guide makes good use of her time.
9 A Guide takes care of her own possessions and those of other people.
10 A Guide is self-controlled in all she thinks, says and does.

BLUEBIRD

Bluebird Promise

I promise I will do my best:
To do my duty to God,
To serve the Queen, my Country
and help other people
and
To keep the Bluebird Law.

Bluebird Law

A Bluebird thinks of others before herself
and does a good turn every day.

Girl Guiding started in Mauritius in 1926 when a unit was opened among English-speaking girls in the army base in Vacoas. They were soon joined by the French-speaking girls of Vacoas. During the following years Guiding gradually spread to other areas of the country, where it centred around various religious institutions. The first Island Council was formed in 1943 and the first constitution of the Association as a Branch Association of the Girl Guides Association of the United Kingdom was approved in 1946.

Girl Guiding is now established in five of the seven districts of the Island, and is open to all races, religions and nationalities. In an attempt to attract more girls from all backgrounds to the Movement, the National Committee is now making efforts to extend Guiding to the schools.

TRAINING

In 1972, a training expert was brought to Mauritius to help adapt the 8-point programme to suit the local needs and circumstances in the island. The programme was readjusted and a modified schedule of activities prepared geared to the badge system. Following the revised badge system, Rangers, Guides and Bluebirds worked at learning new and traditional skills which would ultimately equip them to cope with the demands of modern life.

OUTDOOR ACTIVITIES, CAMPING AND SERVICE

Excursions to local places of interest form an important part of Guiding in Mauritius. Rangers undertake a wide range of outings including, besides the usual excursions, visits to factories and Family Planning units. Camping is another important element of Guiding in Mauritius. It is popular at all levels and many camps are held throughout the year. Service projects include work for orphans and the poor, fund-raising for the sick and care of old people.

Mauritian Guides are encouraged to maintain contacts with Guides in other countries, thereby helping to increase their interest in the international aspect of the Movement.

The Girl Guides Association of Mauritius was recognized as an Associate Member of WAGGGS at the 22nd World Conference (U.K., 1975).

Mexico

Guías de Mexico, A.C.

GUIDE

Promesa	**Promise**
Yo prometo por mi honor hacer cuanto de mi dependa para: cumplir con mi deber hacia Dios y mi Patria; ser útil al prójimo en todas las circunstancias y obedecer la Ley Guía.	I promise on my honour to do my best: to do my duty to God and my country; to help other people in all circumstances and to obey the Guide Law.

	Ley	**Law**
1	Una Guía es persona de honor.	A Guide is a person of honour.
2	Una Guía es leal.	A Guide is loyal.
3	El deber de una Guía es ser útil y ayudar a los demás.	A Guide's duty is to be useful and help all others.
4	Una Guía es amiga de todos y hermana de todas las Guias.	A Guide is a friend to all and a sister to every other Guide.
5	Una Guía es cortés.	A Guide is courteous.
6	Una Guía cuida a los animales y a las plantas y ve en la naturaleza la obra de Dios.	A Guide looks after animals and plants and sees in nature the work of God.
7	Une Guía obedece órdenes.	A Guide obeys orders.
8	Una Guía se enfrenta a las dificultades con entereza y optimismo.	A Guide faces difficulties with fortitude and optimism.
9	Una Guía es ahorrativa.	A Guide is thrifty.
10	Une Guía se guarda pura en pensamientos, palabras y obras.	A Guide is pure in thoughts, words and deeds.

BROWNIE

Motto

Bien preparadas	Be Prepared

Brownie Promise

Yo prometo hacer cuanto de mi dependa para cumplir con mi deber hacia Dios y mi Patria, ayudar a todos, todos los días, especialmente a los de mi casa.	I promise to do my best to do my duty towards God and my country, and to help everyone each day, especially those of my own home.

Brownie Law

Una Hadita dice siempre la verdad.	A Brownie always tells the truth.
Una Hadita es obediente y alegre.	A Brownie is obedient and gay.

Brownie Motto

Dar Ayuda	Help Others

Age Groups

Guía Mayor	Ranger	15–20
Guía	Guide	13–15
Guía Intermedia	Intermediate	9–13
Hadita	Brownie	6–9

The Girl Guide Movement was started in Mexico in 1930, and in 1938 a National Association was formed with a programme adapted to the customs of Mexico, suitable and attractive to Mexican girls. Gradually the work progressed and Mexico was recognized as an Associate Member of the World Association at the 12th World Conference (U.S.A., 1948). It became a Full Member at the 16th World Conference (Brazil, 1957). There are now Guide companies throughout the country.

PROGRAMME

After a study undertaken in 1971 a new programme was drafted introducing a number of changes, one of them being the division of the Guide branch. Since then intensive training has taken place to enable the Guides and adult members to understand the new programme thoroughly.

CAMPING

National camps are held every two years; one year the camp is for the Guides and Intermediate Guides and two years later it is the turn of the Rangers and Leaders. The Brownies also enjoy a National Gathering every two years.

NATIONAL AND INTERNATIONAL EXCHANGES

With the purpose of promoting friendship among Guides throughout the Republic, and in order to get to know the folklore of the different regions, a National Interchange between Districts (INGED) is held each year in which members of the Movement aged between 13 and 25 years participate.

Mexican Guides have many opportunities for international exchange thanks to the proximity of Our Cabaña where members of the Guide Movement from all over the world are welcomed throughout the year.

SERVICE

The most important service project undertaken by the Guías de Mexico is the organization and day-to-day running of the 'Atepec' Literacy Centre. This centre, run by Northern District Girl Guides, has been providing basic education for the underprivileged children of the northern outskirts of Mexico City since 1971. Children attending the centre come from migrant families who have left their home villages to seek employment in Mexico City. Efforts are being made to provide regular medical care for the children and they receive a nutritious meal at the centre every day.

Apart from volunteers who are responsible for various activities at 'Atepec', there is one paid teacher whose salary and transport expenses are covered by the Girl Guides Association. The centre is funded by the UNESCO Co-operative Action Programme 543 (formerly UNESCO Gift Coupon Programme). Donations received so far have been used to buy desks, benches, stools, paint, exercise books and other materials.

Girl Guides of Mexico hope that with public support they might be able to introduce further improvements in 'Atepec': to build walls for the school and to open vocational literacy/cottage industry courses for women to help them develop income-earning skills.

Other national service projects of the Guias de Mexico include helping in orphanages and homes for the aged, participation in the national programme against environmental pollution and various types of community service throughout the country.

ANNUAL CELEBRATIONS

Each year the Association celebrates a national Guide week, during which all members wear their uniforms and give demonstrations of skills acquired. Press, radio and television give special publicity to the Movement, putting emphasis on its contribution to the community.

Another celebration at National level is Thinking Day, in which the Guides of all parts of Mexico remember with love the Founder and sister Guides all over the world.

Also, on 25 September each year the establishment of the Movement in Mexico is commemorated with various activities.

TICALLI

The Association has a headquarters called 'Ticalli' (your house), the main purpose of which is to provide a place in the capital where Guides from all parts of the Republic can meet and stay when necessary. For this reason it has dormitories, meeting rooms and a dining room. The National Office and the Guide shop are also found here. 'Ticalli' is frequently visited by Girl Guides/Girl Scouts of other countries who can stay here and meet and get to know the Guides of Mexico.

Monaco

Association des Guides de la Principauté de Monaco

GUIDE

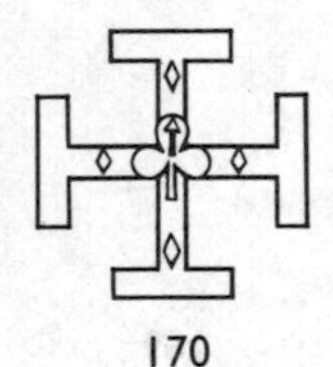

Promesse

Sur mon honneur, avec la grâce de Dieu, je m'engage à servir de mon mieux Dieu, l'Eglise, le Prince, la Patrie; à aider mon prochain en toutes circonstances; à observer la Loi des guides.

Promise

On my honour and with the grace of God, I pledge myself: To do my best to serve God, the Church, the Prince and my country; to help others in all circumstances; to keep the Guide Law.

Ou	or
Sur mon honneur, je m'engage à servir de mon mieux Dieu, le Prince, la Patrie; à aider mon prochain en toutes circonstances; à observer la Loi des guides.	On my honour I pledge myself: To do my best to serve God, the Prince, and my country; to help others in all circumstances; to keep the Guide Law.

Loi	**Law**
1 La guide est loyale.	A Guide is loyal.
2 La guide pense d'abord aux autres.	A Guide thinks first of others.
3 La guide est généreuse: elle est prête à servir.	A Guide is generous; she is prepared to help.
4 La guide est accueillante; elle a l'esprit d'équipe.	A Guide is welcoming; she has the team spirit.
5 La guide, sœur de toute autre Guide, est présente à tous.	A Guide, sister to every other Guide, is available to all.
6 La guide découvre la nature; elle y voit l'œuvre de Dieu.	A Guide explores nature, in which she sees the work of God.
7 La guide sait obéir.	A Guide understands obedience.
8 La guide sourit et chante dans les difficultés.	A Guide smiles and sings under all difficulties.
9 La guide est économe.	A Guide is thrifty.
10 La guide est maîtresse de soi; elle est pure et joyeuse.	A Guide controls herself; she is pure and cheerful.

Motto

Toujours prête	Always ready

Brownie Promise

BROWNIE

Je promets de faire de mon mieux: pour être fidèle à Dieu, au Prince, à mon pays, à mes parents, à la loi de la ronde, et pour faire chaque jour un plaisir à quelqu'un.	I promise to do my best: to be faithful to God, to the Prince, to my parents, to the law of the pack, and to do a good turn to somebody every day.

Brownie Law

Une jeannette est toujours propre.	A Brownie is always neat.
Une jeannette est toujours active.	A Brownie is always active.
Une jeannette est toujours gaie.	A Brownie is always cheerful.
Une jeannette dit toujours vrai.	A Brownie always tells the truth.
Une jeannette pense d'abord aux autres.	A Brownie thinks first of others.

Brownie Motto

De notre mieux	Of our best

Age Groups

Guide Aînée	Ranger	16–20 and over
Guide	Guide	12–16
Jeannette	Brownie	7–12

The first company of Guides was formed in Monaco in 1929. Up until 1956 Girl Guides in Monaco were part of the Guides de France, although they had been working towards independent membership of the World Association since 1953. The Association des Guides de la Principauté de Monaco was recognized as an Associate Member of WAGGGS at the 17th World Conference (Greece, 1960) and became a Full Member at the 18th World Conference (Denmark, 1963). Her Serene Highness Princess Grace is Honorary President of the Association and takes a keen interest in all its activities.

The Association's programme has three main aims: to offer a wide range of interesting activities to girls and young women, thus providing them with a high standard of Guiding; to co-operate with important international projects such as the Freedom from Hunger Campaign and the activities of FAO, UNRWA, Red Cross Society, etc.; and to promote the Movement within the country through Public Relations broadcasts on radio and television. The Association is especially anxious to commit itself to the cause of world peace.

ACTIVITIES

Guide and Brownie meetings are held weekly. Wide-Games, very popular in Monaco, give the girls a chance to put their initiative and self reliance to the test and also to put into practice the skills they have acquired during training. In winter they enjoy trips to the mountains to ski, and both Guides and Brownies camp in summer. The task of recruiting sufficient numbers of Leaders of quality continues to pose problems as demands of school-work and career often prevent young women from assisting in the work of the Movement.

SERVICE

Within the framework of the Freedom from Hunger Campaign and of the campaigns against illness and illiteracy, the Association has made its contribution by undertaking responsibility at national level for organizing the world UNICEF Day, the National Leprosy Day and an important public relations event for the benefit of UNRWA.

Girl Guides in Monaco have also successfully carried out activities during the school year to fight against the pollution of nature both in towns and in the countryside.

INTERNATIONAL CONTACTS

The Association is constantly striving to further develop its international relations by encouraging direct contacts with Guides of other countries by means of international camps, Training courses and joint celebrations of Thinking Day.

Netherlands

Scouting Nederland

HET NEDERLANDSE PADVINDSTERS GILDE

GUIDE

Belofte	Promise
Ik zal ernstig trachten God en mijn land te dienen, of een goed Padvindster te zijn, iedereen te helpen waar ik kan, en de Padvindsterswet na te leven.	I shall earnestly try to serve God and my country, or to be a real Guide, to help others wherever I can, and to live by the Guide Law.

Wet	Law
1 Een padvindster is eerlijk.	A Guide is honest.
2 Een padvindster is trouw.	A Guide is loyal.
3 Een padvindster is hulpvaardig.	A Guide is helpful.
4 Een padvindster is vriendelijk voor iedereen, en een zuster voor alle padvindsters.	A Guide is friendly to everyone and a sister to all Guides.
5 Een padvindster is beleefd en voorkomend.	A Guide is polite and courteous.
6 Een padvindster is goed voor planten en dieren.	A Guide is good to plants and animals.
7 Een padvindster weet te gehoorzamen.	A Guide knows how to obey.
8 Een padvindster draagt teleurstelling met opgewektheid.	A Guide bears disappointment with a smile.
9 Een padvindster is spaarzaam.	A Guide is thrifty.
10 Een padvindster is rein in gedachten, woord en daad.	A Guide is pure in thought, word and deed.

Motto

Wees bereid	Be Prepared

BROWNIE

Brownie Promise

Ik zal mijn best doen een echte Kabouter te zijn, iedereen te helpen waar ik kan, vooral thuis.	I shall try to be a real Brownie to help everybody where I can, especially at home.

Brownie Law

Een Kabouter is eerlijk.	A Brownie is honest.
Een Kabouter is gehoorzaam.	A Brownie is obedient.
Een Kabouter is vriendelijk.	A Brownie is kind.
Een Kabouter is goed voor planten en dieren.	A Brownie is good to plants and animals.

Brownie Motto

Pak maar aan	Lend a Hand

Age Groups

Pionier	Ranger	16–21
Senior Padvindster	Senior Guide	14–16
Junior Padvindster	Junior Guide	10½–14
Kabouter	Brownie	7–10½

DE NEDERLANDSE GIDSEN

GUIDE

Belofte	**Promise**
Op mijn erewoord beloof ik, met de hulp van God's genade, ernstig te zullen trachten: Mijn plicht te doen tegenover God, Kerk en Land; Iedereen te helpen waar ik kan; De Gidsenwet na te leven.	On my honour I promise, with the help of the grace of God, to try: To do my duty to God, the Church and my Country; To help everyone wherever I can; To obey the Guide Law.

	Wet	**Law**
1	Op de eer van een Gids kan men vertrouwen.	The honour of a Guide can be trusted.
2	Een Gids is trouw.	A Guide is loyal.
3	Een Gids weet zich nuttig te maken en anderen te helpen.	A Guide knows how to be useful and to help others.
4	Een Gids is een vriendin voor allen, en een zuster voor alle andere Gidsen.	A Guide is a friend to all and a sister to all other Guides.
5	Een Gids is beleefd en voorkomend.	A Guide is polite and courteous.
6	Een Gids leeft met open oog in God's natuur.	A Guide lives with eyes open in God's nature.
7	Een Gids weet te gehoorzamen.	A Guide knows how to obey.
8	Een Gids lacht en zingt bij alle moeilijkheden.	A Guide smiles and sings in all difficulties.
9	Een Gids is sober en spaarzaam.	A Guide is moderate and thrifty.
10	Een Gids is rein in gedachten, woord en daad.	A Guide is pure in thought, word and deed.

Motto

Wees bereid	Be Prepared

BROWNIE

Brownie Promise

Ik wil graag een echte kabouter zijn en samen met jullie spelen in de . . . kring.	I want to be a real Brownie and play together with you in the . . . pack.

Brownie Law

Een Kabouter is eerlijk.	A Brownie is honest.
Een Kabouter is gehoorzaam.	A Brownie is obedient.
Een Kabouter is vriendelijk.	A Brownie is kind.
Een Kabouter is goed voor planten en dieren.	A Brownie is good to plants and animals.

Brownie Motto

Pak maar aan	Lend a Hand

Age Groups

Sherpa	Senior Guide	14–16
Gids	Guide	10–14
Kabouter	Brownie	7–10

The first groups of Guides appeared in the Netherlands in 1911. In 1916 six of these groups joined together as Het Nederlandse Meisjes Gilde (Netherland Girls Guild) which in 1928 became a Founder Member of WAGGGS. In 1933 it changed its name to Het Nederlandse Padvindsters (Pathfinders) Gilde.

After the Second World War the Netherlands had two Guide Associations: Het Nederlandse Padvindsters Gilde, which was open to everyone wishing to join and had Companies and Packs sponsored by the Ecumenical Council of Youth and the Salvation Army; and De Nederlandse Gidsen, with Roman Catholic membership. Both Associations were represented in WAGGGS by the Nationale Padvindsters Raad (Joint Council).

STRUCTURAL CHANGES

Co-operation between the Girl Guides and Boy Scouts in the Netherlands has been growing since the formation of the Federation Scouting Nederland in 1967. Since 1973 there has been one organization – Scouting Nederland – for Girl Guides and Boy Scouts, which combines elements from all the former associations while remaining constantly open to new developments. H. M. Queen Juliana and H.R.H. Prince Bernhard are patrons of this merged organization.

Scouting Nederland's work is based on the patrol system and, apart from the regular Girl Guiding/Boy Scouting activities, the programmes include service projects, creative drama and handicrafts.

Companies and Packs meet weekly and, in an effort to overcome the present shortage of Leaders, the older Girl Guides help out, thereby achieving an early familiarization with all that Leadership entails.

NEW PROGRAMMES

Senior Guides have their own programme which provides the opportunity to work in small groups on projects chosen by the girls themselves. Such projects could include service to the community or a camp abroad. The Rangers form interest groups, e.g. citizenship, interior decorating, etc. Scouting Nederland also has an Extension Branch (Blauwe Vogels) for handicapped Brownies, Guides and Rangers. New programmes are at present being devised for Brownies, Cub Scouts, Junior and Senior Girl Guides and Boy Scouts.

Some of the highlights of the Girl Guiding/Boy Scouting year are: Thinking Day (celebrated by Scouting Nederland under the name of Baden-Powell Day), the National Water Camp, and the celebration of H.M. Queen Juliana's birthday.

SERVICE

Work with the handicapped and conservation are among the service activities undertaken by Scouting Nederland. An outstanding recent environmental project took place in 1975 when Girl Guides and Boy Scouts from all over the Netherlands helped to create a special 'Scout Forest'. In the the course of this project, carried out in co-operation with the National Society for the Preservation of Historical Monuments and Sites, 3,000 trees were planted by the Girl Guides and Boy Scouts.

New Zealand

The Girl Guides Association New Zealand (Inc.)

GUIDE

Promise

I promise on my honour to do my best:
To do my duty to God;
To serve the Queen and my Country; and
To keep the Guide Law.

Law

1 A Guide is to be trusted.
2 A Guide is loyal.
3 A Guide is useful and helps others at all times.
4 A Guide is friendly to all and a sister to every Guide.
5 A Guide is courteous.
6 A Guide is kind to animals.
7 A Guide is obedient.
8 A Guide is cheerful even under difficulties.
9 A Guide is thrifty.
10 A Guide is self-controlled in all she thinks, says and does.

Motto

Be Prepared

BROWNIE

Brownie Promise

I promise to do my best:
To do my duty to God and the Queen;
To help other people every day, especially those at home.

Brownie Law

A Brownie thinks of others before herself and does a Good Turn every day.

Brownie Motto

Lend a Hand

Age Groups

Ranger Guide	14–19
Guide	10–14
Brownie	7–10

The Girl Guides Association of New Zealand, a Founder Member of the World Association, was incorporated in 1923 from the Girl Peace Scouts which started in 1907. The Association has members on the two main islands of New Zealand – North and South – and it also represents the Girl Guides of the Cook Islands and Western Samoa.

Although Girl Guiding has been popular in New Zealand since the twenties, the greatest expansion has taken place since the early seventies. Numbers, especially in the 14–19 age group, are still increasing, and those involved in Girl Guiding in New Zealand are conscious of the need for continually searching out new avenues of constructive training and service.

PROGRAMME

New Brownie and Girl Guide handbooks have been published with a more extensive programme, and a new Ranger Guide programme, also supported by its own handbook, has given members a broader outlook and a better understanding of the aims of this Branch.

RANGERS

Ranger Guide councils have been formed at all levels and Rangers take their place on Planning Committees for national events and are encouraged to become involved in the Movement in every way possible. Their opinions are listened to and acted upon.

JOINT ACTIVITIES

With the broadening of the programmes, greater co-operation has developed between Ranger Guides and Scout Venturers, with combined camping, shared service projects, joint attendance at flying and drama schools and mixed social activities now a regular part of the Girl Guide programme.

TRAINING

Training plays a major role in Girl Guiding in New Zealand, and with increasing numbers of voluntary Trainers, efforts are being made to keep pace with the needs of both new and experienced Guiders. A new, four-stage training scheme for Leaders has been introduced, with a special Baden-Powell badge awarded on completion of all four stages. Special Leadership courses are held for all Queen's Guide candidates and Duke of Edinburgh Award courses are also well attended.

PUBLICATIONS

The vast distances which separate the people of New Zealand make publications particularly important, and many pamphlets, books and brochures are produced as well as the national Girl Guide magazine *Te Rama*.

LONE GUIDES

In isolated areas Girl Guiding is done by correspondence in the form of a monthly letter or magazine. The *Lone Letter* is posted from one Girl Guide to another throughout a company. Among the more isolated Girl Guides are the Maoris, living in the Cook Islands. Girl Guides and Brownies have been there since 1923, and in spite of communications difficulties in these Pacific islands the Maori Girl Guides and Brownies show tremendous enthusiasm for the Movement.

THINKING DAY AND INTERNATIONAL FRIENDSHIP

Thinking Day takes on a special significance in New Zealand, since this is the first country of the World Association to see the sun rise on 22 February, each year. Very often Girl Guides go to the top of the nearest hill for a service, thus starting the chain of thoughts that ring the world on this day.

International friendship and contacts with other countries are very much encouraged, and delegates from New Zealand attend gatherings, camps and conferences in many overseas countries. Mutual Aid Schemes have been receiving much support from New Zealand Girl Guides.

SERVICE

Community Service is an important part of the Girl Guide programme in New Zealand. Members have raised large sums of money to bring relief to disaster areas and to help countries in need of aid. Girl Guiding and Boy Scouting together continue to work for conservation and anti-litter campaigns, both of which have now become government sponsored. One of the most successful national campaigns was operation 'Greenfingers' during which 20,000 members planted trees and shrubs and undertook a variety of environmental projects.

Special work continues among Polynesian girls and children in the Auckland area and this project has received assistance from Shell Oil NZ Ltd. The Movement has also been involved in activities connected with International Women's Year.

CO-OPERATION WITH OTHER ORGANIZATIONS

The Association is an active member of the National Youth Council of New Zealand and therefore of the World Assembly of Youth, and also co-operates closely with other national and international organizations working in the country.

Nigeria

The Nigerian Girl Guides Association

GUIDE

Promise

I promise, on my honour, that I will
do my best:
To do my duty to God and my
Country;
To help other people at all times;
To obey the Guide Law.

Law

1 A Guide's honour is to be trusted.
2 A Guide is loyal.
3 A Guide's duty is to be useful and to help others.
4 A Guide is a friend to all, and a sister to every other Guide.
5 A Guide is courteous.
6 A Guide is a friend to animals.
7 A Guide obeys orders.
8 A Guide smiles and sings under all difficulties.
9 A Guide is thrifty.
10 A Guide is pure in thought, word and deed.

Motto

Be Prepared

Brownie Promise

I promise to do my best:
To do my duty to God and my Country;
To help other people every day, especially those at home.

Brownie Law

A Brownie is truthful, obedient and cheerful.
A Brownie thinks of others before herself.

Brownie Motto

Lend a Hand

Age Groups

Ranger	19–25
Guide	11–19
Brownie	7–11

BROWNIE

The first Girl Guide company was formed in Nigeria in 1919, and before long Companies were started in several schools. Four years later a committee of interested people was set up to encourage and direct the work of the rapidly spreading Movement. This committee, then known as the Central Nigerian Executive Committee, has now become the Council of the Nigerian Girl Guides Association.

The first Brownie pack was registered in 1927, and in 1929 the first company was formed in a lepers' hospital. Ranger companies made their appearance in Nigeria in 1934 and the further expansion of Girl Guiding led to the formation of Cadet companies. Girl Guiding quickly spread to all parts of the country and numbers increased rapidly. A Constitution was signed in 1947, later to be replaced by the present one drawn up in 1964.

Nigeria was recognized as an Associate Member of the World Association in 1960, and as a Full Member at the 19th World Conference (Japan, 1966).

TRAINING

Great progress has been made in the field of training, with regular trainings organized at national, State and local level, and with National Trainers touring the country to bring Guiding to rural areas.

SERVICE

The Association has increased its efforts to involve members in community service work, especially with regard to the underprivileged groups like the old, the handicapped and the orphans.

Among other service projects undertaken by the Nigerian Girl Guides are a campaign for keeping their country clean, and the establishment in Lagos of a Play Centre for pre-school children. The Centre, which opened with only seven children, now caters for over a hundred.

One of Nigeria's projects for Thinking Day took the form of 'Guide Gardening'. Guides and Brownies planted vegetable seeds and high-yielding maize seeds in their school gardens. The vegetables and maize harvested were donated to Homes both for the handicapped and the aged.

VOCATIONAL TRAINING

The first section of the Vocational Training Centre building for handicapped girls was opened in May 1975. The aim of the Centre is to rehabilitate the disabled girls socially, giving them an opportunity to earn their own living, to live fuller and better lives and to encourage them to make their own contribution towards the development of their country.

Several Girl Guide/Girl Scout Associations have donated to this Centre through the UNESCO Gift Coupon Scheme (now called Co-operative Action Programme), and local non-governmental organizations have also been of assistance. In addition the Nigerian Association held a very successful 'Market Day' to raise funds for the Centre.

'UNITY AND FRIENDSHIP'

An international camp with the theme 'Unity and Friendship' and attended by Olave, Lady Baden-Powell, World Chief Guide, was held to celebrate the Golden Jubilee of the Nigerian Girl Guides Association in 1969. In the same year, two national camps were held at Ibadan and two more for Guiders and Commissioners in 1970.

Members of the Nigerian Girl Guides Association take an active part in international Guiding and have in recent years attended the International Commissioners' Conference in 1973, Juliette Low Seminars in 1974 and the Sub-regional Seminar on Guiding (Africa Group) held in Sierra Leone in 1975. They were also represented at WAGGGS' World Conferences in Canada in 1972 and in the United Kingdom in 1975.

Norway

Fellesrådet for Speiderpiker I Norge

GUIDE

Speiderløftet	**Guide Promise**
Jeg lover etter beste evne:	I promise to the best of my ability:
(Norsk Speiderpikeforbund)	(Norsk Speiderpikeforbund)
I tro på Guds hjelp lover jeg:	Believing in God's help I promise:
(Norges KFUK – Speidere)	(Norges KFUK – Speidere)
Å tjene Gud og mitt land,	to serve God and my country,
hjelpe andre	to help others
og leve etter speiderloven.	and to live according to the Guide Law.

The law and the motto is the same for both associations.

GUIDE

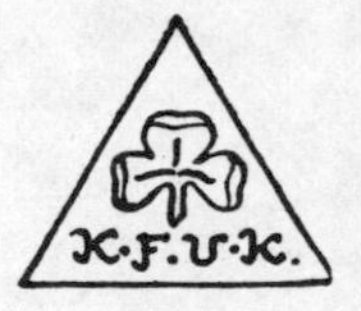

Speiderloven	Guide Law
1 En speider er åpen for Gud og hans ord.	1 A Guide is open to God and His word.
2 En speider kjenner ansvar for seg selv og andre.	2 A Guide accepts responsibility for herself and others.
3 En speider er hjelpsom og hensynsfull.	3 A Guide is helpful and considerate.
4 En speider er en god venn.	4 A Guide is a good friend.
5 En speider er ærlig og pålitelig.	5 A Guide is honest and trustworthy.
6 En speider kjenner naturen og verner om den.	6 A Guide understands nature and protects it.
7 En speider tenker og handler selvstendig og prøver å forstå andre.	7 A Guide thinks and acts independently.
8 En speider gjør sitt beste i motgang og vansker.	8 A Guide does her best in adversities and difficulties.
9 En speider er nøysom og prøver å klare seg selv.	9 A Guide is thrifty and tries to manage on her own.
10 En speider arbeider for fred og forståelse mellom mennesker.	10 A Guide works for peace and understanding (between men/peoples).

Motto

Vaer beredt	Be prepared

BROWNIE

Brownie Promise

Jeg lover å gjøre mitt beste for:	I promise to do my best:
(Norsk Speiderpikeforbund)	(Norsk Speiderpikeforbund)
I tro på Guds hjelp lover jeg:	Believing in God's help I promise:
(Norges KFUK – Speidere)	(Norges KFUK – Speidere)
å være lydig og hjelpsom hjemme og ute.	to be obedient and helpful at home and elsewhere.

Brownie Motto

Gjør ditt beste	Do your best

BROWNIE

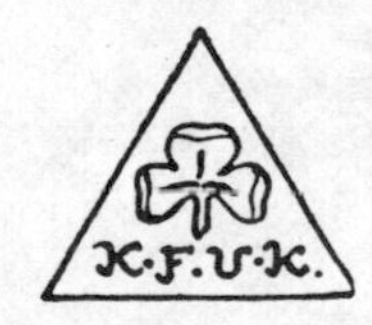

Age Groups

Rangere	Rangers	16–19
Vandrere	Guides	13–15
Stifinnere	Guides	10–12
Småspeidere/meiser	Brownies	7–9

Girl Guides were active in Norway before the First World War and the oldest companies have records that go back as far as 1912, but no national organization existed until the end of 1920 when the Norges KFUK Speidere (YWCA Guides of Norway) was established. The Norsk Speiderpikeforbund (Norwegian Girl Guides Association) was founded in 1921, and seven years later Norway became a Founder Member of the World Association. The Girl Guide programme is identical in both Associations, and their activities are co-ordinated by a committee, the Fellesrådet for Speiderpiker I Norge, with headquarters in Oslo. This committee represents Norway in the World Association.

STRUCTURE AND PROGRAMME

A characteristic feature of the structure of Girl Guiding in Norway is the groupings at local level, which usually include one unit (seldom more) from each age-group. Each grouping has a leader who co-ordinates its activities and acts as a liaison with other groupings. The patrol system adapted according to the needs of the different age-groups is maintained within the units. The programme is divided into two parts – compulsory and voluntary. The first part, which is different every year, is based on certain themes essential to Girl Guiding; the second consists of 'studies' and proficiency badges and includes special activities such as preparation for camps. Apart from their ordinary Girl Guide activities, both Associations organize Guiding for Lone and for handicapped Guides; extension branches include girls who are deaf, blind or mentally disabled.

To accommodate the changes in programme and structure both associations have published new handbooks for girls; and a handbook for Leaders was issued in 1974.

EXPANSION OF THE MOVEMENT

Both associations have seen considerable growth in membership over the years. Particularly noticeable is the increased number of adults joining the Movement. Many who have never been Guides recognize the need for Guiding in their local communities and join as leaders. This has created a great demand for Leadership training, and the number of training courses held in recent times has more than tripled, thanks partly to the increased grants to youth organizations from the Norwegian authorities. Training is constantly being revised in an effort to make it as effective as possible for Leaders of the youth of today.

CO-OPERATION WITH BOY SCOUTS

Another important feature of the Girl Guide work over the last few years has been the growing co-operation with the Boy Scouts. In 1972, a formal agreement to co-operate was concluded between the two Girl Guide Associations and the Norwegian Boy Scouts Association. As a result, the Norska Speideres Fellesrad (the Joint Council of the Norwegian Girl Guides and Boy Scouts) has been established, which, when desirable, co-ordinates plans and activities and represents Norwegian Girl Guiding and Boy Scouting to the public. The three associations have also set up a 'co-operation plan' which gives guidelines for the development of co-operation between associations at the unit, district and national levels.

CAMPS

Camps in Norway are truly international in scope and are attended by visitors from abroad. Norwegian Girl Guides wear badges on their belts, each representing attendance at one camp.

Thousands of Girl Guides participated in national camps which stressed physical fitness and outdoor life, with all campers taking part in overnight hikes in the nearby mountains.

FUND-RAISING

The Associations have raised money for many overseas projects, such as a Children's Home in Uganda, medicines and food for Vietnamese refugees and for victims of natural disasters in all parts of the world.

The annual 'Speiderjobben' campaign raises large sums of money to fund national as well as international projects of special interest to the Girl Guides.

One such fund-raising drive provided money for the publication of Braille books for the blind.

CO-OPERATION WITH OTHER ORGANIZATIONS

Norway co-operates with UNICEF and in 1976 Norwegian Brownies and Cubs raised the record sum of half a million kroner for the Children's Fund.

Pakistan

Pakistan Girl Guides Association

GUIDE

Waada *Urdu*	**Promise**
Mein waada karti hun ke mein poori koshish karoongi ke, Khuda aur mulk ke ahkam per paband rahoon.	1 I promise to do my duty to God and Pakistan, and participate in nation-building activities.
Baninau insaan ki madad aur tamir-e-Pakistan ke kamon mein hissa loon.	2 To help other people at all times.
Guide ke qawanin ki pabandi karoon.	3 To obey the Guide Laws.

N.B. For Buddhist Guides the words 'My religion' may be substituted for 'God' in the first part of the Promise.

Qanoon *Urdu*	**Law**
1 Guide qable aitemad hoti hai.	A Guide can be trusted.
2 Guide wafadar hoti hai.	A Guide is loyal.
3 Guide milansaar aur tamam doosri Guides ki behan hoti hai	A Guide is friendly and a sister to all other Guides.
4 Guide khosh akhlag aur doosrum ka khiyal rakhti hai.	A Guide is polite and considerate.
5 Guide janwaron se acha selaouk karti hai aur har jandar chiz ka khiyal rakhti hai.	A Guide is kind to animals and respects all living things.
6 Guide hukam ki taamil karti hai aur apne naffas per qaboo rakhti hai.	A Guide is obedient and self-disciplined.
7 Guide madadgar hoti hai aur woqt ka sehi istemal karti hai.	A Guide is helpful and makes good use of her time.
8 Guide mesaib aur mushkilat ka hosla mandi se mukabla karti hai.	A Guide is courageous and cheerful in all difficulties.
9 Guide kifayat sauaar hoti hai, woh apni aur doosron ki chizon ki hifazat karti hai.	A Guide is thrifty and takes care of her own and other people's possessions.
10 Guide apne qual-o-fail aur khiyalat mein pakiza hoti hai.	A Guide is pure in thought, word and deed.

Motto

Teyar raho *Urdu* Be Prepared

JUNIOR GUIDE

Junior Guide Promise

Mein waada karti hun ke mein puri koshish karoongi ke,
Khuda ke ahkam ki taamil karoon.
aur Pakistan se muhabat karoon
Hamesha doosran ki madad karoon
khas kar apne ghar walon ki,
Chhotee Guide ke qanoon ki taamil karoon.

I promise to do my best, to obey God, to love Pakistan, to help other people every day, especially those at home, and to keep the Junior Guide Law.

Junior Guide Law

Chhotee Guide baron ka kehna manti hai,
Chhotee Guide her rose eik achta kam karti hai,
Chhotee Guide apni mun mani nahein karti.

A Junior Guide obeys her elders and tries to do a good turn every day.

Motto

Hath batana

Lend a Hand

Age Groups

Senior Guide	16 and above
Guide	11–16
Junior Guide	7–11

Girl Guides have been active in the area which is now Pakistan since 1911. In 1928, this area along with that of present-day India and Bangladesh became a Founder Member of the World Association under the name of India. In 1948 the Pakistan Girl Guides Association was welcomed as a separate member of the World Association.

The policy making is the responsibility of the General Council of Pakistan Girl Guides; the Association has its National Headquarters in Lahore.

Girl Guiding is the most popular extra-curricular activity among school girls, who have the choice of three branches: Junior Guides, Girl Guides and Senior Guides. Girl Guiding is much respected in Pakistan and its activities, especially in the field of youth and women's welfare work, receive much public support.

PROGRAMME

A study has been undertaken to assess the programme of the Association, as a result of which a new programme has been drawn up to meet the needs and aspirations of both rural and urban girls. New handbooks for Junior Guides and Girl Guides have been prepared offering a wider selection of activities and opening new opportunities for girls.

SERVICE

The Association is recognized for its outstanding service to the community both in normal times and in times of emergency. Four areas of social service are now permanently featured in Guide activities: literacy and on-going education; food and nutrition; health and environment; and economic development of rural areas.

Women's welfare service camps are held in villages and slum areas in different parts of the country, and one of the most successful community development projects, 'Health and Nutrition for Healthy, Happy Families', was undertaken by the Association in a village in Punjab. Girl Guides run numerous literacy centres and with their help some 30,000 women have become literate since 1957.

Guides work on a 'Grow More Food' project by making vegetable gardens in their schools and homes, and tree plantation campaigns have been launched with more than 2,000 trees planted in the provinces.

Magnificent relief work was carried out by the Association during the disastrous floods and earthquake in 1974/75. Girl Guides worked at rehousing victims, distributed relief supplies and gave medical aid to 1,468 people, mostly women and children.

Interest in Guiding with the handicapped continues among Guides and Rangers and camps for handicapped Girl Guides are held annually.

INTERNATIONAL WOMEN'S YEAR

Many successful events were held to promote International Women's Year: Workshops with the theme 'Girl Guiding for Rural Areas' and 'Adult Education' were held for the adult members of the Association in Sind and Punjab. Another event was the National Conference 'Women – A Vital Force in Development'. Delegates from the Pakistan Girl Guides Association also attended the International Women's Year Conference organized by the Girl Scouts of the U.S.A.

Plans have been drawn up for the contribution of the Movement to the Decade for Women and Development, 1975–85, and a special committee formed to implement a five-year plan of action in which emphasis is put on improving the lot of women by working on projects for development. These projects are both imaginative and practical. They include: improved agricultural methods which would shorten women's working day; the promotion of health and sanitation as factors of community development; setting up rural health centres for mothers and children; family planning; environmental hygiene and control of epidemics and infectious diseases.

Vocational training and functional literacy for women have been chosen as special Girl Guide projects in many parts of Pakistan.

NATIONAL EVENTS

Two national events of major significance took place in 1974: the 6th All Pakistan Camp attended by about 1,000 Girl Guides from the four provinces of the country; and the opening of the National Training Centre at Islamabad. This centre will provide residential facilities for trainings, camps, conferences, etc.

PARTICIPATION IN INTERNATIONAL EVENTS

Efforts have been made to promote the international aspect of Girl Guiding in Pakistan. Members of the Movement have successfully represented Pakistan in many international events, among them the 22nd World Conference of WAGGGS (U.K., 1975), and the International Commissioners' Conference in Ghana. A member of the Association served on the Planning Committee of the Asian Seminar, 'Guiding for the Whole Country'. Among the other events attended were: the Asia Pacific Camp in Japan, the Juliette Low Seminar on Development at Olave House and the National Girl Guide Camp held in Iran.

Republic of Panama

Asociación Nacional de Muchachas Guías de Panama

GUIDE

Promesa

Con la gracia de Dios, yo prometo por mi honor, hacer cuánto de mi dependa para:
Cumplir mis deberes para Dios y mi Patria,
Ser útil al prójimo en todas las circunstancias,
Obedecer la Ley Guía.

Promise

With the help of God I promise on my honour to do my best:
To fulfil my duty to God and my country,
To be useful in all circumstances,
To obey the Guide Law.

Ley

1 La Guía es persona de honor.
2 La Guía es leal.
3 La Guía es útil y ayuda al prójimo.
4 La Guía es amiga de todos, y hermana de las demás Guías.
5 La Guia es cortés.
6 La Guía ama las plantas y los animales y ve la obra de Dios en la Naturaleza.
7 La Guia es obediente y disciplinada.
8 La Guía sonrie en las dificultades.
9 La Guía es económica.
10 La Guia es pura en sus pensamientos, palabras y obras.

Law

A Guide is honourable.
A Guide is loyal.
A Guide is useful and helps others.
A Guide is a friend to all and a sister to other Guides.
A Guide is courteous.
A Guide loves plants and animals and sees in nature the work of God.
A Guide is obedient and self-controlled.
A Guide smiles at difficulties.
A Guide is thrifty.
A Guide is pure in her thoughts, words and deeds.

Motto

Siempre listas

Always ready

BROWNIE

Brownie Promise

Prometo hacer todo lo mejor que me sea posible para cumplir con mis deberes hacia Dios y mi Patria.
Ayudar todos los días a los demás, especialmente a los de mi casa.

I promise to do my best to do my duty to God and my country, to help others every day, especially those at home.

Brownie Law

La Alita siempre cede a los deseos de sus mayores.
La Alita nunca cede a si misma.

A Brownie always gives in to the wishes of her elders.
A Brownie never gives in to her own wishes.

Brownie Motto

Ayudar	Give help

Age Groups

Cadete	Cadet	17–19
Guía Mayor	Ranger	15–17
Guía Intermedia B	Guide	12–14
Guía Intermedia A	Guide	10–12
Alita	Brownie	7–9

Guiding began in the Republic in 1950, and Panama became an Associate Member of the World Association at the 14th World Conference (Norway, 1952). By 1966 the Asociación Nacional de Muchachas Guías de Panamá had Guides in 14 localities and it established its headquarters in Panama City. In 1966, the 19th World Conference held in Japan granted the Association Full Membership of WAGGGS.

STRUCTURE AND TRAINING

The Association is divided into regions, the work of which is co-ordinated by Management Committees. These meet annually at a conference to review the current programmes and methods used and to outline changes and improvements for the future. The Association holds its General Meeting in January of each year which representatives of the different regions attend.

Leadership training is given high priority and Leaders' conferences have been held regularly since the first National Conference of Leaders in 1966. Every two years the Association organizes a training, which is occasionally attended by members from other countries. In addition, trainings are organized at regional level for Guiders and young Leaders.

In order to help meet the shortage of Leaders, the Association has formed groups of Cadets (aged 17–19) who while pursuing their Girl Guide programmes are in charge of Brownie packs. This system has enabled adult Guiders to devote more time and attention to Intermediate and Senior Guides.

EXPANSION OF THE MOVEMENT

Activity within the organization is steadily increasing and it has been recognised by the Government which has allocated a grant to the Movement. At the moment the Ministry of Education is financing the salary of three teachers who work full-time for the Girl Guides Association. This has resulted in an increased number of Guides and Guiders in new areas and the strengthening of the Movement in established areas.

Thinking Day, International Friendship Day and the Girl Guide Week (celebrated in June of each year) help, as do the various Seminars and Round Tables, to promote the development of Girl Guiding and to keep the Movement in the public eye.

The Association is very conscious of the need for good Public Relations, and activities in this field have included: publicity on radio, TV and in the press; the publication of a bulletin, *La Voz del Comité Nacional*; and visits to Government officials, directors of business firms and of civic bodies.

INTERNATIONAL GUIDING

The Lady Baden-Powell Committee, established in 1959, ensures liaison between

Girl Guides of Panama, Girl Scouts of the U.S.A. and the International Girl Scouts of the Panama Canal Zone. The Association participates in international meetings and gatherings and entertains Guides from many other countries who attend training or camping events in their country.

SERVICE

The Association is extremely active in several fields of service, and is in the process of setting up a literacy project in conjunction with the Ministry of Education. Girl Guides are also deeply involved in ecology and the 'Year of Ecology' has been promoted through a series of conferences, seminars, TV programmes and film shows. An ecology pamphlet for children has been produced and some of the projects have included anti-litter campaigns and tree-planting.

INTERNATIONAL WOMEN'S YEAR

A national programme, '25 Years of Guiding in Panama', was especially developed to promote IWY goals. The Girl Guides Association was awarded the first prize for the best contribution to IWY as a result of a national survey carried out by the Soroptimist Club of Panama among 45 non-governmental organizations (NGOs).

Paraguay

Asociación Guías Scouts del Paraguay

GUIDE

Promesa

Por mi honor y con la gracia de Dios prometo hacer todo lo posible para cumplir mis deberes para con Dios, mi Patria y la Humanidad.
Servir al prójimo en todas las cicunstancias y cumplir con las leyes Guías.

Promise

On my honour and with the grace of God I promise to do my best to do my duty to God, my country and humanity.
To serve other people in all circumstances and to observe the Guide Laws.

Ley

1 Una Guía es digna de toda confianza.
2 Una Guía es leal.
3 Una Guía es útil y ayuda a los demás.
4 Una Guía es amiga de todos y hermana de las demás Guías.
5 Una Guía es cortés.
6 Una Guía ve en la naturaleza la obra de Dios, por éso la admira y la respeta.

Law

A Guide is to be trusted.
A Guide is loyal.
A Guide is useful and helps others.
A Guide is a friend to all and a sister to all other Guides.
A Guide is courteous.
A Guide admires and respects nature for in it she sees the work of God.

7 Una Guía acepta consejos y sugerencias.	A Guide accepts advice and suggestions.
8 Una Guía sonrie y canta en las dificultades.	A Guide smiles and sings under difficulties.
9 Una Guía es económica.	A Guide is thrifty.
10 Una Guía se conserva pura en pensamientos, palabras y obras.	A Guide keeps herself pure in thoughts, words and deeds.

Motto

Siempre Lista	Always ready

Brownie Promise

BROWNIE

Prometo hacer todo lo posible para cumplir mis deberes para con Dios y mi patria. Ayudar siempre a los demás, especialmente a los de mi casa y cumplir con Ley de la Ronda.	I promise to do my best to fulfil my duties towards God and my country. To help others always, especially those at home and to obey the Law of the Round.

Brownie Law

Una Alita obedece a sus mayores.	A Brownie obeys her elders.
Una Alita hace la buena acción diaria.	A Brownie does the daily good turn.

Brownie Motto

Ayudar a todos	Help everyone

Age Groups

Mayor	Ranger	14–18
Mediodia	Guide (noon)	12–13
Amanecer	Guide (dawn)	10–11
Alita	Brownie	6–9

Girl Guiding started in Paraguay in 1959 and in 1960 the National Association was founded. During the years that followed the Association expanded rapidly thanks to the friendly co-operation of Guides in Brazil and Argentina, who sent Trainers and provided useful information on organizing Guide activities.

In 1962 the Association received official recognition by the government, and the Association was recognized as an Associate Member of WAGGGS at the 19th World Conference (Japan, 1966).

PROGRAMME

In the early 1970s the Association undertook the reorganization of the programme and training committee, bringing the programme up to date by dividing the different levels on the basis of a new system of age groups and through activities aimed at living Guiding more deeply.

PUBLICATIONS

The Association publishes several books and manuals on Guiding plus a monthly magazine on training.

TRAINING AND INTERNATIONAL EVENTS

There are regular information courses for Guiders and Patrol Leaders and one-day training courses are also held.

Guides in Paraguay have also taken part in the 'Our Friend' project of international exchange and in other international events which included: international gathering for Commissioners and Trainers in Salta (Argentina); international camp for Senior Guides in Argentina; first Latin-American gathering for religious assistants and national Commissioners (Brazil); a gathering for Senior Guides, a Training for Trainers and the Young Adults Seminar in Mexico; a Training for Trainers (Buenos Aires) and the international Jubilee camp held in Brazil.

CO-OPERATION WITH INTERNATIONAL ORGANIZATIONS

INTERNATIONAL WOMEN'S YEAR

The Association organized a special competition for Senior Guides based on the theme of IWY. Special attention was paid to the promotion through Guide magazines of the status of women.

UNICEF

The Association co-operates with UNICEF in celebrating International Children's Day.

SERVICE

In the context of keeping their city clean, Guides in Asunción put transfers in buses and trams urging people to avoid litter and help keep the city as they would like it to be.

An important project in recent years has been a campaign for recruiting blood donors among members of the Movement.

Peru

Asociación Nacional de las Guías-Scouts del Perú

GUIDE

Promesa	**Promise**
Prometo por mi honor, hacer todo lo posible, para cumplir mis deberes, para con Dios y mi patria Ayudar a mis semejantes en todo momento y obedecer la Ley Guía.	I promise on my honour, to do everything possible, To accomplish my duties towards God and my country To help all human beings at any time and to obey the Guide Law.

Ley	**Law**
1 Una Guía es digna de confianza.	A Guide is trustworthy.
2 Una Guía es leal.	A Guide is loyal.
3 Una Guía debe ser útil.	A Guide must be useful.

4 Una Guía es amiga de todos y hermana de toda Guía.	A Guide is a friend to all and a sister to every Guide.
5 Una Guía es cortés.	A Guide is courteous.
6 Una Guía proteje a los animales y plantas y ve en la Naturaleza la Obra de Dios.	A Guide protects animals and plants and sees in Nature the work of God.
7 Una Guía es obediente.	A Guide is obedient.
8 Una Guía tiene valor, afronta y sonrie ante las dificultades.	A Guide is courageous, faces difficulties with a smile.
9 Una Guía hace buen uso de su tiempo y es económica.	A Guide makes good use of her time and is thrifty.
10 Una Guía es pura de pensamiento, palabra y obra.	A Guide is pure in thought, word and deed.

Motto

Estar preparadas	Be Prepared

Brownie Promise

BROWNIE

Prometo hacer lo posible por cumplir mis deberes para con Dios y mi patria.	I promise to do everything possible to do my duty to God and my country.
Ayudar a otras personas cada día especialmente a los de casa.	To help other people every day especially those at home.

Brownie Law

Una Alita se da a los mayores.	A Brownie thinks first of her elders.
Una Alita no se da a sí misma.	A Brownie does not think of herself.

Brownie Motto

Ayudar	To Help

Age Groups

Guía de Servicio	Service Guide	19–25
Guía Mayor	Ranger	14–18
Guía Intermedia	Guide	10–13
Alita	Brownie	7–9

Girl Guiding has existed in Peru since 1916, but it was not until 1945 that the National Association was set up under the sponsorship of the Ministry of Education. With the help of the World Association Travelling Commissioner for the Western Hemisphere, Girl Guiding was reorganized in 1953 as an autonomous Movement continuing to be officially recognized by the Ministry of Education and chartered by Congress.

The National Association was recognized as an Associate Member of WAGGGS at the 17th World Conference (Greece, 1960) and became a Full Member at the 18th World Conference (Denmark, 1963). The Association's headquarters, which includes hostel accommodation for visiting members of the Movement, is situated in San Isidro, Lima.

PROGRAMMES AND TRAINING

All four age-groups have been instrumental in the planning of programmes in accordance with their needs and wishes. Service has been intensified and trainings, Round Tables and discussions have been held on various aspects of Girl Guiding. The Association is at present engaged in the organization of a Nation-wide training on all levels and it is hoped that this will soon be established on a permanent basis.

STRUCTURE

Since the National Assembly of 1975 there have been some changes in the structure of the Association. A President of the National Association is now elected along with five Directors of specific areas: International Section, Training, Programme, Finance and National Centres. Each of these Directors also takes a turn as Vice-President. They work with the help of a team composed of Members of the National Council and the Executive National Committee. An advisory National Committee has also been set up composed of Past Presidents of the Association, two legal advisers and two spiritual advisers. This Committee, whose President is the National Adviser, meets three times a year and brings its reports and suggestions to the National Council.

SERVICE

Among the best known service projects undertaken by the Girl Guides of Peru is the Pamplona project for Youth Recreation in Young Towns which started as far back as 1962. This project, organized within the WAGGGS/UNESCO Gift Coupon Scheme benefited girls in underdeveloped areas of the country by providing an educational centre with organized recreation.

After ten successful years the Centre was entrusted to the Ministry of Education to be used within the new reformed educational system and the scheme has now been replaced by a new mobile recreational project involving hundreds of children in young towns.

Another important Girl Guide project is a 'Youth to Youth' Nutrition Campaign undertaken with the help of financial assistance from their colleagues in the Scandinavian countries. This scheme, in which FAO Lima has co-operated, was launched in 1974 and involves Senior Girl Guides working with mothers and children in several localities in Peru.

LA CASTELLANA GUIDE CENTRE

In 1966 Peru celebrated the fiftieth anniversary of the founding of the first Guide company. On this occasion the government, through the National Youth Council, donated a large sum of money towards building an outdoor activity centre. With the help of private donations and Guide contributions it opened a year later under the name of 'National Programme Centre La Castellana'. The Centre was extensively used during the earthquake which hit Peru in 1970, providing shelter for mothers and their children whose homes were destroyed in the disaster. A four-month programme of health, education and nutrition work for the refugees followed, gaining for the Association a Special Mention Award from the Ministry of Health.

CO-OPERATION WITH OTHER ORGANIZATIONS

The Asociación Nacional de las Guías-Scouts del Perú is regularly represented at meetings organized in the country by the United Nations Development Programme (UNDP) and other UN Agencies.

Under the auspices of the Municipality of San Isidro, Girl Guides run a local Children's Centre in co-operation with two other NGOs, the Association of

Alumnae of the Sacred Heart and the Business and Professional Women's Association.

INTERNATIONAL WOMEN'S YEAR

The Association has participated in all activities organized to celebrate International Women's Year. Seminars and Round Tables on current women's affairs have been held in Lima and Girl Guide delegates have attended events organized by the Committee on Co-operation of the Inter-American Commission of Women of the Organization of American States. The Association's legal Adviser was a member of the official Peruvian delegation to the UN International Women's Year Conference, and Girl Guide Leaders attended the International Women's Year Tribune held in Mexico.

INTERNATIONAL UNDERSTANDING

The Asociación Nacional de las Guías-Scouts del Perú arranges valuable exchange programmes with the Girl Scouts of the U.S.A. and with other organizations, welcomes girls from other countries and attends all World Association events.

Philippines

Girl Scouts of the Philippines

GIRL SCOUT

Promise

On my honour, I will fulfil my duty:
To serve God
My country and mankind
And to abide by the Girl Scout Law.

Law

As a Girl Scout and a true Filipino, I will be
- clean in thought, word and deed
- compassionate
- disciplined
- industrious
- law-abiding
- loyal
- ready to help others
- respectful of all living things
- self-reliant
- and trustworthy.

Motto

Laging Handa   Be Prepared

STAR SCOUT

Star Scout Promise

Ipinangangako ko na sisikapin kong:	I promise to do my best:
Ibigin ang Diyos at ang aking bansa;	To love God and my country;
Tumulong sa ibang tao araw-awaw, lalong-lalo na sa mga kasama sa bahay.	To help other people every day; especially those at home.

Star Scout Law

Ang Star Scout ay matapat.	A Star Scout is truthful.
Ang Star Scout ay masunurin.	A Star Scout is obedient.

Star Scout Motto

Maging matulungin	Lend a Hand

Star Scout Slogan

Magpaligaya ng kapwa araw-araw.	Make someone happy every day.

Age Groups

Senior Scout	13–15
Junior Scout	9–12
Star Scout	6–9

Girl Scouting began in the Philippines as early as 1918, but it was not until 1939 that the Girl Scout Movement was formally launched. In 1940, the Girl Scouts of the Philippines was chartered as a national organization.

The first National Girl Scouts' rally and the first Leaders' Training Conference were held in 1941, and during the Second World War, although the Association suspended its activities, Girl Scout Leaders committed themselves to humanitarian service to victims and prisoners of war. After the war, the task of the Movement's reconstruction became the most urgent job for the Leaders, and with public support it had reached such a state of development that in 1946 at the 11th World Conference of WAGGGS in France the Philippines was recognized as an Associate Member of the World Association. Girl Scouts of the Philippines became a Full Member of the World Association at the 12th World Conference of WAGGGS in U.S.A. in 1948.

INTERNATIONAL GIRL GUIDING/GIRL SCOUTING

The Association hostessed the Regional Centenary World Camp in 1957, which Girl Guides/Girl Scouts from 22 countries attended, and the Asian Trainers' Conference in 1958, with participants from 14 Asian countries. The 1971 WAGGGS-sponsored Public Relations-Finance Seminar attended by Leaders from 13 Member Organizations of WAGGGS was also held in the Philippines. In 1973 the first Asia-Pacific Regional Jamboree was held there to celebrate the Golden Jubilee of Philippine Scouting and was attended by 20,000 Boy and Girl Scouts from 12 countries.

'FOCUS ON THE PERFORMING ARTS'

The Girl Scouts of the Philippines celebrated their 35th anniversary in 1975 with the Third National Girl Scout Gathering whose theme was 'Focus on the

Performing Arts'. The gathering was attended by some 800 Girl Guides and Girl Scouts from Australia, Hong Kong, Japan, Malaysia, the Republic of China and the Philippines, and had four main aims: to stress the role of Girl Scouts in preserving the cultural heritage and identity; to provide a venue for establishing a meaningful relationship between the girls of the various regions of the Philippines and Asia-Pacific countries; to emphasize the service ideal of Girl Scouting and to underline the informal educational character of the Girl Scout Movement.

Workshops on drama, dance and music were organized throughout the camp by specialists assisted by Girl Scout Camp Counsellors, and what was learnt was immediately put to practical use as part of a service project to bring entertainment to guests and the local population. Also included in the programme of the camp were: visits to places of historical interest and an international festival of song, dance and drama.

SERVICE

Girl Scouts have for years been partners in the national development programmes. A food production campaign, known as the 'Green Revolution' which was started in 1974 has proved especially popular with Filipino Girl Scouts, 127,000 of whom are now engaged in food production, setting up vegetable gardens, poultry and pig farms as well as developing small-scale fisheries. These projects make a substantial contribution to the economic growth of the country, improve nutritional habits of the population, and in general help to mobilize both community participation and untapped resources.

Out-of-school young people represent another area of major involvement for the Association which, among other things, holds annual hikes to raise funds that enable these young people to enjoy the benefits of Girl Scouting. The scheme in the first four years has benefited thousands of girls who have learned basic camping and training skills.

Other areas of Girl Scout service include visiting homes for old people, assistance to hospitals and to victims of natural disasters, forest conservation and ecology.

Handicrafts, culture and the arts also play an important part in the Girl Scout programme in the Philippines.

Portugal

Associacao das Guias de Portugal

GUIDE

Promessa	**Promise**
Cumprir os seus deveres para com Deus-e a Pátria.	To do one's duty to God and Country.
Ajudar o próximo em todas as ocasiões.	To help other people at all times.
Obedecer à Lei das Guías.	To obey the Guide Law.

Lei	Law
1 O sentimento de honra da Guia é sagrado, a sua palavra merece toda a confiança.	A Guide's honour is sacred and her word worthy of complete trust.
2 A Guia é leal.	A Guide is loyal.
3 A Guia é útil e practica diàriamente uma Boa Acção.	A Guide is useful and does a Good Deed every day.
4 A Guia é amiga de todos e irmã de todas as outras Guias.	A Guide is a friend to all and a sister to every other Guide.
5 A Guia é atenciosa e delicada.	A Guide is courteous.
6 A Guia vê a obre de Deus na natureza e protege as plantas e os animais.	A Guide sees the hand of God in Nature and protects plants and animals.
7 A Guia é obediente.	A Guide is obedient.
8 A Guia tem sempre boa disposição de espírito.	A Guide is always cheerful.
9 A Guia é económica, amiga do arranjo e da ordem e respeitadora do bem alheio.	A Guide is thrifty, likes good order and respects the property of others.
10 A Guia é pura em pensamentos, palavras e acções.	A Guide is pure in thought, word and deed.

Motto

Sempre Alerta	Always Prepared

BROWNIE

Brownie Promise

Eu prometo fazer o possível por: Cumprir o meu dever para com Deus e a Pátria e ajudar sempre o próximo, especialmente todos em minha casa.	I promise to do my best: To do my duty to God and country and to help others, especially those at home.

Brownie Law

A Avesinha é obediente.	A Brownie is obedient.
A Avesinha anda sempre limpa e arranjada.	A Brownie is always clean and tidy.
A Avesinha está sempre alegre.	A Brownie is cheerful.
A Avesinha diz sempre a verdade.	A Brownie always tells the truth.

Brownie Motto

A Avesinha ajuda sempre	A Brownie always helps

Age Groups

Senior	Ranger	17+
Junior	Junior	14–17
Guia	Guide	10–14
Avesinha	Brownie	6–10

The first Guide companies were started in Oporto in 1919 and the Movement later spread to Lisbon. In 1930, Brownie packs and Guide companies were started on the Portuguese island of Madeira.

The Guias de Portugal became a recognized national movement in 1934; but, by

1938, all Guiding had been suspended in Portugal and it was not until 1952 that the Movement restarted, as interest in the Movement grew. Guías de Portugal was recognized as an Associate Member of the World Association at the 18th World Conference (Denmark, 1963) and as a Full Member at the 22nd World Conference (United Kingdom, 1975).

TRAINING

One of the main problems in Portugal is that of recruiting leaders, and great efforts have been made to meet this need. A correspondence course was started, aimed especially at leaders in the provinces. In 1969, a leaders' training course was held in the Lisbon area with twenty-six participants. It was followed, a year later, by a similar course which thirty-five girls attended. With support from the educational section of the Gulbenkian Foundation, a team was set up to study and revise the programmes so that the needs of young people could be more effectively met.

After many years of financial difficulties, a subsidy of 180,000 escudos (approximately £2,600) was allocated to the Association by the Ministry of National Education in 1971. This grant made it possible to rent a headquarters building and, in view of the expansion of the Movement, to pay the salary of a secretary. In addition, it covered the cost of travel expenses for a team of trainers to visit the provinces and to engage the assistance of three ex-leaders responsible for training and counselling leaders in the Lisbon area. This financial assistance also made it possible to give efficient help to the units already formed, and to facilitate the establishment of new units.

SERVICE

The Association is at present concentrating on alleviating the problems of migrants. Among the various schemes under way is a programme of resettlement and re-education for migrants returning home to Portugal.

CO-OPERATION

The Guias de Portugal have established a system of friendly co-operation with the official Youth Movement for Women, 'Mocidade Portuguesa Feminina', and are also collaborating more closely with the Boy Scout Association. The possibility of setting up training centres for use by both Girl Guide and Boy Scout leaders is being studied.

Rhodesia

Girl Guides Association of Rhodesia

GUIDE

Promise

I promise that I will do my best
To do my duty to God,
To serve my country, and other people
and
To keep the Guide Law.

Law

1 A Guide is loyal and can be trusted.
2 A Guide is helpful.
3 A Guide is polite and considerate.
4 A Guide is friendly and a sister to all Guides.
5 A Guide is kind to animals and respects all living things.
6 A Guide is obedient.
7 A Guide has courage and is cheerful in all difficulties.
8 A Guide makes good use of her time.
9 A Guide takes care of her own possessions and those of other people.
10 A Guide is self-controlled in all she thinks, says and does.

Motto

Be Prepared

BROWNIE

Brownie Promise

I promise that I will do my best:
To do my duty to God;
To serve my country and other people;
and
To keep the Brownie Law.

Brownie Law

A Brownie is truthful, obedient and cheerful.
A Brownie thinks of others before herself.

Brownie Motto

Lend a Hand

Age Groups

Ranger	14–21
Guide	11–14
Brownie	7–11

THE GIRL GUIDES ASSOCIATION OF RHODESIA

Girl Guiding was started in Rhodesia in 1912. The special needs of rural girls led to the formation, in 1926, of the Wayfarer Movement, and it ran on parallel lines to the Girl Guide Movement until 1940 when a process of fusion between the two began. This process was completed in 1950, since which time only one Girl Guide Movement with fully multi-social and multi-racial membership has been in operation.

The Girl Guides Association of Rhodesia became an Associate Member of WAGGGS at the 20th World Conference (Finland, 1969) and was recognized as a Full Member at the 21st World Conference (Canada, 1972).

Over the years the Association has been active in all-African conferences sponsored by the World Association, one of which was held in Rhodesia in 1956 (the second such conference ever held), and more recently in sub-regional gatherings in Africa.

TRAINING

Training is naturally of great importance to the Association and Members are continually working to increase the number of qualified Trainers in the country. They have also been assisted by visiting Trainers whose work has resulted in a significant raising of standards of Girl Guiding in Rhodesia.

CAMPING AND NATIONAL TRAINING CENTRES

The Rhodesian Girl Guides Association has two National Training and Camping Centres: Pax Park near Salisbury and Rowallan Park near Bulawayo in the Matapos Hills; and four permanent camping sites are maintained in other parts of the country.

PUBLICATIONS

Guide publications include: Handbooks for Brownies, Guides and Rangers and, for their respective Guiders, a *Commissioners' Handbook*, a *Games and Activities Book* and a *Brownie Painting Book*. *News and Views* is published once a term, as is *Guigest*, a magazine for the children.

JUBILEE CELEBRATIONS

Rhodesian Girl Guiding celebrated the Diamond Jubilee of World Guiding in 1972 with the establishment of the National Endowment Fund. Six bicycles ridden by successive teams of Senior Guides and Rangers covered some 800 miles around the country as a public relations exercise to raise money for the Fund.

SERVICE

Service is an extremely important part of Guiding in Rhodesia and Guides and Rangers endeavour to respond to their country's needs, even at short notice, as for example in the case of the drought which struck the country in 1965. Their prompt and untiring service during that disaster was recognized by the award of the Walter Donald Ross Certificate of Merit.

There are, of course, more long-term projects, such as the work Guides carry out with children in crèches, nursery schools, clinics and special camps which they organize for underprivileged children.

Every section of the Association is involved and concerned with the protection of the environment. The 'Year of the Tree' (1975) was celebrated in Rhodesia by vast tree-planting campaigns and other tree-related projects, while Girl Guide Headquarters is registered as a reclamation depot for scrap glass as part of the CARE campaign (CARE = clean air, rivers and environment).

Other areas of concern to Girl Guides in Rhodesia include: the welfare of the aged; world population control and the problems of the handicapped (they try as far as possible to integrate handicapped Guides into regular units).

CONFERENCES, CAMPS, SEMINARS AND 'GUIDE FRIENDS'

Two representatives of Rhodesian Guiding attended the International Commissioners' Conference in 1973, further to which they arranged for an International Friendship Camp to be held in their country in 1974.

Young Adult Seminars were held in Rhodesia in 1974 and 1975 and a group entitled 'Guide Friends' came into being in 1975. Its aim? To provide a link between former members of the Movement and help them to 'keep in touch' with each other and with the Movement. A similar idea was behind the setting up of the first Venture Club in 1971, which provides social contact and involvement in a variety of interests and social projects for present and past senior Girl Guides and Boy Scouts.

Sierra Leone

The Sierra Leone Girl Guides Association

GUIDE

Promise

I promise on my honour that I will
do my best
To do my duty to God,
To serve my Country and help other
people
And to keep the Guide Law.

Law

1 A Guide is loyal and can be trusted.
2 A Guide is helpful.
3 A Guide is polite and considerate.
4 A Guide is friendly to all and a sister to all Guides.
5 A Guide is kind to animals and plants and sees in Nature the work of God.
6 A Guide is obedient.
7 A Guide has courage and is cheerful in all difficulties.
8 A Guide makes good use of her time, money and talents.
9 A Guide takes care of her own possessions and those of other people.
10 A Guide controls herself and is clean in all she thinks, says and does.

Motto

Be Prepared

Brownie Guide Promise

I promise that I will do my best
To do my duty to God,
To serve my Country and help other people
And to keep the Brownie Guide Law.

BROWNIE

Brownie Guide Law

A Brownie Guide thinks of others before herself and does a Good Turn every day.

Brownie Guide Motto

Lend a Hand

Age Groups

Ranger	19 and over
Guide	12–18
Brownie	6–11

Guiding was started in Sierra Leone in 1924 and before long spread throughout the country. The first African commissioner was appointed in 1947.

The Sierra Leone Girl Guides Association was recognized as an Associate Member of WAGGGS at the 18th World Conference (Denmark, 1963) and as a Full Member at the 21st World Conference (Canada, 1972).

TRAINING

The Association has made rapid progress in the field of Training, with increasing numbers of Guiders willing to undergo training for their local trainer's certificate. This has enabled Guiding to expand to the rural areas where several new Guide companies have been formed.

ORGANIZATION

In an effort to improve organization within the Association, the Executive Council has set up new committees for finance, training and programme, badges and awards, and publications.

PARTICIPATION IN EVENTS

Celebrations for the Diamond Jubilee of World Guiding in Sierra Leone were many and varied and included a picnic where 700 Girl Guides assembled. The World Association helped a delegate from Sierra Leone to participate in the Young Adults seminar held at Our Chalet in 1971, and two delegates from Sierra Leone also attended the celebrations for the Golden Jubilee of Guiding in Nigeria.

Delegations from the Association were present at the 20th, 21st and 22nd WAGGGS World Conferences, and in 1976 Sierra Leone was hostess to one of the African Sub-regional gatherings.

SERVICE

Guides give service in Cheshire homes, children's homes, hospitals and private nursing homes. They also help during national festivals and other public events.

In two districts Guides have provided more food by growing and selling vegetables. Other activities include a literacy campaign, a keep clean and beautify the city campaign and work on community development.

EXPANSION OF THE MOVEMENT

Improved communications have made it easier for the Movement to reach remote parts of the country. The expansion of Guiding has been helped by the establishment of secondary schools in provincial towns, and also by greater recognition on the part of parents and the Government.

Singapore

The Singapore Girl Guides Association

GUIDE

五　女童軍組之組織及行政

女童軍矢言

我願：對上蒼盡我的本分。
我願：爲我的國家及人民服務。
我願：遵守女童軍規律。

Promise

I promise to do my best: to do my duty to God,
To serve my country and help other people and
To keep the Guide Law.

女童軍規律

1 女童軍是忠心誠實的。
2 女童軍是樂於助人的。
3 女童軍是溫文有禮，尊敬長輩的。
4 女童軍是友善的，視每位女童軍如姊妹。
5 女童軍是愛護動物的。
6 女童軍是服從的。
7 女童軍是不畏困難的。
8 女童軍是愛護公物的。
9 女童軍是勤勉的，珍惜光陰的。
10 女童軍是三思而行的。

Law

1 A Guide is loyal and can be trusted.
2 A Guide's duty is to be useful and to help others.
3 A Guide is polite, considerate and respects her elders.
4 A Guide is friendly and a sister to all Guides.
5 A Guide is kind to all living things.
6 A Guide is obedient.
7 A Guide has courage and is cheerful in all difficulties.
8 A Guide takes care of her own possessions and those of other people.
9 A Guide is diligent, and makes good use of her time.
10 A Guide is self-controlled in all she thinks, says and does.

Motto

Selalu Sedia

Be Prepared

BROWNIE

Brownie Promise

I promise to do my best: to do my duty to God,
To serve my country and help other people, and
To keep the Brownie Law.

Brownie Law

A Brownie always obeys and respects her elders.
A Brownie always thinks of others before herself.
A Brownie always tells the truth.
A Brownie is always neat and tidy.
A Brownie always plays and works cheerfully.

Brownie Motto

Tolong Orang Selalu	Lend a Hand

Age Groups

Ranger	Ranger	16–21
Pemandu Perempuan	Guide	11–16
Brownie	Brownie	7–11

Girl Guiding began in Singapore in 1917 as part of the Girl Guide Association of the Federation of Malaya. In 1934 the first Extension pack was started, and in 1940 the first Land Ranger company was formed. From 1953 the Movement in Singapore was a separate entity having administrative links with the Commonwealth Girl Guide Headquarters.

With the formation of Malaysia in 1963, Singapore became a State Member in the Malaysian Girl Guide Association. In 1965, as an independent nation, Singapore applied for Associate Membership of the World Association and received recognition at the 19th World Conference (Japan, 1966). In 1972 at the 21st World Conference in Canada, Singapore became a Full Member of the World Association.

STRUCTURE

The National Council, which is a policy-making body, consists of uniformed and 'lay members', and has as its Chairman the President of the Association. The Council's decisions are implemented by the Executive Committee, which consists of uniformed members of the Association. The Executive Committee is responsible for the day-to-day administration of the Association. Standing Committees have been set up to deal with such matters as Organization and Membership Training, Camping, International Division, Finance, General Administration, Programme and Publications, etc.

A review of the Constitution in 1969 and an increased participation of younger members in administration and programming have contributed to the increased efficiency of the Movement in recent years.

MEMBERSHIP

There are now five Divisions headed by a Division Commissioner and several District Commissioners, each Division having its own Local Association. Companies and packs, where Guides of different races meet together, use English as the medium for test-work, games, songs, etc. 'Open Packs' are run, on similar lines to those in the schools, with office workers, nurses and housewives as Guiders.

PROGRAMME

A general desire to revise and further develop the programme for all three branches has led to the formation of a Programme and Publications Committee. A Brownie Handbook emphasizing training in self-development has been published in both Chinese and English. A lot of attention is being paid to the organization and contents of the training sessions for Guiders to ensure a high quality of the Movement in the country. One of the most successful events in this category was a seminar 'Guiding towards a better Singapore'.

HANDICAPPED

The Extension Branch of the Girl Guides Association has a pack and company in both the School for the Deaf and the School for the Blind. Camps are also held for handicapped girls.

JOINT ACTIVITIES AND INTERNATIONAL CONTACTS

The Singapore Girl Guides Association co-operates closely with the Boy Scouts Association and through the annual Boy Scout/Girl Guide Week celebrates Thinking Day/World Friendship Day with rallies, camp fires and service projects undertaken jointly throughout the week.

Guiders and Guides from Singapore have participated in seminars, trainings and camps in India, New Zealand, Japan, Malaysia and at Our Chalet in Switzerland.

PARTICIPATION IN NATIONAL EVENTS

The Association participates fully in national projects such as National Day and the Youth Festival Rally. They also respond to invitations issued by other organizations, especially the United Nations, to participate in events organized by them. The celebration of the Diamond Jubilee of Singapore Guiding will have as its highlight the National Seminar 'Guiding for the Girls', with participation from countries throughout the Asia-Pacific Region.

South Africa

The Girl Guides Association of South Africa
Die Dogtergidsvereniging van Suid Afrika

GUIDE

Belofte

Ek belowe om my bes te doen:
Om my plig teenoor God en my land na te kom;
Om te alle tye my medemens te help;
En om aan die Gidswet te voldoen.

Promise

I promise that I will do my best:
To do my duty to God and to my country;
To help other people at all times;
And to keep the Guide Law.

Wet

1 'n Gids is betroubaar.
2 'n Gids is getrou.
3 'n Gids is hulpvaardig.
4 'n Gids is vriendelik.
5 'n Gids is hoflik en dink aan ander.
6 'n Gids sorg vir die aarde en lewende dinge.
7 'n Gids is gehoorsaam.
8 'n Gids is dapper en blymoedig.
9 'n Gids is spaarsaam.
10 'n Gids is rein in alles wat sy dink, sê en doen.

Law

A Guide is to be trusted.
A Guide is loyal.
A Guide is helpful.
A Guide is friendly.
A Guide is polite and thoughtful for others.
A Guide cares for the earth and living things.
A Guide is obedient.
A Guide is brave and cheerful.
A Guide is thrifty.
A Guide is pure in all that she thinks, says and does.

Motto

Wees Gereed

Be Prepared

BROWNIE

Brownie Promise

Ek belowe om my bes te doen:
Om my plig te doen teenoor my God en my land;
Om elke dag ander te help, veral diegene in die huis.

I promise to do my best:
To do my duty to God and my country;
To help other people every day, especially those at home.

Brownie Law

'n Brownie het die waarheid lief, is gehoorsaam en opgeruimd.
'n Brownie dink aan ander voordat sy aan haarself dink.

A Brownie is truthful, obedient and cheerful.
A Brownie thinks of others before herself.

Brownie Motto

Wees Hulpvaardig

Be Helpful

Age Groups

Pionier	Ranger	15–20
Gids	Guide	$10\frac{1}{2}$–16
Brownie	Brownie	7–11

Girl Guiding started in Johannesburg in 1910 and soon spread throughout the whole country. When, in 1928, the World Association of Girl Guides and Girl Scouts was formed, South Africa became one of its Founder Members.

The Association has Brownies, Guides and Rangers with sections Air, Land, Sea, Home and Cadets. Besides these there are companies for Lone Guides and a section for handicapped Guides.

TRAINING

In spite of both lack of finance and language barriers, the Association carries out an intensive and enthusiastic training programme. South Africa has several permanent Training Centres and national training weeks are held annually at which Guiders from all over the country gather, taking back what they have learnt to Guides in their own areas. In addition each province organizes its own provincial trainings throughout the year. A Guider's training magazine *Look Wide* is published quarterly. Many South African Guiders visit Training Centres abroad and South Africa has welcomed Trainers from other countries. A number of Guiders took part in the scheme of interchange of personnel with Canada and Holland, which was sponsored by the Juliette Low World Friendship Fund.

CAMPING

Camping retains its popularity in South Africa, and there are many beautiful campsites, some of them permanent ones, all over the country. National camps are held regularly and are attended by Guides from the whole of South Africa.

EXPANSION OF THE MOVEMENT

Girl Guiding in South Africa goes from strength to strength with membership figures continually increasing, and enthusiasm reflected in the many varied activities of the Association. Due to this growth, it was necessary to rearrange the administrative section and there are now eleven 'Guiding' provinces as compared with seven previously.

DIAMOND JUBILEE

The Girl Guides Association of South Africa celebrated its Diamond Jubilee in 1970, and was lucky enough to have the World Chief Guide present, not only for some of their celebrations but also for her 80th birthday on 22 February (Thinking Day). Besides the usual company and district camps, national Jubilee camps were held during 1970 strengthening ties of friendship between girls all over South Africa.

PROGRAMME AND PUBLICATIONS

The Brownie Story has been adapted to incorporate South African animals and traditions. The Guide Laws have been reworded, and the Constitution updated. The Publications Department has also been busy with revising and reprinting the policy, organization and rules, and test cards have been translated into several African languages. New handbooks have been published and old ones revised, and a new and updated programme for both Brownies and Guides has recently been introduced.

INTERNATIONAL WOMEN'S YEAR

A three-part project was undertaken by Rangers as their contribution to IWY, consisting of a survey to establish a complete list of women's organizations in the country, followed by an effort to contact members of these other organizations which led to an exchange of information and a series of joint activities. The project gave a valuable insight into the activities undertaken by the world's women for the benefit of society as a whole. The Association also took part in IWY exhibitions.

HANDICAPPED

South Africa has introduced a breakthrough in activities with the handicapped, training the handicapped Rangers themselves to help out at the Alexandra Institute in Cape Town by bathing, dressing and feeding children who are unable to look after themselves.

SERVICE

Service to the community continues to be a keynote of the organization. Rangers have assisted hospital patients by adapting programmes to suit their needs, while toys, clothing and food have been donated by the Association to various welfare organizations.

Girl Guides are very much involved in environmental issues, and in 1974 many units in Cape West took part in the 'Clean-Up of Table Mountain'. Also numerous trees planted during Green Heritage Year are still being cared for by the Guides. In 1974 Girl Guides became members of the Council for the Habitat set up by the Department for the Environment.

Spain

Comité de Enlace del Guidismo en España

Comprising:
ASOCIACIÓN GUÍAS DE ESPAÑA
GUIATGE CATALÀ
Comprising: **Escoltes Catalans**
Guies Sant Jordi
Noies i Nois Escoltes

ASOCIACIÓN GUÍAS DE ESPAÑA

GUIDE

Promesa	**Promise**
Con la ayuda de Dios, yo prometo hacer cuanto de mi dependa para amar a Dios y a mi país, ser útil a mi familia y al prójimo en todo momento y vivir la Ley Guía.	With the help of God, I promise to do all within my power to love God and my country, to be useful at all times to my family and to other people and to live the Guide Law.
Ley	**Law**
La Guía:	The Guide
1 Es leal y digna de confianza.	Is loyal and trustworthy.
2 Es consciente de los derechos de los demás y de sus propios deberes.	Is conscious of the rights of others and of her own duties.
3 Es generosa.	Is generous.
4 Es abierta a todos y hermana de las demás guías.	Is friendly to all and is a sister to other Guides.
5 Es amable.	Is amiable.
6 Ama la naturaleza y ve en ella la obra de Dios.	Loves nature and sees in it the work of God.
7 Aprende a obedecer para saber colaborar.	Learns to obey so that she knows how to collaborate.
8 Afronta las dificultades con alegría.	Cheerfully faces difficulties.
9 Es austera, limpia y ordenada.	Is frugal, clean and tidy.
10 Sabe dominarse: es pura y alegre.	Knows how to control herself: is pure and cheerful.

BROWNIE

Motto

Bien preparada	Be Prepared

Brownie Promise

Con la ayuda de Dios, prometo hacer todo lo posible para vivir según la Ley de las Alitas.	With the help of God, I promise to do my best to live according to the Brownie Law.

Brownie Law

La Alita está siempre alegre.	The Brownie is always cheerful.
La Alita es limpia y trabajadora.	The Brownie is clean and industrious.
La Alita es amiga de todos y les ayuda.	The Brownie is a friend of others and helps all people.
La Alita piensa primero en los demás y procura llevarles su alegría.	The Brownie thinks first of others and brings them her cheerfulness.
La Alita ama la Naturaleza y es observadora.	The Brownie loves nature and observes it.
La Alita dice siempre la verdad.	The Brownie always tells the truth.
La Alita dice siempre SI a Dios y a los demás.	The Brownie always says YES to God and others.

Brownie Motto

Haremos lo mejor	We shall do our best

Age Groups

Guía mayor	Ranger	16–18
Pionera	Pioneer	14–16
Guía	Guide	11–14
Alita	Brownie	7–11

GUIATGE CATALÀ

Escoltes Catalans

Text of Promise and Law not available at time of going to Press.

Guies Sant Jordi

Promesa	Promise
Pel meu honor i amb la gracia de Déu, jo prometo fer tot el que pugui per complir els meus deures envers Déu, l'Església i la Pátria; ajudar tothora l'altra gent, y obeir la Llei Guia.	On my honour and by the Grace of God, I promise to do my best to do my duty to God, the Church and my country; to help others at all times, and to obey the Guide Law.

Llei	Law
La Noia Guia:	The Girl Guide:
1 Estima la veritat i la viu.	Loves and lives the truth.
2 Es lleial.	Is loyal.
3 Es servicial, pensa primer en els altres.	Is useful and likes to help others.
4 Germana de tots els escoltes, es oberta a tothom.	Is a friend to all and a sister to all Scouts.
5 Es generosa i austera.	Is generous and self-disciplined.
6 Protegeix la vida perquè ve de Déu.	Protects life, because life is given by God.
7 Aprèn a obeir per saber collaborar.	Learns to obey so that she may learn to co-operate.

8 Estima l'esforç i no fa res a mitges.	Does not fear endeavour and does nothing by halves.
9 Es treballadora i previsora.	Is industrious and thrifty.
10 Sap dominar-se per pura i alegre.	Controls herself to be pure and cheerful.

Motto

Sempre a punt	Always ready

Brownie Promise

Jo prometo fer tot el que pugui per estimar Déu, l'Església i la Pàtria i obeir la Llei de l'Aplec.	I promise to do my best to love God, the Church and my country, and to obey the Brownie Law.

Brownie Law

La Daina diu sempre la veritat.	The Brownie always tells the truth.
La Daina creu als grans.	The Brownie obeys the grown-ups.
La Daina és neta i endreçade.	The Brownie is clean and tidy.
La Daina és valenta i alegra.	The Brownie is courageous and cheerful.
La Daina ajuda a tothom.	The Brownie helps others.

Brownie Motto

Tant com puc	To do my best

Age Groups

Truc	Truc	15–18
Caravella	Caravelle	14–16
Pioneer Noia Guia	Pioneer Guide	11–14
Daina	Brownie	8–11

GUIDE

Noies i Nois Escoltes

Text of Promise and Law not available at time of going to Press.

WAGGGS' Member Organization in Spain comprises the Asociación de Guias de España and the Guiatge Català (a Federation of three Catalan associations: Escoltes Catalans, Guies Sant Jordi and Noies i Nois Escoltes).

Asociación de Guias de España started its activities in San Sebastian in 1929, and soon afterwards groups of Guides made their appearance in Barcelona, Zaragoza, Murcia and Madrid.

In Catalonia, the Germanor de Noies Guies was developing in much the same way as the Guías de España, and as early as 1932 some girls had approached Boy Scout Leaders who gave them training and in a short time Guide companies were formed, followed by Brownie packs and a Ranger section. During the Civil War all Guide activities ceased in Spain, and it was not until 1947 that Girl Guiding restarted throughout the country.

By 1955 Guiding had developed throughout Spain, and in the same year the Guías de España and the Germanor de Noies Guies joined together to form the Federación Guía de España, which in January 1959 became an Associate Member of the World Association. In 1962 the Federación was replaced by the Comité de Enlace del Guidismo en España thereby extending membership of the national organization, through the newly created Guiatge Català, to more Guides in Catalonia. At the 20th World Conference (Finland, 1969) the Comité de Enlace became a Full Member.

Since 1957 the Comité de Enlace has been represented at all of WAGGGS' World Conferences and at many International or European Conferences and Gatherings, at the UN World Youth Assembly, etc. Several Senior Guides and Guiders have taken part in international camps in different countries and there is a growing interest in international exchanges.

In 1974 the Germanor de Noies Guies, which in 1969 had become co-educational and changed its name to Germanor de Nois i Noies Guies, joined with two other Catalan lay co-educational associations and formed the Escoltes Catalans.

In recent years Guides have been active in the field of service, working with gypsies, helping a group of about 50 girls to become self-reliant, to work together with team spirit and to develop a sense of responsibility. Guides are also helping in an effort to integrate those who migrate from one area of the country to another.

ASOCIACIÓN GUÍAS DE ESPAÑA

One of the chief aims of the Association is to develop Guiding throughout the country in such a way as to group the various provinces according to their affinities. Each province has its Guide team and these provincial teams hold annual meetings in preparation for the National Guide Assembly. These meetings review progress within the Association and underline the importance of the task of those concerned as educators of young people.

At national level the Association regularly organizes meetings for Branch and Unit Leaders.

Brownie and Guide Handbooks are published and there is a national quarterly Guide magazine which includes notes on modern Guide methods and techniques.

Escoltes Catalans

Escoltes Catalans has grown out of the union of several Catalan lay co-educational associations, in an attempt to concentrate efforts in one strong association.

The Escoltes Catalans was constituted in Montserrat, at the end of 1974, the culmination of two years' work and collaboration to adapt Girl Guiding and Boy Scouting, strengthening it both ideologically and pedagogically. At present the work of the Association is directed towards three basic aims:

(*a*) To develop Guiding to the utmost and ensure its future.

(*b*) To evolve educational systems suited to the needs of young people and to their circumstances.

(*c*) To train Leaders. Very high priority is given to Leadership training, and new methods are constantly being used to bring this training up to date. More than 10 training camps were held in 1976.

Guies Sant Jordi

This Association, which emphasizes the Christian viewpoint in its policy and activities, covers the following zones: Gerona, Lleida, Tarragona, Vic/Manresa and Barcelona, all of which have a vote at the National Assembly. The governing body is the General Commissariat and is composed of the general commissioners, the general counsellor and members of the training team, public relations team, etc.

The Association works closely with its male counterpart, the 'Minyons Escoltes' and both associations have common objectives.

The training of Leaders is the responsibility of each zone in accordance with the wishes of the General Commissariat. A Leadership Training camp held in 1975 and attended by 700 Leaders of the Guies Sant Jordi/Minyons Escoltes, raised such points as: the Evaluation of present-day Girl Guiding/Boy Scouting; what it is like to belong to an organized movement; the present and future structure of the Movement and the task of Leaders.

Guies Sant Jordi continues to participate in all the work of the Guiatge Català and maintains contact with the Guías de España.

Noies i Nois Escoltes

Present-day problems of young people are among the main preoccupations of the Association, and commissioners regularly hold meetings to carry out studies on the best programme methods to meet the needs of young people. They work in close co-operation with specialists in education, psychology, sociology, etc.

In 1976 the Association held a 'Boom Sant Jordi' where three days were spent in sports, literacy competitions, technical workshops and recreational activities. There were also activities for non-Guides; these included a snow-camp, an indoor camp for young children, excursions for adolescents and a course on communications techniques.

Sri Lanka

Sri Lanka Girl Guides Association

GUIDE

Porondhuwa	Promise
Maage aagama saha rata kerehee maage yuthukam etukiree-matath, hama vitama anunata pihitaveematath, Baladhakshika neethiyata keekaruveematath mata pilivan tharamin dhiri dhareemata mama gaurawa peradhariva perendhu vemi.	I promise on my honour to do my best: To do my duty to my religion and country; To help other people at all times; And to obey the Guide Law.

Neethi	Law
1 Baladhakshikava vishvasa kata yuthuya.	A Guide's honour is to be trusted.
2 Baladhakshikava pakshapathaya.	A Guide is loyal.
3 Baladhakshikavage yuthukam nam anunata prayojanavath veemath upakara veemathya.	A Guide's duty is to be useful and to help others.

4	Baladhakshikava sama geyma mithuriyeki ann hema Baladhakshikavakage, a sohoyuriyeki.	A Guide is a friend to all and a sister to every other Guide.
5	Baladhakshikava karunasheeliya.	A Guide is courteous.
6	Baladhakshikava sathunge mithuriyeki.	A Guide is a friend to animals.
7	Baladhakshikava anata kee-karuvei.	A Guide obeys orders.
8	Baladhakshikava apahasukam madha sinahavemin gee gayai.	A Guide smiles and sings under all difficulties.
9	Baladhakshikava sakasuruvam sahithaya.	A Guide is thrifty.
10	Baladhakshikava sithinuth, vatchanayenuth, kriyavenuth pivithuruya.	A Guide is pure in thought, word and deed.

Motto

Sudhanamva sittinna — Be Prepared

LITTLE FRIEND

Little Friend Promise

I promise on my honour to do my best:
To do my duty to my religion and country;
To help other people every day, especially those at home.

Little Friend Law

A Little Friend gives in to Older Folk.
A Little Friend does not give in to herself.

Little Friend Motto

Lend a Hand

Age Groups

Ranger	16–21
Guide	12–16
Brownie (Little Friend)	7–11

Girl Guiding started in Sri Lanka (formerly Ceylon) in 1917 with the opening of the first Girl Guide company in the historical hill town of Kandy. Throughout the last sixty years the Girl Guide Movement has engendered and strengthened ties between the country's multi-social, multi-lingual and multi-religious population. The present headquarters of the Association in Colombo was opened in 1933, and the Girl Guides Association, Ceylon, became a Full Member of the World Association of Girl Guides and Girl Scouts in 1951 following a decision of the 13th World Conference held in the United Kingdom in 1950.

TRAINING

The most important activity of the Association continues to be training and the development of the girl. All-island Trainers' Conferences are held annually, and with a new angle now given to training, subjects such as conservation and population awareness have been introduced and training methods include drama and puppetry. Each Division and District through its Training Unit System helps to promote Guiding all over the island. The development and continuity of the training programme is ensured through regular training sessions for prospective Trainers, enabling them to qualify for Trainers' Certificates and Diplomas in the various branches. Publications on various aspects of Guide work appear in the three official languages Sinhala, Tamil and English, and are instrumental in keeping standards high.

SERVICE

In recent years the accent has been laid more and more on service and especially on service programmes geared to the needs of the country. For example, badges have been introduced to help cultivate skills which will entail the use of indigenous material for economic purposes.

Rangers' service programmes include community development projects and population awareness schemes and the work with underprivileged children continues as before. Ranger Service Projects (many of them encouraged by challenges and trophies) include assisting in road-building; socio-economic surveys; teaching food-preservation, first-aid, health and sanitation and child-welfare in villages. Guides also do some very significant work with delinquent girls in Detention Homes.

The Association identifies itself with national efforts in food growing and economic development. Rural development through the Guide programme is going ahead, as a follow-up to the Asia-Pacific Regional Seminar 'Guiding for the Whole Country' hostessed in 1974 by the Sri Lanka Girl Guides Association on behalf of WAGGGS.

INTERNATIONAL WOMEN'S YEAR

The Association organized a seminar for Non-Governmental Organizations on the 'Role of Women in the Domestic Sphere in Urban Areas' in March 1975, while the theme of the All-island Trainers' Conference held in August 1975 was 'Developing through the Guide programme the scope of women in their own habitat'. A special workshop (with the participation of other NGOs) was organized on the theme 'Economic Development for Women through Self-Employment'.

CO-OPERATION AT NATIONAL AND INTERNATIONAL LEVELS

The Association co-operates with other voluntary Non-Governmental Organizations such as the Family Planning Association in their Population Awareness Programme, with the YWCA in Family Life Education, with the Sarvedaya Sangamaya for rural improvement, and with the Suukyadana Movement at the Medical Aid Centre during Pilgrim seasons and religious festivals.

Members of the Sri Lanka Girl Guides Association have represented WAGGGS at various international events organized during World Population Year in 1974, and have also participated in International Women's Year conferences.

Sudan

Sudan Girl Guides Association

Promise

GUIDE

On my honour, I promise that I
will do my best
To do my duty to God, my
Country and President of the
Republic
To help other people at all times
To obey the Girl Guides Law.

Law

1. A Guide's honour is to be trusted.
2. A Guide is loyal.
3. A Guide's duty is to be useful and to help others.
4. A Guide is a friend to everybody and a sister to every other Guide, no matter to what country, class or creed, the other may belong.
5. A Guide is courteous.
6. A Guide is a friend to animals.
7. A Guide obeys orders.
8. A Guide smiles and sings under all difficulties.
9. A Guide is thrifty.
10. A Guide is pure in thought, words and deed.

Motto

Be Prepared

Bluebird Promise

BLUEBIRD

I promise to do my best
to do my duty to God, my
Country and the President
To help other people every day,
especially those at home and to
obey the Bluebird Law.

Bluebird Law

1. A Bluebird always does her best.
2. Thinks of others, before herself.
3. Does a good turn every day.

Bluebird Law

Lend a Hand

Age Groups

Raaidat	Ranger	16–20
Mursheda	Guide	12–16
El Taira el Zarga	Brownie (Bluebird)	7–11

The Girl Guide Movement started in Sudan in 1928, but ceased activity shortly afterwards. It was restarted some years later with people of many different nationalities working together in the name of Guiding and friendship. Today there are companies and flocks in all parts of Sudan with a national headquarters in the capital, Khartoum.

The Sudan Girl Guides Association was recognized as an Associate Member of the World Association at the 16th World Conference (Brazil, 1957). It became a Full Member at the 22nd World Conference (U.K., 1975).

PROGRAMME

Sudanese Guides work side by side with their people, keeping alive the traditions and customs of the country, and as a result have gained widespread recognition and sympathy. The programme covers a wide variety of activities such as cookery, needlework, home nursing, first aid, hiking and camping. Members of the Association also take part in national parades. Once a year they hold a gala to show their work and raise funds for the Association. Many different fund-raising projects have been organized in order to improve the financial situation of the Movement.

The Association also works in co-operation with the Boy Scouts and with other women's organizations in Sudan.

TRAINING

Great emphasis is laid on the training of leaders. As there is a shortage of trained Guiders in the country, leaders meet weekly for training.

In 1976 two leaders from the Sudan Girl Guides Association visited the Pakistan Girl Guides Association to study training methods. This visit was part of the exchange programme among regions of WAGGGS.

SERVICE

Sudanese Guides help in any emergency in the hospitals and collaborate in other community activities. They have also set up emergency first-aid classes for women in towns and villages throughout the country which has won them the appreciation of the general public. On Thinking Day Guides carry out special welfare activities such as helping the poor and sick.

An important service project was undertaken in Sudan in 1976. It involved Sudanese Girl Guides and Boy Scouts in a joint poultry-farm project with Girl Guides and Boy Scouts from Denmark and is a long-term undertaking which, it is hoped, will bring prosperity to Sudan and at the same time consolidate the links of friendship and international understanding between the two Associations.

Surinam

Surinaamse Padvindsters Raad

HET SURINAAMSE PADVINDSTERS GILDE

GIRL SCOUT

Promise

I promise to do my very best to serve
God and my country, to help others
as much as possible and to live up
to the Girl Scout Law.

Law

1 A Girl Scout is honest and to be trusted.
2 A Girl Scout is helpful.
3 A Girl Scout is polite and considerate.
4 A Girl Scout is friendly and a sister to other Girl Scouts.
5 A Girl Scout is good to animals and has respect for Nature.
6 A Girl Scout is obedient.
7 A Girl Scout is courageous and remains cheerful in setbacks.
8 A Girl Scout spends her time usefully.
9 A Girl Scout takes care of her own possessions and those of other people.
10 A Girl Scout keeps control of her thoughts, words and deeds.

Motto

Be Prepared

GIDSEN SURINAME

GUIDE

Promise

On my honour, I promise, with the
help of God, that I will do my best:
to do my duty to God, Church and
country,
to help other people at all times,
to obey the Guide's Law.

Law

1 A Guide's honour is to be trusted.
2 A Guide is loyal.
3 A Guide's duty is to be useful and to help others.
4 A Guide is a friend to all and a sister to every other Guide.
5 A Guide is courteous.
6 A Guide is appreciative of Nature.
7 A Guide is obedient.
8 A Guide smiles and sings under all difficulties.
9 A Guide is thrifty.
10 A Guide is pure in thought, word and deed.

Motto

Be Prepared

BROWNIE

Brownie Promise

I shall do my best, with the help of
God, to be a good Brownie,
to help other people at all times,
especially at home.

Brownie Law

A Brownie is honest.
A Brownie is obedient.
A Brownie is friendly.
A Brownie takes good care of
plants and animals.

Brownie Motto

Tackle the job

Age Groups

Ranger	18+
Guide (senior)	15–18
Guide (junior)	11–14
Brownie	8–11

Surinaamse Padvindsters Raad, composed of two Associations, Het Surinaamse Padvindsters Gilde and Gidsen Suriname, was recognized as an Associate Member of the World Association at the 21st World Conference (Canada, 1972).

HET SURINAAMSE PADVINDSTERS GILDE

Het Surinaamse Padvindsters Gilde was started in Paramaribo in May 1947 and since then has spread to other areas of the country.

PROGRAMME

Following study of the U.K. eight-point programme, a programme was drawn up in 1969 to meet the requirements of the girls, based on the need to develop self-reliance.

Activities included in the programme are outings, cycling and boat trips for leaders, and camps for all branches of the Association. Each year special celebrations are held to mark Thinking Day.

TRAINING

Much emphasis is placed on training, and regular Trainings are held, including ones for group leaders and assistant group leaders, and also for Brownie leaders. Guide leaders are trained in hiking, and in first-aid in co-operation with the Surinam Red Cross.

SERVICE

Service to others is stressed in the programme and many service activities are organized. Gifts of food and flowers have regularly been taken to a home for underprivileged children and to an old people's home.

GIDSEN SURINAME

In 1945 'the Grail' in the Netherlands started Guiding for girls. As a result of its ties with the Netherlands, Surinam joined with the Catholic Young Women and the Catholic Young Girls Association to form Gidsen Suriname. In 1947 one of the older Grail leaders came to Surinam to train leaders and on 15 August 1948 the first leaders were installed and the first Chief Commissioner for Surinam appointed. This marked the official start of Gidsen Surinam. The membership was then about 600.

TRAINING

The training of leaders continues to get priority in the Gidsen Suriname and thanks to help from various sources has been able to continue without interruption in spite of several setbacks in recent years. One of these sources was the Catholic Boy Scouts in Surinam who gave valuable assistance in camp training.

Swaziland

The Swaziland Girl Guides Association

GUIDE

Setsembiso	**Promise**
Ngetsembisa kwenta lokusemandleni ami:	I promise to do my best:
Kukhonta Nkhulunkhulu,	To do my duty to God,
Kusebentela iNgwenyama nokusita labanye bantfu,	To serve the King and help other people,
Nokugcina umtsetfo wema Gaidi.	And to keep the Guide Law.

Umtsetfo Wemagaidi	**Guide Law**
1 LiGaidi letsembekile katsi futsi lingetsentjwa.	A Guide is loyal and can be trusted.
2 LiGaidi linelusito.	A Guide is helpful.
3 LiGaidi linenhlonipho, liyacabangelana.	A Guide is polite and considerate.
4 LiGaidi lingumngani nadzadze wawo onke emaGaidi.	A Guide is friendly and a sister to all Guides.
5 LiGaidi liphatsa kahle tilwane, nato tonkhe tintfo letiphilako.	A Guide is kind to animals and respects all living things.
6 LiGaidi liyalalela.	A Guide is obedient.
7 LiGaidi linesibindzi, libeketelela bonkhe bumatima.	A Guide has courage and is cheerful in all difficulties.
8 LiGaidi lisisebentisa kahle sikhatsi salo.	A Guide makes good use of her time.
9 LiGaidi liphatsa kahle timphahla talo, netalabanye.	A Guide takes care of her own possessions and those of other people.

10 LiGaidi liyatibamba kuko konkhe lelikucabangako, lelikushoko nalelikwentako.	A Guide is self-controlled in all she thinks, says and does.

Motto

Hlala Ulungele	Be Prepared

BLUE JAY

Blue Jay Promise

Ngetsembisa kwenta lokusemandleni ami:	I promise to do my best:
Kukhonta Nkhulunkhulu,	To do my duty to God,
Kusebentela iNgwenyama nokusita labanye bantfu,	To serve the King and help other people,
Nokugcina umtsetfo wemaFemfe.	And to keep the Blue Jay Law.

Blue Jay Law

LiFemfe licanga ngalabanye ngaphambi kokutsi liticabange lona; futsi lenta sento Lesihle onkemalanga.	A Blue Jay thinks of others before herself and does a Good Turn every day.

Blue Jay Motto

Sita labanye	Lend a Hand

Age Groups

Ranger/Cadet	15–21
Girl Guide	10½–15
Blue Jay	7–10½

Girl Guiding started in Swaziland in 1924, but only really began to spread throughout the country after the visit of the World Chief Guide in 1950.

The Swaziland Girl Guides Association became an Associate Member of the World Association at the 20th World Conference (Finland, 1969).

The Ranger section of Guiding was started in Swaziland in 1963, and five years later a Cadet company was formed in one of the two training colleges in the country. In the same year, Brownies and Sunbeams were amalgamated into one section called Blue Jays. The Blue Jay is the Royal Bird of Swaziland, and the national emblem of the Association.

PROGRAMME

The programme of the Swaziland Girl Guides Association has, over the years, been revised and brought up to date, and division committees have been formed in order to effect a more decentralized structure. Another sphere of development is a social and cultural one; the Guides are actively involved in Swazi culture and custom, and there is increasing co-operation between the Girl Guides Association and other youth organizations in the country.

TRAINING

Special attention has been given to training adult members of the Movement; trainings are held throughout the country, including trainings for commissioners and future commissioners.

SERVICE

Swaziland Guides visit hospitals, clinics and centres for the handicapped, and undertake community projects. For example, they planted trees near bus stops along the main roads to provide shade for travellers. Much research has gone into involving Guides in agricultural pursuits. They visit experimental farms and learn better ways of cultivation. Rangers have also taken a leading part in the national literacy scheme. Brownies, too, do some social service such as holding a flower-show to raise money to buy presents for children in hospital.

Sweden

Svenska Scoutrådet

UNION BADGE

FRÄLSNINGSARMENS SCOUTFÖRBUND FA
KFUK:s och KFUM:s SCOUTFÖRBUND KFUK-KFUM
NYKTERHETSRÖLSENS SCOUTFÖRBUND NSF
SMU:s SCOUTVERKSAMHET SMU
SVENSKA SCOUTFÖRBUNDET SSF

Löfte	Promise
Jag lovar att efter bästa förmåga följa scoutlagen.	I promise to do my best to follow the Guide Law.

Lag	Law
1 En scout visar vördnad för Gud och hans ord.	A Guide reveres God and His word.
2 En scout är ärlig och pålitlig.	A Guide is honest and reliable.
3 En scout är vänlig och hjälpsam.	A Guide is friendly and helpful.
4 En scout visar hänsyn och är en god kamrat.	A Guide is considerate to others and trustworthy as a friend.
5 En scout möter svårigheter med gott humör.	A Guide faces difficulties without complaining.
6 En scout lär känna och vårdar naturen.	A Guide learns about nature and is concerned with its conservation.
7 En scout känner ansvar för sig själv och andra.*	A Guide feels responsibility for herself and others.*

* The word 'andra' (others) is a Swedish expression for society, and the clause as a whole means responsibility to the communities in which we live.

GUIDE

Motto

Var redo	Be Prepared

Minior Law

En miniorscout vill vara ärlig och hjälpsam och försöker göra sitt bästa.	A Minior Guide/Scout is honest and helpful and tries to do her/his best.

BROWNIE

KFUK
KFUM

Age Groups

Leaders	18+
Senior Guide/Scout	15–18
Guide/Scout	12–14
Junior Guide/Scout	10–11
Minior Guide/Scout	8–9

The first groups of Girl Guides were formed in Sweden as early as 1910, and by 1913 the foundations of the Swedish Girl Guide Movement had been laid. When the World Association of Girl Guides and Girl Scouts was formed in 1928, Sweden became one of its Founder Members. By the end of the 1950s as many as six Girl Guide and six Boy Scout Associations were active in Sweden. Following the trend towards co-education in the 1960s the Girl Guide and Boy Scout Associations amalgamated to form six Joint Associations within the Svenska Scoutrådet (The Swedish Guide and Scout Federation). Later, two of these associations became one, and there are now five Joint Associations working in Sweden. The structural changes which have taken place in Swedish society and especially the increasing emphasis on adult education, nature conservation and ecology have influenced the planning of programmes and activities.

NSF

PROGRAMME AND TRAINING

In the late 1960s a new Guide and Scout programme was adopted by most of the Associations. The former three-part programme was replaced by a programme with four stages: Minior Scouting (replacing Brownies and Cubs), Junior Scouting (ages 10–12), Patrol Scouting and Senior Scouting. All units are open to both boys and girls but there are also units entirely made up of girls or entirely of boys. The aim of the programme is individuality – introducing projects based on the principles of individual requirements instead of the former tests which were based on absolute standards (the same requirements for all).

Joint Leadership Training takes place at local, regional and national levels.

FS

CAMPING AND OUTDOOR ACTIVITIES

Outdoor activities play an important role in Swedish Guiding and Scouting. Many companies own forest huts used by Guides and Scouts at week-ends. Guides and Scouts are also trained in tracking and orienteering, skills necessary for survival in Swedish forests.

Summer camping is, of course, very popular and camps vary in size from twenty participants to sometimes several thousand. The Association also organizes camps for the handicapped. A poster publicizing the outdoor activities of the Swedish Guides and Scouts is circulated to schools throughout the country.

SMU

EXTENSION GUIDING

Extension Guiding is now an established part of the Movement in Sweden, and constant efforts are made to integrate handicapped girls into regular units.

A special feature over the past twenty years has been the fund-raising campaigns undertaken jointly by Girl Guides and Boy Scouts. These have enabled research work on the handicapped to be done, and special homes and schools to be opened.

SERVICE

During the period 1972–4 the Guides and Scouts of Sweden have worked on a project called 'Jambo Tanzania'. The purpose was to give information about Tanzania to the Guides and Scouts of Sweden and to raise money for the work of the Guides and Scouts of Tanzania.

An important part of the project was 'Pamoja', a study excursion to Tanzania for Guides, Scouts and Leaders in the summer of 1974. The trip was organized in co-operation with the Girl Guide and Boy Scout Associations of Tanzania and governmental and other organizations within the country.

An increasing number of immigrants to Sweden has resulted in the Associations starting activities for the immigrants' children and inviting them to become members of the Movement.

Switzerland

Fédération des Eclaireuses Suisses
Bund Schweizerischer Pfadfinderinnen
Federazione delle Esploratrici Svizzere
Lia Svizra da Battasendas

French

GUIDE

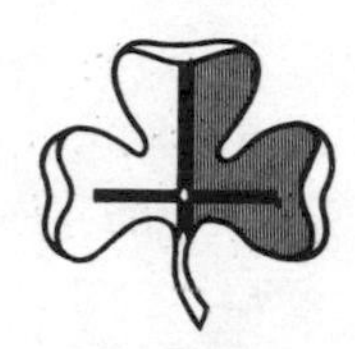

Promesse	**Promise**
Sur mon honneur, je promets de faire tout mon possible pour: Servir Dieu, ma famille et ma Patrie;	I promise on my honour to do my best: To do my duty to God, my family and my country;
ou	*or*
Sur mon honneur et avec la grâce de Dieu, je promets de faire tout mon possible pour: Servir Dieu, l'Eglise, ma famille et ma Patrie; aider mon prochain en tout temps; obéir à la loi de l'éclaireuse.	I promise on my honour and by the grace of God to do my best: To do my duty to God, the Church, my family and my country; to help other people at all times; to obey the Girl Scout Law.
(L'éclaireuse qui ne veut pas affirmer ses sentiments religieux promet de servir sa famille et sa Patrie.)	(The Girl Scout who does not wish to express religious beliefs promises to serve her family and her country.)

German	*Italian*
Versprechen	**Promessa**
Auf mein Ehrenwort verspreche ich, mein Möglichstes zu tun, um Gott, meiner Familie und meinem Vaterland zu dienen;	Prometto sul mio onore di fare tutto il mio possible per: Servire Dio, la famiglia e la patria;
oder	o
Auf mein Ehrenwort und mit Gottes Gnade verspreche ich, mein Möglichstes zu tun, um Gott, der Kirche, meiner Familie und meinem Vaterland zu dienen; andern jederzeit zu helfen; dem Gesetz der Pfadfinderinnen zu gehorchen.	Prometto sul mio onore e con la grazia di Dio di fare tutto il mio possible per: Servire Dio, la Chiesa, la famiglia e la patria; aiutare ognora il prossimo; obbedire alla legge dell'Esploratrice.
(Die Pfadfinderin, die das religiöse Versprechen nicht ablegen will, verspricht nur, ihrer Familie und ihrem Vaterland zu dienen.)	(L'Esploratrice che non voglia affermare i sui sentimenti religiosi, promette di servire solamente la famiglia e la patria.)

French

Loi	**Law**
Nous voulons:	*We wish:*
1 Etre vraies.	To be true/truthful.
2 Aider avec simplicité.	To give help quietly.
3 Surmonter les difficultés avec humour.	To overcome difficulties with a laugh.
4 Choisir et nous engager.	To choose and to commit ourselves.
5 Partager.	To share.
6 Respecter la vie.	To respect life.
7 Nous réjouir de tout ce qui est beau.	To rejoice in all that is beautiful.
8 Accueillir et comprendre les autres.	To receive/welcome/greet and understand others.

German

Gesetz	**Law**
1 Sei aufrichtig.	Be sincere.
2 Hilf wo du kannst.	Help where you can.
3 Ueberwinde Schwierigkeiten.	Vanquish difficulties.
4 Wähle und setze dich ein.	Choose and pledge yourself.
5 Sei zuverlässig.	Be reliable.
6 Schütze die Natur.	Protect Nature.
7 Suche und bringe Freude.	Seek and convey joy.
8 Verstehe und achte.	Understand and pay heed.

Italian

Legge	**Law**
1 Sono leale.	I am loyal/faithful/sincere/fair/true.

2	Aiuto spontaneamente.	I help spontaneously/without being asked.
3	Affronto serenamente le difficolta.	I face difficulties calmly.
4	So scegliere e mi impegno.	I know how to choose and I pledge myself.
5	Sono generosa.	I am generous.
6	Amo la vita e proteggo la natura.	I love life and protect nature.
7	Cerco e dono la gioia.	I seek and give joy.
8	Comprendo e accettto gli altri.	I understand and accept other people.

Romansh

		Law
1	Esser vardaivels	Be sincere.
2	Güdar plü pussibel	Help where you can.
3	Survendscher las difficultats da buna glüna	Vanquish difficulties.
4	Tscherner ed ans impegnar	Choose and pledge yourself.
5	Esser generus	Be reliable.
6	Respettar la vita e proteger la natüra	Protect Nature.
7	Portar algrezcha a tuot e dapertuout	Seek and convey joy.
8	Incleger ed acceptar ils oters sco chi sun	Understand and pay heed.

These eight clauses set out the Law which is common to all. A Girl Scout may, when she makes or renews her Promise, add one or two personal Laws of her own.

Motto

French	*German*	*Italian*	*Romansh*	*English*
Sois prête	Allzeit bereit	Sempre pronta	Adüna pront	Be Prepared

BROWNIE

Brownie Promise

German

Ich will mir Mühe geben,
Gott und meine Familie zu lieben,
das Bienli-Gesetz zu befolgen
und täglich andern eine Freude zu bereiten

French

Je veux faire de mon mieux
pour aimer Dieu et ma famille
suivre la loi
et faire chaque jour plaisir à chacun.

Romansh

Eu am less dar fadia ed
avair jent a Dieu ed a mia famiglia,
am tgnair vi da la ledscha d'aviöl
e far minchadi ün plaschair ad oters.

Italian

Voglio fare del mio meglio
per amare Dio e la mia famiglia
seguire la legge e fare ogni giorno
un piacere a qualcuno

English

I promise to try to do my best to
love God and my family, to follow
the law of the Brownies and to do a
good turn to somebody every day.

Brownie Law

German	*French*
An andere denken	Penser d'abord aux autres
mit offenen Augen um sich schauen	regarder autour de soi
die Wahrheit sagen	dire vrai
den andern helfen	être propre
	savoir aider et sourire

Romansh	*Italian*
ün aviöl	Pensare prima agli altri
fa per cumond e disch la vardà	Guardarsi attorno
ün aviöl guarda in intuorn	Dire la verità
sai cun ögls averts	Saper aiutare e sorridere
ed es adüna pront da güdar.	

English

The Brownie thinks of others,
keeps her eyes open,
tells the truth and
helps cheerfully

Brownie Motto

German	*French*	*Romansh*	*Italian*
Freudig hälfe!	De notre mieux!	Güdar jent	Aiuta allegramente

English

Helps gladly

Between 1913 and 1916 nine groups of Girl Scouts were formed independently in different parts of Switzerland. In 1919 all these groups joined together and became one Association, the Fédération des Eclaireuses Suisses (FES), a Founder Member of the World Association of Girl Guides and Girl Scouts.

PROGRAMME

Within the framework of the FES the Roman Catholic and the Salvation Army Girl Guides have their own special programme of religious and training activities.

Much attention has been given to the programme for each age group. Girls have a considerable amount of choice as regards the groups they join between the ages of 10 and 16. As regards Rangers and Guides, many activities and contacts are offered at national level, as well as opportunities for personal development and international exchange. During 1975 and 1976 efforts have been made to achieve the Association's main objectives, i.e. a well-adapted programme for each branch put into practice by a well-informed Leader.

Migrant girls are welcomed into the units of the FES. Wherever possible handicapped girls are integrated in ordinary packs and companies. For others, Post companies and groups in institutions are maintained.

TRAINING

With such a programme, training naturally takes on great importance. While the Patrol Leaders' training is the responsibility of the individual cantons and local groups, the training of Guiders is mainly the responsibility of the FES. Trainings are organized during holidays with the main training camps held at the Association's two mountain chalets in southern Switzerland, for two weeks in the summer. This camp is attended by the entire national staff, and all the professional and volunteer Trainers. Each year a new group of Leaders are involved in helping to organize workshops for girls from 14 upwards where they can acquire cooking skills, learn about first-aid and have a chance to become involved in some practical conservation work.

This national training camp also provides an opportunity for Leaders to do their training course and obtain their camper's licence at the same time.

PROMISE AND LAW

Much useful work has gone into the study of the wording of the Association's Promises and Laws. Everyone has been involved, and the discussions have been extremely beneficial since they have given members a deeper understanding of the real importance of the Promise and Law.

OUTDOOR ACTIVITIES

Company camps take place in summer in the mountains or in the autumn at lower levels. In winter many companies have skiing camps. Hiking too is popular with older Guides and Rangers. Hike camps permit them to explore an unknown part of the country and to get to know the inhabitants.

CO-OPERATION WITH BOY SCOUTS

The FES maintains good relations with the Boy Scouts Federation of Switzerland and collaboration between the two is increasing. Members of both federations participate in Gilwell courses, summer and winter hikes in the mountains, folk-festivals, etc. Together they publish the Leaders' magazine *Trèfle/Kim* and Leaders of the two federations meet regularly to organize joint events and discuss public relations.

GOLDEN JUBILEE

In 1969 the Fédération des Eclaireuses Suisses celebrated its Golden Jubilee. The Jubilee had as its theme 'Loyalty to the past and looking to the future'. The FES also wanted to celebrate the occasion under the sign of international friendship. The culminating point of the year was the Golden Jubilee camp, which both Swiss Eclaireuses and foreign Girl Guides/Girl Scouts attended. The Brownies also had Jubilee celebrations, meeting in three groups on the banks of the three Swiss lakes.

SERVICE

Ranger activities are based mainly on service and studying social problems while Girl Scouts and Little Bees (Brownies) give help and service wherever they are needed. Service camps are very popular, as is service given in hospitals and institutions.

INTERNATIONAL RELATIONS

The FES encourages international contacts and exchanges and each year an increasing number of Swiss Girl Scouts and Leaders go abroad or receive guests from other countries. Where necessary Swiss Trainers have gone abroad to help promote Guiding in other countries.

Tanzania

Tanzania Girl Guides Association

GUIDE

Ahadi za maskauti wa kike

Natoa ahadi kuwa nitafanya bidii
kutimiza yote yanipasayo kwa
Mwenyezi Mungu na Taifa langu;
kuwasaidia watu wote siku zote;
nakutii kanuni za Maskauti wa kike.

Guide Promise

I promise on my honour to do my best:
To do my duty to God and my Nation;
To help other people at all times;
And to obey the Guide law.

Kanuni za Maskauti wa kike

1 Skauti ni mwaminifu.
2 Skauti ni raia mwema.
3 Wajibu wa Skauti wa kike ni kuwa mtu wa kufaa na kuwasaidia watu kwa hiari.
4 Skauti ni rafiki kwa watu wote na ndugu kwa maskauti wote.
5 Skauti huwa na adabu na heshima.
6 Skauti huwahurumia na kuwapenda wanyama na viumbe vyote vyenye uhai.
7 Skauti hutii amri kwa furaha.
8 Skauti huchangamka hata katika shida taabu yoyote.
9 Skauti ni mwangalifu, na mtuzaji pia huweka akiba.
10 Skauti ni safi kwa mawazo maneno na matendo.

Guide Law

A Guide's honour is to be trusted.
A Guide is a good citizen.
A Guide's duty is to be useful and help others.
A Guide is a friend to all and a sister to every other Guide.
A Guide is courteous.
A Guide is kind to animals and all creation.
A Guide obeys orders cheerfully.
A Guide is courageous and cheerful.
A Guide is thrifty.
A Guide is pure in thought, word and deed.

Guide Motto

Uwe Tayari

Be Prepared

BROWNIE

Ahadi ya Kiangaza

Natoa ahadi kuwa nitafanya bidii
Kutimiza wajibu wangu kwa
kumtumikia Mungu na Taifa langu.
Kuwasaidia watu wengine kila siku,
hasa wale wa nyumbani.

Brownie Promise

I promise to do my best:
To do my duty to God and my Nation.
To help other people every day
especially those at home.

Kanuni ya Kiangaza

Kiangaza huwaheshimu wakubwa wake.
Kiangaza hajipendelei mwenyewe.

Brownie Law

A Brownie respects her elders.
A Brownie thinks of others before herself.

Neno Kubwa la Kiangaza	Brownie Motto
Kuwasaidia wengine.	Lend a Hand.

Age Groups

Ranger/Cadet	16–21
Guide	10–16
Brownie	6½–10

The first Guide company was started in Tanganyika in 1928 but it was not until 1935, when the Founder and the World Chief Guide visited the country, that Guiding really became firmly established. A Territorial Council and a local Association were formed in 1938. Between 1940 and 1950 Guiding spread to all areas of the country. The first executive committee was formed in 1957 and in the same year a constitution was approved. The Tanganyika Girl Guides Association became an Associate Member of the World Association at the 18th World Conference (Denmark, 1963) and the Tanzania Girl Guides Association was welcomed as a Full Member at the 20th World Conference (Finland, 1969).

TRAINING

Training has played an increasing part in the programme in Tanzania. International Leadership Training Camps are held, as are local Trainers' Camps.

SERVICE

The Association is involved in a wide variety of service projects. Guides give blood, help in hospitals and dispensaries and ensure that public grounds are well kept. Work continues on a Girl Guide/Boy Scout farm; sugar-cane and fruit trees have been planted. Evening classes for women are run by the Association and a brick-making/bricklaying project has been undertaken as part of the very successful programme of the Cottage Industry Centre at Dar-es-Salaam, where school leavers receive vocational training to enable them to become independent wage-earners and more responsible citizens.

The Association is at present working on a project to build a hostel in Dar-es-Salaam to house young Tanzanian girls coming to live in town for the first time.

Another of the Association's projects is a literacy campaign for slum children. It is intended to extend this campaign to the rural areas.

During International Women's Year (1975) the Association was a member of a special committee whose programmes focused on the promotion and rights of women in society.

The Association was represented at a seminar on Social and Economic Development and Population Change in Tanzania, organized by the Ministry of Labour and Social Welfare.

CO-OPERATION WITH OTHER ORGANIZATIONS

The Association co-operates with the YWCA, the YMCA, the Tanzanian Boy Scouts and the Salvation Army.

Thailand

The Girl Guides Association of Thailand

GUIDE

Kum Patiyan

Duey giat kapajow kaw patiyan:
Kapajow ja patibat na-tee un pueng mee taw chart, sassana, pra mahakasat;
Kapajow ja chuey luer poo uen smer;
Kapajow chuer lae ja patibat tam goht kong kana poo bumpen prayote.

Promise

On my honour I promise:
To do my duty to my country, my religion and the King;
To help other people at all times;
To obey the Guide Law.

Goht

1 Tum ton hai pen tee chuer tue lae wai wang jai dai.
2 Suesat.
3 Tam ton hai pen prayote lae chuey luer poo uen smer.
4 Pen mit gub kon tung lai lae tue pen pee nong gub poo bumpen prayote ruam kana.
5 Supab on nom.
6 Metta karuna taw sut.
7 Chuer fung lae patibut tam kumsung.
8 Oht ton taw kwam yark lumbark duey jai ra rerng.
9 Muttayut.
10 Sujarit prom gai vaja jai.

Law

1 A Guide's honour is to be trusted.
2 A Guide is loyal.
3 A Guide's duty is to be useful and to help others.
4 A Guide is a friend to all and a sister to every other Guide.
5 A Guide is courteous.
6 A Guide is a friend to animals.
7 A Guide obeys orders.
8 A Guide smiles and sings under all difficulties.
9 A Guide is thrifty.
10 A Guide is pure in thought, word and deed.

Motto

Triam prom smer

Be Prepared

BLUEBIRD

Bluebird Promise

Kapajow ja patibut na-tee un pueng mee taw chart, sassana, pra mahakasat.
Kapajow ja chuey luer poo uen took wun doye chapaw kon nai bahn.

I promise to do my best to do my duty to my country, my religion and the King.
I promise to help other people every day.

Bluebird Law

Nok seefar chuer pu tee toe gwa.
Nok see far mai tarm jai tua eng.

The Bluebird gives in to older people.
The Bluebird does not give in to herself.

Bluebird Motto

Chuey luer poo uen smer — Lend a Hand

Age Groups

Senior Guide	17–21
Guide	11–16
Bluebird (Brownie)	7–10

Girl Guiding first made its appearance in Thailand in March 1957 when a representative of WAGGGS visited the country, and a month later the first group received training from the World Association Travelling Commissioner. The Association was registered as the Girl Guides Association of Thailand in June 1958. Other visits from Travelling Commissioners followed, and Guiding expanded rapidly, with Guide companies being formed all over the country. In January 1962 the Association was granted Royal Patronage by Her Majesty Queen Sirikit.

The Girl Guides Association of Thailand was recognized as an Associate Member of the World Association at the 18th World Conference (Denmark, 1963), and became a Full Member at the 21st World Conference (Canada, 1972).

The Association's Headquarters in Bangkok was opened in 1967 and consists of an administrative block with a hostel attached, providing dormitories for trainers, guest rooms, and a swimming pool.

PROGRAMME

The programme for both Guides and Bluebirds focuses on four points – character building, health, handicrafts and service. Every effort is made to put across to the girls the idea conveyed in the fundamental principles. The Senior Branch programme is in five sections, laying stress on service, duty to religion and country, development of skills useful to society and the individual, and international understanding. A number of books on the programmes for the different age-groups are available in Thai and English.

The Association has good Press, radio and TV coverage and its relations with NGOs are excellent.

TRAINING

A training department has been set up at headquarters, and a full-time trainer is included in the staff members there. In 1972 an experienced World Association trainer visited Thailand to conduct trainings and assist in strengthening the department.

A Home Economics Course is conducted by members of the Association and this is seen as a real contribution to national development. The course lasts eight months and is designed to bring girls aged between 18 and 25 from rural areas to be trained as Senior Girl Guides. Emphasis is laid on Home Economics and Leadership Training. At the end of the course the girls go back and help with Community Development work in their villages.

The Association also carries out Home Aid Training for underprivileged girls. This course aims to train girls aged between 14 and 18 in simple vocational skills in order to help them to be able to work and support themselves. The Association helps to find permanent employment for Home Aid trainees when they have completed the course.

SERVICE

Service to the community is included in the programmes of all the branches and large-scale service projects are undertaken.

Guides render service whenever the opportunity arises, they help in hospitals, with the handicapped and leprosy patients, in orphanages and day nurseries. They also give service during emergencies and epidemics such as Asian flu and cholera.

Annual service camps for underprivileged girls are run by Senior Guides and those from the home economics courses. These camps help give young girls from poor families and with little education a broad general training. The girls have a chance to enjoy themselves, to see new things and to acquire a simple knowledge of their own country.

A special literacy programme is being carried out for girls who do not receive a formal education. During the course the girls learn reading, writing, handicrafts, hygiene, etc. The Association intends to develop this programme in the rural areas.

The Girl Guides Association of Thailand runs a national campaign with reference to urban and rural population growth. Training in population awareness is given in many villages.

ENVIRONMENT

In common with other Girl Guide Associations throughout the world the Girl Guides Association of Thailand is conscious of the threat of pollution and the necessity of protecting the fabric of our environment. The Association has held meetings on this subject jointly with other youth organizations in the country and has produced anti-pollution stickers.

INTERNATIONAL WOMEN'S YEAR

To celebrate International Women's Year – 1975 – the Girl Guides Association of Thailand expanded its home-economics training programme, opening new training centres in the north and south of Thailand in order to train more girls from each region.

Togo

Scoutisme Féminin du Togo

GUIDES DU TOGO

GUIDE

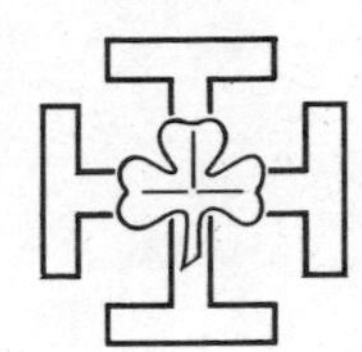

Promesse

Sur mon honneur, avec la grâce de Dieu, je m'engage:
A servir de mon mieux Dieu, l'Eglise et la Patrie;
A aider mon prochain en toutes circonstances;
A observer la loi des guides.

Promise

On my honour and with the grace of God, I pledge myself:
To do my best to serve God, the Church and my Country;
To help others in all circumstances;
To observe the Guide Law.

Loi

1 La guide est loyale.
2 La guide pense d'abord aux autres.
3 La guide est généreuse: elle est prête à servir.
4 La guide est accueillante: elle a l'esprit d'équipe.
5 La guide, sœur de toute autre guide, est présente à tous.
6 La guide découvre la nature; elle y voit l'œuvre de Dieu.
7 La guide sait obéir.
8 La guide ne craint pas l'effort; elle ne fait rien à moitié.
9 La guide aime son travail et respecte celui des autres.
10 La guide est maîtresse de soi; elle est pure et joyeuse.

Law

A Guide is loyal.
A Guide thinks first of others.
A Guide is generous: she is prepared to help.
A Guide is welcoming: she has the team spirit.
A Guide, sister to every other Guide, is available to all.
A Guide explores nature, in which she sees the work of God.
A Guide understands obedience.
A Guide does not fear endeavour; she does nothing by halves.
A Guide likes her work and respects that of others.
A Guide controls herself; she is pure and cheerful.

Motto

Toujours prête

Always ready

BROWNIE

Brownie Promise

Je promets de faire de mon mieux: pour être fidèle à Dieu, à mon pays, à mes parents, à la loi de la ronde, et pour faire chaque jour un plaisir à quelqu'un.

I promise to do my best: to be faithful to God, to my Country, to my parents and to the law of the pack, and to do a good turn to somebody every day.

Brownie Law

Une jeannette est toujours propre.	A Brownie is always neat.
Une jeannette est toujours active.	A Brownie is always active.
Une jeannette est toujours gaie.	A Brownie is always cheerful.
Une jeannette dit toujours vrai.	A Brownie always tells the truth.
Une jeannette pense d'abord aux autres.	A Brownie thinks first of others.

Brownie Motto

De notre mieux	Of our best

Age Groups

Guide Aînée	Ranger	17 and over
Guide	Guide	12–17
Jeannette	Brownie	7–12

ECLAIREUSES UNIONISTES DU TOGO

GUIDE

Promesse

Avec l'aide de Dieu, je promets sur mon honneur de faire tout mon possible pour:
Servir Dieu, la Patrie, la famille;
Aider les autres en tout temps;
Obéir à la Loi des éclaireuses.

Promise

With the help of God, I promise on my honour to do all I can to:
Serve God, my Country, my Family;
Help others at all times;
Obey the Girl Scout Law.

Loi	Law
1 L'éclaireuse est loyale, on peut compter sur elle, elle ne ment jamais.	A Girl Scout is loyal, one can rely upon her, she never lies.
2 L'éclaireuse est disciplinée, elle est exacte et ordonnée.	A Girl Scout is self-disciplined, she is punctual and tidy.
3 L'éclaireuse est calme, elle sait se dominer.	A Girl Scout is composed, she knows how to control herself.
4 L'éclaireuse est énergique et travailleuse. Elle ne craint pas les difficultés.	A Girl Scout is energetic and industrious. She does not fear difficulties.
5 L'éclaireuse est bonne, elle est obligeante et polie.	A Girl Scout is kind, she is obliging and polite.
6 L'éclaireuse est l'amie de tous et la sœur des autres éclaireuses.	A Girl Scout is a friend of everyone and a sister to other Girl Scouts.
7 L'éclaireuse est sobre dans ses goûts et sa parure.	A Girl Scout is moderate in her tastes and dress.
8 L'éclaireuse est l'amie des animaux et des plantes.	A Girl Scout is a friend to animals and plants.
9 L'éclaireuse est toujours de bonne humeur, elle s'efforce de faire régner la paix autour d'elle.	A Girl Scout is always cheerful, she tries to create peace around her.
10 L'éclaireuse est pure dans ses pensées, ses paroles et ses actes.	A Girl Scout is pure in her thoughts, words and deeds.

Motto

Sois prête	Be ready

Brownie Promise

Je promets de faire de mon mieux pour obéir à Dieu, aimer mon pays, prêter la main chaque jour.	I promise to do my best to obey God, to love my Country, and to help someone every day.

Brownie Law

Les Petites Ailes écoutent les cheftaines.	The Brownies always obey their Leaders.
Les Petites Ailes s'aiment comme des sœurs et ne se disputent pas.	The Brownies love other Brownies as their sisters and never quarrel.

Brownie Motto

Prêter la main	To lend a hand

Age Groups

Eclaireuse Aînée	Ranger	16–20 and over
Eclaireuse	Girl Scout	11–16
Petite Aile	Brownie	7–11

The Fédération du Scoutisme Féminin du Togo is composed of two Guide Associations; the Eclaireuses Unionistes du Togo started in 1942, and the Guides du Togo for Catholic girls started in 1956. While the Eclaireuses Unionistes are to be found throughout the rural areas of Togo, membership of the Guides du Togo is mainly concentrated on schools in the capital, Lomé.

Both Associations try to co-operate as closely as possible but contact is often difficult due to the different areas in which the Movement has taken root.

Togo gained independence in 1960 and following this the Scoutisme Féminin du Togo was recognized as an Associate Member of the World Association at the 18th World Conference (Denmark, 1963).

ECLAIREUSES UNIONISTES DU TOGO

TRAINING

There is no national programme for Eclaireuses. Each organizer establishes her own programme on a chosen theme. The main activities centre on knowledge of the Promise and Law, sewing, gardening, the sale of garden produce, and service projects such as helping to improve the lives of old people.

Much attention is centred on Brownies, and special events are held for them where they learn to know their environment, their families and their village better. These events are sometimes combined with Training for Leaders.

The events are of a special interest to the girls since this is where they make new friends but it is very difficult, once back in the villages, to find Leaders to carry on the work undertaken during the events.

THINKING DAY

Thinking Day is widely celebrated in Togo. The Eclaireuses are encouraged to mark this day by giving special thought to Girl Guides/Girl Scouts throughout the world and especially to those in other African countries.

GUIDES DU TOGO

TRAINING

Each year the Guide programme has a special theme. In 1969 a training camp for Guiders and team leaders was held with the theme 'Girl Guides and Development'. Included in the activities was a programme designed to broaden the Guides' knowledge of their country. A report of their findings was produced at the end of the programme.

The following year (during which a training camp was held) was devoted to 'Discovery'. Another training took place a year later with the theme 'Responsibility and Participation'. One item of the programme was the setting-up in Lomé of workshops producing decorations, greeting cards and paper hats for the children as well as publicizing the Movement.

THINKING DAY

Thinking Day is celebrated each year when activities include selling Thinking Day stamps and giving information about Guiding to the press and over the radio. In 1972 an outing was arranged for the Guides and Eclaireuses Unionistes of Lomé, and a collection was made for the Thinking Day Fund.

Trinidad and Tobago

The Girl Guides Association of Trinidad and Tobago

GUIDE

Promise

I promise that I will do my best
To do my duty to God,
To serve my country
and help other people,
And to keep the Guide Law.

Law

1 A Guide is loyal and can be trusted.
2 A Guide is helpful.
3 A Guide is polite and considerate.
4 A Guide is friendly and a sister to all Guides.
5 A Guide is kind to animals and respects all living things.
6 A Guide is obedient.
7 A Guide has courage and is cheerful in all difficulties.
8 A Guide makes good use of her time.
9 A Guide is careful of her own belongings and respects those of others.
10 A Guide is self-controlled in all she thinks, says and does.

Motto

Be Prepared

Brownie Guide Promise

I promise that I will do my best
To do my duty to God,
To serve my country
and to help other people,
And to keep the Brownie Law.

Brownie Guide Law

A Brownie thinks of others before
herself,
And does a good turn every day.

Brownie Guide Motto

Lend a Hand

BROWNIE

Age Groups

Ranger	14–21
Guide	10½–16
Brownie	7–11

Girl Guiding started in Trinidad and Tobago in 1914. One of the highlights in its history was in 1930 when the Founder and the World Chief Guide visited the country and laid the foundation-stone of the Girl Guide headquarters. Trinidad and Tobago was a branch Association of the United Kingdom Girl Guides Association until 1963 when it was recognized as an Associate Member of the World Association at the 18th World Conference (Denmark, 1963). It became a Full Member of WAGGGS at the 20th World Conference (Finland, 1969). Trinidad and Tobago is a member of the Caribbean Link of Guiding. The present Constitution provides for a President who is the overall head of the Association and a Chief Commissioner responsible for the uniformed branches.

JUBILEE CELEBRATIONS

The Association celebrated its Golden Jubilee in 1964 with a camp held in Trinidad, and its Diamond Jubilee in 1974 with one held in Tobago. Both camps were attended by Girl Guides and Girl Scouts from numerous Member Organizations of the World Association.

ATTENDANCE AT INTERNATIONAL EVENTS

Links with abroad, of great importance to Trinidad and Tobago, have been strengthened through participation in international events. The Association was represented at the International Commissioners' Conference in Ghana in 1973 and at the Western Hemisphere Regional Gathering in Peru in the same year. Rangers and Guides have camped in the United Kingdom and in Canada in 1974 and participated in Conferences on International Women's Year in the United States in 1975. The President, Chief Commissioner, International Commissioner and a young Guider attended the 22nd World Conference in the United Kingdom in 1975.

INTERNATIONAL WOMEN'S YEAR

An essay-writing competition was organized for age groups 14–16 and 17–19 on the subject: 'Being a woman. What it means to me.' A workshop on the role of women both at home and outside the family took place in 1975.

SERVICE

The Association holds 'Career Guidance Seminars' which are open to everyone. The seminars are held at local centres where an expert gives a talk and answers questions on choice of career.

POPULATION AWARENESS

Conscious of the problems of world population, Guides are taking an active part in a Population Awareness programme supported by the government family planning agency. A delegate from Trinidad and Tobago represented WAGGGS at the International Youth Population Conference in Bucharest in 1974.

Turkey

The Girl Guide Section of the Scouts and Guides of Turkey

GUIDE

And	**Promise**
Tanriya, vatanima karşi vazifelerimi yerine getireceğime, izcilik türesine uyacağima, Başkalarina her zaman yardimda bulunacagima, Kendimi bedence sağlam, fikirce uyanik ve ahlâkça dürüst tutmak için elimden geleni yapacağima şerefim üzerine and içerim.	On my honour, I will try: To do my duty to God and my country, To obey the Girl Guide law, To help other people at all times, To keep myself physically fit, mentally awake and morally honest.

Türe	**Law**
1 İzci sözünün eridir, şeref ve haysiyetini her şeyin üstünde tutar.	A Girl Guide's honour is to be trusted.
2 İzci, yurduna, milletine, ailesine ve izci liderlerine sadiktir.	A Girl Guide is loyal to her country, her parents and her leaders.
3 İzci, başkalarina yardimci ve yararli olur.	A Girl Guide's duty is to be useful and to help others.
4 İzci, herkesin arkadaşi ve bütün izcilerin kardeşidir.	A Girl Guide is a friend to all and sister to all other Guides.

5 İzci, herkese karşi naziktir.	A Girl Guide is courteous.
6 İzci, bitki ve hayvanlari sever ve korur.	A Girl Guide is a friend to animals and plants.
7 İzci, büyüklerin sözünü dinler, kücüklerini sever ve korur.	A Girl Guide obeys orders of her parents and loves and helps those who are younger than herself.
8 İzci, cesurdur her türlü şartlar içinde neşeli ve güler yüzlüdür.	A Girl Guide is brave. She smiles under all difficulties.
9 İzci, tutumludur.	A Girl Guide is thrifty.
10 İzci, fikir, söz ve hareketlerinde açik ve dürüsttür.	A Girl Guide is clean in thought, word and deed.

Motto

İzci daima hazirdir	Be Prepared

Brownie Promise

BROWNIE

Tanriya, vatanima karşi vazifelerimi yerine getireceğime, Yavrukurt türesine uyacağima, Başkalarina her zaman yardimda bulunacağima, Kendimi bedence sağlam, fikirce uyanik ve ahlâkça dürüst tutmak için elimden geleni yapacağima şerefim üzerine and içerim.	On my honour, I will try: To do my duty to God and my country, To obey the Brownie law, To help other people at all times, To keep myself physically fit, mentally awake and morally honest.

Brownie Law

Yavrukurt, izcinin izinde gider ve her gün bir iyilik yapar.	A Brownie lives like a Guide and does a good turn every day.
Yavrukurt çaliskandir, isinde bikkinlik ve bezginlik göstermez.	A Brownie is industrious and never never shows boredom or laziness.

Brownie Motto

Yavrukurt çok çalişir	Lend a Hand

Age Groups

Ergin İzci	Venture	16–21
İzci	Guide	12–16
Yavrukurt	Brownie	8–12

Girl Guiding first started in Turkey just after the foundation of the Turkish Republic in 1923 following a request from the Ministry of Education that the Movement be started in several of the girls' schools. These troops continued their activities until 1936 when the Directorate of Scouting and Guiding was founded. This Directorate acted as the central governing body for both the Girl Guides and Boy Scouts.

In 1968 in line with current trends in Girl Guiding and Boy Scouting, a new organization was set up and new regulations adopted. Under the new organization, the Boy Scouts and Girl Guides were accepted as one self-governing mixed organization with joint administrative committees at both national and regional level. Men and women have equal rights of election to these committees, but activities and programmes for Girl Guides and Boy Scouts remain separate. The Girl Guide section of the Scouts and Guides of Turkey was recognized as an Associate Member of the World Association at the 21st World Conference (Canada, 1972).

STRUCTURE, PROGRAMME AND TRAINING

The Girl Guide section has both professional Executive Commissioners and volunteer Trainers working on training for the girls. The provincial committees consist of Scouters and Guiders who work with an elected committee. The programme for girls emphasizes the spiritual and moral values of Guiding as outlined in the Promise and Law. It concentrates on giving them an interest in other people and in service to the community in which they live. It also enables them to learn practical skills and crafts. The Girl Guide section is free to decide and carry out its own training programmes and to determine administrative matters.

SERVICE

Turkish Guides are involved in many different fields of service. They organize literacy classes for adults and are active in hygiene and cleanliness campaigns. During the disastrous earthquake which hit Turkey in 1975, Girl Guides gave valuable assistance, providing clothing and shelter for the victims.

Uganda

The Uganda Girl Guides Association

GUIDE

Promise

I promise, on my honour, to do my best:
To do my duty to God and my Country;
To help other people at all times; and
To obey the Guide Law.

Law

1 A Guide is reliable and speaks the truth.
2 A Guide is loyal.
3 A Guide's duty is to be useful and to help others.
4 A Guide is a friend to all and a sister to every other Guide.
5 A Guide is polite and considerate.
6 A Guide respects God's creation and protects plants and animals.
7 A Guide obeys orders.
8 A Guide smiles and sings under all difficulties.
9 A Guide makes good use of time, talents and possessions.
10 A Guide is pure in thought, word and deed.

Motto

Be Prepared

Brownie Promise

I promise to do my best:
To do my duty to God and my Country;
To help other people every day, especially those at home.

Brownie Law

A Brownie is truthful, obedient and cheerful.
A Brownie gives in to the older folk.
A Brownie thinks of others before herself.

Brownie Motto

Ready and helpful

Age Groups

Ranger	17 and over
Guide	11–17
Brownie	7½–11

BROWNIE

Guiding was first started in a girls' school in Uganda between 1914 and 1918, but it was not until 1922 that the first Guide company was officially recognized and the Movement firmly established. Over the following years Guide companies started throughout the country. In 1946 the Uganda Girl Guides Association's constitution was registered and the first full-time Trainer appointed.

In 1961 the Uganda Girl Guides Association was chosen by WAGGGS to hostess an All-Africa Conference whose theme was 'How Guiding can help Africa'. The Uganda Girl Guides Association was recognized as an Associate Member of the World Association at the 18th World Conference (Denmark, 1963).

TRAINING

Training is considered of great importance and much progress has been made in training over the last seven years. A World Association Trainer visited Uganda in 1970 and in 1971 a national Trainer was appointed and a training committee formed.

ACTIVITIES WITH A FOCUS ON YOUTH

A Youth Council was formed in Uganda with the aim of strengthening and co-ordinating the activities of all youth organizations in the country. It also acts as a forum for the discussion of problems relating to youth and representation on statutory and other bodies on matters affecting youth in consultation with the National Council of Social Services of Uganda.

SERVICE

Guides have become involved in an agricultural project established on land given by local authorities. The Association plans to build an Arts and Crafts training centre on this land. A very successful poultry project was started some years ago and continues to flourish. Its aim is to encourage the girls to become independent and to serve the community.

PUBLIC RELATIONS

The Association has broadcast both on Ugandan radio and television.

United Kingdom of Great Britain and Northern Ireland

The Girl Guides Association

GUIDE

Promise

I promise that I will do my best;
To do my duty to God,
To serve the Queen and help other people,
and
To keep the Guide Law.

Law

1 A Guide is loyal and can be trusted.
2 A Guide is helpful.
3 A Guide is polite and considerate.
4 A Guide is friendly and a sister to all Guides.
5 A Guide is kind to animals and respects all living things.
6 A Guide is obedient.
7 A Guide has courage and is cheerful in all difficulties.
8 A Guide makes good use of her time.
9 A Guide takes care of her own possessions and those of other people.
10 A Guide is self-controlled in all she thinks, says and does.

Motto

Be Prepared

BROWNIE

Brownie Guide Promise

I promise that I will do my best;
To do my duty to God,
To serve the Queen and help other people,
and
To keep the Brownie Law.

Brownie Guide Law

A Brownie thinks of others before herself and does a Good Turn every day.

Brownie Guide Motto

Lend a Hand

Age Groups

Ranger Guide	14–18
Guide	10–15
Brownie Guide	7–10

The Girl Guides Association of Great Britain and Northern Ireland comprises membership in England (divided into six Regions each with its own Chief Commissioner), Scotland, Wales and Ulster. It also represents twenty-six Branch Associations throughout the world, the Chief Commissioner of the Association providing a liaison between the independent countries of the Commonwealth.

The Girl Guides Association was officially recognized in 1910. A year later the first Lone Guides appeared, and in 1914 the Brownie Branch was formed, while Senior Guides, later renamed Rangers, made their appearance in 1916. Handicapped children were brought into Guiding as early as 1909 with the formation of a hospital company, although the Extension Group as such was not formed until 1919. Olave, Lady Baden-Powell, was appointed as the first Chief Commissioner for England in 1916 and became Chief Guide two years later.

During the Association's life, spanning nearly seventy years, many notable events have taken place, among them the establishment of the World Association in 1928, of which the Girl Guides Association was a founder member. The Diamond Jubilee of United Kingdom Guiding was celebrated in 1970, and the Association acted as hostess to the 22nd World Conference of the World Association in 1975, during which thousands of Brownies and Guides actively participated in events organized for the delegates. In that year, too, the Commonwealth and Caribbean Conferences were held in the United Kingdom.

ROYAL PATRONAGE

The Royal Family has always taken a great personal interest in the Guide Movement and H.R.H. the Princess Margaret is President of the Association. H.M. the Queen and H.M. Queen Elizabeth the Queen Mother are both Patrons.

EIGHT-POINT PROGRAMME

The present eight-point programme, instituted in 1968, is common to Brownies, Guides and Rangers. Worked out differently for each section, it is designed to provide opportunities for each girl to develop as a complete person physically, mentally and spiritually, and in so doing to grow in her understanding of the Promise and her ability to keep it.

The particular interpretation for each section is presented in the handbooks, of which each girl and adult Leader has her own copy. On the basis of the interpretation and material given in the handbooks, a unit's own eight-point programme is planned and carried out by the girls themselves with the help of their Guiders. Through participation in group activities and individual challenges, and preparation for Interest and Service Badges, and Certificates, camping, pack holidays and outdoor activities, a girl is encouraged to make personal effort in varied directions, and to take full part in the unit's programme.

LEADERS' CERTIFICATE

In 1973 the Adult Leaders' Certificate was instituted to ensure that no Guider can be warranted to a Unit without undertaking a course of basic training. A Young Leaders' scheme, started in the same year, provides leadership training for 16–18-year-olds who may or may not also be members of an active Ranger Unit.

TRAINING CENTRES

The two Commonwealth Headquarters residential training centres, Foxlease and Waddow, continue to serve known needs as do also the training centres for Scotland, Wales and Northern Ireland. Many counties organize their own residential week-ends and the counties/regions also use the centres for courses. Trainers from the United Kingdom have also worked in very many countries and islands overseas.

SERVICE

Service has always been emphasized in the programme and the Guides play an active part in the life of the community taking care of the aged, the handicapped and the lonely. They have also helped in hospitals and children's centres. Outdoor activities have, in recent years, stimulated awareness of the needs of the environment. Members of the Movement have joined in conservation campaigns and fund-raising drives for the protection of wild life. One of the special service projects connected with European Architectural Heritage Year in 1975 included fund-raising for the repair and restoration of architectural monuments and the beautification of historic English villages.

INTERNATIONAL ACTION

The interest in assisting Guiding in other countries continues and substantial funds have been donated for this purpose through the Girl Guides Association's World Friendship Fund and WAGGGS' Mutual Aid Scheme. Members of the Association help in service projects in countries throughout the world and delegates have attended international gatherings and seminars.

United States of America

Girl Scouts of the United States of America

GIRL SCOUT

Promise

On my honour, I will try
To serve God,
My country and mankind
And to live by the Girl Scout Law

Law

I will do my best:
- to be honest
- to be fair
- to help where I am needed
- to be cheerful
- to be friendly and considerate
- to be a sister to every Girl Scout
- to respect authority
- to use resources wisely
- to protect and improve the world around me
- to show respect for myself and others through my words and actions.

Motto

Be Prepared

Age Groups

Senior Girl Scout	14–17
Cadette Girl Scout	12–14
Junior Girl Scout	9–11
Brownie Girl Scout	6–8

BROWNIE GIRL SCOUT

Girl Scouting was started in the U.S.A. by Juliette Gordon Low, who brought the idea from England after meeting Lord Baden-Powell and working with Guide companies in England and Scotland. Her first troop meeting of twelve girls was held in Savannah, Georgia, on 12th March 1912. Under her leadership the idea spread quickly so that by 1915 a national organization was formed. Girl Scouts of the United States of America is a Founder Member of the World Association.

Today, Girl Scouts of the U.S.A. serves 352 chartered councils covering 50 states, Puerto Rico, the Virgin Islands, the Canal Zone, Guam, and American Samoa, with nearly 3½ million members. Girl Scout headquarters is in New York City, and four National Centers are: Juliette Gordon Low Center in Savannah, Georgia; Edith Macy Center in Briarcliff Manor, New York; National Center West in Ten Sleep, Wyoming; and Rockwood Center in Potomac, Maryland.

AIMS AND OBJECTIVES OF THE PROGRAMME

Based on the purpose of the organization and the expressed needs and interests of girls and young women, the direction and goal of all programme efforts are to help each girl:

. . . deepen her awareness of self as a unique person of worth,
. . . develop values to give meaning and direction to her life,
. . . relate to others with increasing skill, maturity and satisfaction,
. . . contribute to her society through her own talents and in co-operative efforts with others.

These four emphases reflect the intent and the potential of the Movement to play a vital, meaningful role in the lives of girls and women.

NEW TRENDS

Efforts are made through the programme to reach all girls in rural or urban settings. New flexible ideas are being tried in councils across the country to find better ways of:

– reaching girls and increasing minority participation.
– recruiting and training leaders.
– using resources to best advantage.
– finding means to support the programme financially.

INVOLVEMENT WITH GLOBAL ISSUES

An increased awareness of our environment has emphasized the importance of global issues to which we must all contribute . . . conservation, combating hunger and poor nutrition, increasing literacy, etc., and girls are helped to become more aware of how Girl Scout experience carries over into other aspects of life.

In 1975, the United Nations provided a meaningful focus for activities to enhance the status of women. At the national level, a *Leader* magazine issue was devoted to International Women's Year; Girl Scouts of the U.S.A. co-operated with the U.S. Center for IWY and two mini-conferences were held to further the International Women's Year goals . . . Equality, Development and Peace.

PUBLICATIONS

A variety of books, pamphlets, films, filmstrips and other resources are produced by Girl Scouts of the U.S.A. for girls of all four age levels. Periodicals published are: *American Girl*, for ages 12–17; *Daisy*, for ages 6–11; and the *Girl Scout Leader*, for adults and Senior Girl Scouts.

THE JULIETTE LOW WORLD FRIENDSHIP FUND

The Juliette Low World Friendship Fund was established in Mrs Low's memory in 1927. Voluntary contributions from girl and adult members in Girl Scouting go towards . . .

– the Thinking Day Fund – to strengthen and extend the Girl Guide/Girl Scout Movement.
– bringing together Girl Guides and Girl Scouts for home living, camps, and special events for person-to-person experiences in international exchange.
– the Mutual Aid Scheme to share with others in helping National Associations with specific needs, and in providing training opportunities for adults.

Upper Volta

L'Association des Guides de Haute-Volta

GUIDE

Promesse

Sur mon honneur, et avec la grâce de Dieu, je m'engage:
A servir de mon mieux Dieu, . . . (l'Eglise)* et la Patrie;
A aider mon prochain en toutes circonstances;
Et à observer la Loi des Guides.

**Note:* si la Guide n'est pas chrétienne, elle ne pronounce pas le mots, l'Eglise, dans le texte de la promesse.

Promise

On my honour and with the grace of God, I pledge myself:
To do my best to serve God, (the Church)* and my Country;
To help others in all circumstances;
To observe the Guide Law.

**Note:* if the Guide is not a Christian, she does not say the words, the Church, in the promise.

Loi

1. La guide est loyale.
2. La guide pense d'abord aux autres.
3. La guide est généreuse: elle est prête à servir.
4. La guide est accueillante; elle a l'esprit d'équipe.
5. La guide, sœur de toute autre guide, est présente à tous.
6. La guide découvre la nature; elle y voit l'œuvre de Dieu.
7. La guide sait obéir.
8. La guide ne craint pas l'effort; elle ne fait rien à moitié.
9. La guide aime son travail et respecte celui des autres.
10. La guide est maîtresse de soi; elle est pure et joyeuse.

Law

A Guide is loyal.
A Guide thinks first of others.
A Guide is generous, she is prepared to help.
A Guide is friendly, she has the team spirit.
A Guide, sister to every other Guide, is prepared to help all.
A Guide explores nature in which she sees the work of God.
A Guide knows how to obey.
A Guide does not fear endeavour; she does nothing by halves.
A Guide likes her work and respects that of others.
A Guide practices self-control; she is pure and cheerful.

Guiding was started in Upper Volta in 1955. For approximately fifteen years Guiding was confined to towns, where it existed mostly in schools. It wasn't until 1971 that rural Guiding began to become established and the Association was organized into provinces, districts and companies. The National Headquarters is in Ougadougou. The Association des Guides de Haute-Volta was recognized as an Associate Member of the World Association at the 21st World Conference (Canada, 1972).

PROGRAMME

The Association's programme is based on the 'Four Signposts' formulated as follows: (1) giving young people the opportunity to become active and happy citizens, (2) involving them in the life of their community, (3) strengthening the bonds of solidarity with one's country and (4) creating international goodwill. The Association's programme is reviewed annually.

TRAINING

Qualified training advisers carry out training at special camps. A national or international leaders' training camp has been held every year since 1969.

SERVICE

Guides in Upper Volta are involved in many different areas of service to the community. They help with hygiene campaigns, first-aid and child-care, and organize market-gardening projects throughout their country.

The role of women is understandably of particular concern to them. International Women's Year, 1975, was marked by the creation of a new sub-region which has about forty rural Guide units. A series of training camps was organized to enable the maximum number of Guides to participate. Guides also carried out research on customs affecting women throughout their lives. Responding to UNESCO's appeal, a group of Rangers from Upper Volta prepared an audio-visual presentation on African women.

Uruguay

Asociación Guías Scout del Uruguay

GUIDE

Promesa	Promise
Con la gracia de Dios, prometo por mi honor, hacer cuanto de mi dependa para servir a Dios y a la Patria, ayudar al prójimo en toda circunstancia y cumplir la Ley Guía.	With God's grace, I promise on my honour, to do what I can to serve God and my country, to help other people at all times and to obey the Guide Law.

Ley	Law
1 La Guía cifra su honor en merecer confianza.	A Guide's honour is to be trusted.
2 La Guía es leal.	A Guide is loyal.
3 La Guía tiene el deber de ser útil y ayudar al prójimo.	A Guide's duty is to be useful and to help other people.
4 La Guía es buena con todos y hermana de las demas Guías.	A Guide is kind to all and a sister to all other Guides.
5 La Guía es cortés.	A Guide is courteous.
6 La Guía ve en la Naturaleza a la obra de Dios.	A Guide sees in Nature the work of God.
7 La Guía es obediente y disciplinada.	A Guide is obedient and disciplined.

8 La Guía es fuerte ante el sufrimiento y se sobrepone a las dificultades.	A Guide is brave in suffering and overcomes difficulties.
9 La Guía es económica, limpia y ordenada.	A Guide is thrifty, clean and tidy.
10 La Guía es pura en pensamientos, palabras y obras.	A Guide is pure in thought, word and deed.

Motto

Siempre lista	Always ready

Brownie Promise

BROWNIE

Prometo hacer todo lo que puedo para ser fiel a Dios, a mi patria, a los de mi casa y a la Ley de la Colmena;	I promise to do my best to be true to God, to my country, to those at home, and to the Law of the Hive;
y para darle cada día una alegría a alguien.	and to give pleasure to somebody every day.

Brownie Law

La Abeja piensa primero en los demás.	A Brownie thinks first of others.
La Abeja dice siempre la verdad.	A Brownie always tells the truth.
La Abeja es siempre alegre.	A Brownie is always gay.
La Abeja es siempre trabajadora.	A Brownie is always busy.
La Abeja es siempre obediente.	A Brownie is always obedient.
La Abeja es siempre limpia.	A Brownie is always neat.

Brownie Motto

Siempre Ayuda	Always helps

Age Groups

Guía Mayor	Ranger	14–20
Guía	Guide	10–13
Abeja	Brownie (Bee)	7–10

Guiding started in Uruguay in 1924, with the formation of the 1st Montevideo Company of British Guides. It was not until March 1955 that the National Association for Uruguayan Guides was established and the first packs and companies set up. Much help was given to the new Association during its formative years by Guiders from foreign companies in Uruguay.

At the request of prominent Roman Catholics in the community, an Association of Catholic Guides was formed in 1961, which incorporated all the existing companies, with one exception. That company became a separate group, but in 1964, as a result of much close co-operation between the two groups, they joined together under the name 'Asociación de Guías del Uruguay'. In 1965 the first national elections were held and a National Executive Council officially elected.

Asociación Guías del Uruguay was recognized as an Associate Member of WAGGGS at the 19th World Conference (Japan, 1966). In 1974 the name of the Association was changed to Asociación Guías Scout del Uruguay.

SERVICE

Rangers give service in schools for crippled and mentally retarded children by preparing material for work and play; they also entertain children in slum areas of the country.

The Association co-operates with the Red Cross in training young people to be aware of the needs of the country and to take action to meet them.

Interest in nature conservation is fostered and in 1971 'Nature Day' was held, and has continued to be held each year since. Studies have been undertaken on the theme of 'Nature' and performances given to illustrate important points related to this theme.

TRAINING AND CAMPS

Increased emphasis is being placed on the value of training, and Trainers have attended two international training seminars at Our Cabaña and have also participated in training courses in Argentina and Brazil.

Guides and Rangers attend camps and Brownies have pack holidays. A number of Guiders, Rangers and Guides have attended camps in other parts of South America.

The Association has a young and enthusiastic leadership and every effort is being made to expand the Movement to the interior of the country and attract more young people by means of more challenging and interesting activities. Programmes are continually being revised to bring them up to date.

INTERNATIONAL ACTIVITIES

Members of the Association regularly attend special activities of other local Associations working with youth and of non-governmental organizations operating in Latin America.

In 1975, representatives of the Uruguayan Association joined representatives of the Federação das Bandeirantes do Brazil and of the Western Hemisphere Committee at the First Interagency Consultation on the Collaboration of Programmes for Youth in Latin America and at the Interagency Meeting on the Child and Family. Both conferences were held in Montevideo under the sponsorship of the Organization of American States, the Interamerican Children's Institute and UNICEF.

In July 1976, Asociación Guías Scout del Uruguay hostessed a Latin American Encounter of Guiders, organized by the International Catholic Conference of Guiding.

Venezuela

Asociación de Guías Scouts de Venezuela

GUIDE

Promesa	**Promise**
Yo prometo por mi honor hacer cuanto de mi dependa para: Cumplir con mi deber hacia Dios y mi Patria, Ser útil al prójimo en todo momento y obedecer la Ley Guía.	I promise on my honour to do my best: To fulfil my duty to God and my Country, To help my fellow-creatures at all times and to obey the Guide Law.

Ley	**Law**
1 La Guía es leal y merece confianza.	A Guide is loyal and merits trust.
2 La Guía es útil y ayuda a otros.	A Guide is useful and helps other people.
3 La Guía es comprensiva y generosa.	A Guide is understanding and generous.
4 La Guía es hermana de toda muchacha Guía.	A Guide is a sister to every Girl Guide.
5 La Guía es cortés.	A Guide is courteous.
6 La Guía ve en la naturaleza la obra de Dios.	A Guide sees in nature the work of God.
7 La Guía sabe obedecer.	A Guide knows how to obey.
8 La Guía es valiente y animosa en las dificultades.	A Guide is courageous and faces up to difficulties.
9 La Guía es económica y ordenada.	A Guide is thrifty and methodical.
10 La Guía es pura en lo que piensa. dice y hace.	A Guide is pure in thought, word and deed.

Motto

Siempre lista	Always ready

BROWNIE

Brownie Promise

Prometo hacer cuanto pueda por cumplir mis deberes para con Dios y para con la Patria, observar la Ley de la Ronda y hacer un servicio a alguien cada día.	I promise to do my best to do my duty to God and my country, to keep the law of the pack and to do a good turn every day.

Brownie Law

La Alita obedece y escucha a sus mayores.	The Brownie obeys and heeds her elders.
La Alita no se da gusto a si misma.	The Brownie does not give in to herself.

Brownie Motto

La Alita ayuda siempre	The Brownie always helps

Age Groups

Guía Mayor	Ranger	15–17
Guía Menor	Guide	10–15
Alita	Brownie	6–10

Guiding started in Venezuela in 1958 with the foundation in Caracas of the Asociación de Muchachas Guías de Venezuela. In the following year various companies were formed around the country, and the first Venezuelan Guide rally was held in 1959. Also in 1959 the Asociación de Muchachas Guias de Venezuela held its first National Assembly. Venezuela became an Associate Member of WAGGGS at the 17th World Conference (Greece, 1960) and was recognized as a Full Member at the 19th World Conference (Japan, 1966). Since 1972 the Association has been known as the Asociación de Guias Scouts de Venezuela.

The Venezuelan Association hostessed a Western Hemisphere Regional Conference held in Caracas in 1968 and made the most of this event for public relations purposes. Venezuelan Guiding has a good image in the community and the Public Relations Committee is aware of the need to make known the work of the Association and its value for the children of the country.

The Association's National Headquarters is based in Caracas and it also has its own school camp at Curupao, complete with swimming pool and other facilities. It is enjoyed by Girl Guide visitors from all over the country. Courses for the adult personnel as well as for the girls of the three branches of the Movement are also given here.

SERVICE

The Association attaches great importance to service to the community, an area where much enthusiasm has been shown by the girls. Girl Guides have undertaken a literacy project lasting two years, with the aim of helping people in the suburbs of large cities. First-aid, life-saving and safety are other areas in which many Girl Guides have become efficient in order to better serve the community in which they live. They have also organized an exchange project with a group of North American Girl Scouts specializing in work with the blind, and studied Braille in order to be able to translate Spanish textbooks into meaningful material for the blind.

Venezuelan Girl Guides have also worked in programmes of conservation and environmental protection and the Association has pioneered the promotion of public awareness of this problem.

TRAINING

Training sessions and camps are held regularly for Rangers, Guiders and Patrol Leaders. Members of the Association attend trainings, and training courses for future Guiders are held periodically at colleges. This has resulted in better leadership and has led to new groups being formed in schools.

Representatives of the Association attend national events for Rangers with international participation, Guide conferences for Latin-American countries and international meetings as well as WAGGGS' World Conferences.

PUBLICATIONS

El Trébol, the attractive quarterly magazine of the Association, gives information on Guiding at home and abroad. New Guide Handbooks were published in 1975 and new programme aids are being developed for the Guiders and Trainers.

Zambia

Girl Guides Association of Zambia

GUIDE

Promise

I promise that I will do my best:
To serve God;
To serve my country and other
people
and
To keep the Guide Law.

Law

1 A Guide is to be trusted.
2 A Guide is loyal.
3 A Guide is helpful.
4 A Guide is a friend to all and a sister to all Guides.
5 A Guide considers other people.
6 A Guide is kind to animals and respects all living things.
7 A Guide is obedient.
8 A Guide is cheerful and brave, even in difficulties.
9 A Guide is thrifty.
10 A Guide controls herself in all she thinks, says and does.

Motto

Be Prepared

LECHWE

Lechwe Promise

I promise that I will do my best:
To serve God;
To serve my country and other
people
And to keep the Lechwe Law.

Lechwe Law

A Lechwe is truthful, obedient
and cheerful.
A Lechwe thinks of others
before herself.

Lechwe Motto

Wide Awake

Age Groups

Guide Cadet	18+
Ranger	14–21
Guide	11–16
Lechwe Guide	7½–11

Girl Guiding began in Zambia in 1924 when the first Guide company was registered in Livingstone, capital of what was then Northern Rhodesia. A Ranger company was opened within the same year and the first Brownie pack followed two years later. In 1935 the first National camp was held near Lusaka. There were originally two groups within the Association, Girl Guides and Brownies, and Wayfarers and Sunbeams, but in 1948 (following a referendum) the name 'Wayfarer Guides' was dropped and from 1952 all girls under 11 years of age were called Brownies. The Movement was unified under one Commissioner.

When Zambia became an Independent Republic within the Commonwealth in 1964, the Girl Guides Association of Zambia (previously a branch of the Girl Guides Association, U.K.) was established as a self-governing organization. In September 1966 the first Zambian Chief Commissioner was appointed and the newly built National Headquarters opened in Lusaka. In the same year Zambia was granted Associate Membership of the World Association at the 19th World Conference (Japan, 1966).

INTERNATIONAL CONTACTS AND GOLDEN JUBILEE

International contacts are extremely important in Zambian Guiding and Guiders and Rangers travel to many other countries in a continual effort to 'look wide'. In 1974 the Association celebrated its Golden Jubilee with an international camp whose participants came from as far away as the United States and the Philippines.

Camping and outdoor skills are special favourites with the girls and membership of the Association continues to rise in spite of the lack of adult Leaders.

To mark her fifty years of Guiding Zambia adopted her own badge and changed the name of her Brownies to Lechwe Guides – Lechwe being a species of brown antelope found only in Zambia.

SERVICE

The concept of service to the community is not new to Girl Guides in Zambia. As far back as the Second World War they were sending clothes to the troops, raising money for a Mobile Canteen which was given to the Army and donating to the Guide International Service.

Present-day Guides in Zambia have launched a pilot project in literacy/Guide leadership training for young married women in shanty townships and rural areas and have been able to publish booklets and charts in the major local languages.

HANDICAPPED

The Association now produces some of its publications in Braille and there are companies and packs for blind Guides and Brownies and also for leper children. Many girls with lesser handicaps are attached to ordinary companies and packs.

INTERNATIONAL WOMEN'S YEAR

To further the aims of International Women's Year the Association is establishing a training centre in Lusaka with vocational and recreational facilities for teenage girl trainees from rural areas.

Supplement to Seventh Edition

Hong Kong

Hong Kong Girl Guides Association

GUIDE

Promise

(a) I promise that I will do my best,
To do my duty to God,
To serve the Queen and help other people, and
To keep the Guide Law.

or

(b) I promise that I will do my best,
To do my duty to God,
To serve Hong Kong, and help other people, and
To keep the Guide Law.

Law

1 A Guide is loyal and can be trusted.
2 A Guide is helpful.
3 A Guide is polite and considerate.
4 A Guide is friendly and a sister to all Guides.
5 A Guide is kind to animals and respects all living things.
6 A Guide is obedient.
7 A Guide has courage and is cheerful in all difficulties.
8 A Guide makes good use of her time.
9 A Guide takes care of her own possessions and those of other people.
10 A Guide is self-controlled in all she thinks, says and does.

BROWNIE

Brownie Guide Promise

(a) I promise that I will do my best,
To do my duty to God,
To serve the Queen and help other people, and
To keep the Brownie Guide Law.

or

(b) I promise that I will do my best,
To do my duty to God,
To serve Hong Kong, and help other people, and
To keep the Brownie Guide Law.

Brownie Guide Law

A Brownie thinks of others before herself and does a Good Turn every day.

Age Groups

Ranger Guide	15–21
Guide	11–15
Brownie Guide	7–11

Girl Guiding started in Hong Kong in 1916 with the opening of a Girl Guide Company in the Victoria British School. In 1919 the Association was formally organized and registered as a Branch Association of The Girl Guides Association of the United Kingdom. The first Colony Commissioner of The Girl Guides Association was appointed the following year. Membership increased steadily and by 1926 it had reached 190.

In 1939 the first company in the New Territories was opened at the Taipo Rural Home. Membership had now increased to 385, but in 1941 Girl Guiding was forbidden. However, Girl Guides continued to meet and the spirit of Girl Guiding remained alive. The first post-war meeting on record was held by Guiders of the Association in Hong Kong on 8 December 1945 where all present renewed their Promise.

In 1948, a rally was held in the grounds of Government House and in the same year, the Association was invited to join the newly formed Social Welfare Council. This marked the beginning of the Association's involvement in the growth of social welfare in Hong Kong.

The publication, *Guide to Guiding*, was translated into Chinese in 1958, making it possible to extend Girl Guiding into all areas of the country.

In 1975 the Association made successful efforts to extend Girl Guiding into the low-cost housing estates with the hope that the girls living there would join the Movement.

Hong Kong Girl Guides Association was recognized as an Associate Member of the World Association of Girl Guides and Girl Scouts at the 23rd World Conference (Iran 1978).

PROGRAMME

The Eight-Point Programme, introduced in 1969, is common to all three branches, but is adapted to the needs of each age group. The object of the Programme is to encourage girls to undertake a balanced range of activities and to help them see Girl Guiding as a whole, with a continual progression from one stage to the next.

SERVICE

All members are encouraged to participate in service projects at Company or National level. A Service Badge is awarded to Girl Guides giving forty hours of service. Girl Guides help in the City Hall Library, in the children's wards of hospitals, and participate in national projects such as 'Walk for a Million' and 'Keep Hong Kong Clean'. During the summer, Girl Guides carry out a varied programme for underprivileged children. Funds have been raised by Girl Guides and Brownies towards the Kidney Transplant Fund.

PARTICIPATION IN INTERNATIONAL EVENTS

During 1977, Girl Guides, Rangers and Leaders attended three Regional and National events held in other Asian countries, and four Rangers attended the World Association Juliette Low Gathering at Sangam. The Association organized its first International Camp in 1976 to celebrate its Diamond Jubilee.

Lesotho

Lesotho Girl Guides Association

GUIDE

Promise

I promise on my honour to do my best
To do my duty to God and my country
To help other people at all times
And to obey the Guide Law.

Law

1 A Guide is to be trusted.
2 A Guide is loyal.
3 A Guide is helpful.
4 A Guide is friendly and is a sister to all Guides.
5 A Guide considers other people.
6 A Guide is kind to animals and respects all living things.
7 A Guide is obedient.
8 A Guide is brave and cheerful in all difficulties.
9 A Guide is thrifty.
10 A Guide controls herself in all she thinks, says and does.

Sunbeam Promise

I promise to do my best
To do my duty to God and my country
To help other people every day
Especially those at home.

Sunbeam Law

A Sunbeam thinks of others before herself.

Age Groups

Ranger	17+
Guide	12–16/17
Sunbeam	7–11

Girl Guiding was introduced into the Kingdom of Lesotho (then known as Basutoland) in 1925 by the Chief Commissioner of The Girl Guides Association of South Africa. As the membership was small the Association was attached to The Girl Guides Association of South Africa. This continued until 1961 when, after South Africa left the Commonwealth of Nations, Basutoland was administered as a Branch Association of The Girl Guides Association of the United Kingdom. Following Lesotho's political independence, a Chief Commissioner and Deputy Chief Commissioner were appointed. Guiding continued to grow and spread to many areas of the country. Trainers from the United Kingdom visited on several occasions to conduct trainings. In 1975, the Association was reorganized and a World Association Trainer/Adviser visited there in 1976 to assist them.

At a meeting of the Executive Committee of The Girl Guides Association of the United Kingdom in December 1977, a deed of transfer was signed, making the

Lesotho Girl Guides Association an independent Association. The Lesotho Girl Guides Association was recognized as an Associate Member of the World Association of Girl Guides and Girl Scouts at the 23rd World Conference (Iran 1978).

PROGRAMME

A Planning Committee is responsible for the programme development. The programme is based on those of The Girl Guides Association of South Africa and The Girl Guides Association of the United Kingdom with adaptations suited to the needs and cultural traditions of the Basuto girl. The programme is designed to help the girl become a useful and loyal citizen of her country. Since Lesotho is an agricultural country, training in agricultural skills is an important part of the overall programme.

SERVICE

Service plays an important part in the life of the Girl Guides in Lesotho. Many community development projects are undertaken and Girl Guides frequently participate in the building of wells, community centres and roads, in tree planting, in cleaning roads and in work camps in the villages.

Nepal

Nepal Scouts (Girl Scouts' Section)

GUIDE

Promise

On my honour I promise that I will do my best
(1) to do my duty to God/Dharma, my Country and my King
(2) to help other people at all times
(3) to obey the Girl Scout law.

Law

1 A Girl Scout's honour is to be trusted.
2 A Girl Scout is loyal to her country, her King and her employers.
3 A Girl Scout's duty is to be useful and to help others.
4 A Girl Scout is a friend to all and a sister to every other Scout no matter to what country, class or creed the other may belong.
5 A Girl Scout is courteous.
6 A Girl Scout is a friend to animals.
7 A Girl Scout obeys orders of her King, parents, Patrol Leaders, Scout Leaders, without question.
8 A Girl Scout smiles and sings under all difficulties.
9 A Girl Scout is thrifty.
10 A Girl Scout is clean in thought, word and deed.

Motto

Be Prepared

Ranger Motto

Do service

Brownie Promise

I promise to do my best
(1) to do my duty to God/Dharma, my Country and my King
(2) to help other people at all times
(3) to keep the laws of the Brownie pack.

Brownie Law

The Brownie gives in to her elders.
The Brownie is courteous and clean.
The Brownie utilizes her time properly.

Brownie Motto

Do your best

Age Groups

Ranger	15–21
Girl Scout	13–15
Brownie	7–12

Girl Scouting first began in Nepal in 1952, within the Boy Scout Association, when the Nepal Minister of Education invited a group of Girl Guide and Boy Scout Trainers from India to conduct Trainings for teachers in colleges and schools. The teachers then opened Girl Scout and Boy Scout Companies in and around Kathmandu. This was followed by the official inauguration of the Nepal Boy and Girl Scouts on 18 June 1952; the King of Nepal was appointed the Chief Patron. During the early years, the Association received help from the Bharat Scouts and Guides, who often sent Trainers to assist Nepal and invited Nepal Boy Scout and Girl Scout Leaders and Trainers to participate in national Trainings and other events organized in India.

In 1969 a separate Girl Scout Section was formed but Girl Scouting existed only in a few towns. In 1975 a new Constitution was adopted and the name changed to Nepal Scouts. A five-year development programme was launched to introduce Girl Scouting into all seventy-five districts by 1980.

Nepal Scouts is a joint association and some of its activities are undertaken by the boys and girls together while others are carried out by girls only. Due to the traditions of the country, Girl Scouting is still confined to schools. The Association works closely with the Education Ministry and receives help in its efforts to reach the more remote areas.

The Girl Scouts' Section of the Nepal Scouts was recognized as an Associate Member of the World Association at the 23rd World Conference (Iran 1978).

PROGRAMME

The programme emphasizes handicrafts, camping, hiking, nature conservation and community development. Efforts are being made to revise the programme according to the needs of the Nepalese girl.

SERVICE

Community service projects have included tree planting, relief operations during earthquakes, floods, landslides and forest fires, and manning first aid posts, information centres and lost property offices during festival times. The Association has recently approached the Nepal Blind and Disabled Association in order to introduce Girl Scouting to the handicapped.

PARTICIPATION IN INTERNATIONAL EVENTS

The Association has sent delegations to events in India and, during the past five years, to Regional and World events.

Netherlands Antilles

Da Padvindstersvereniging van de Nederlandse Antillen

Promise

I will earnestly try:
(1) To do my duty to God and my country
(2) To help all people where possible
(3) To obey the Guide Law.

Law

1 A Girl Guide is honest.
2 A Girl Guide is loyal.
3 A Girl Guide is willing to help.
4 A Girl Guide is a friend to all and a sister to all Guides.
5 A Girl Guide is courteous and attentive.
6 A Girl Guide cares for plants and animals.
7 A Girl Guide is obedient.
8 A Girl Guide accepts disappointments with cheerfulness.
9 A Girl Guide is thrifty.
10 A Girl Guide is pure in thought, in word, and in deed.

Age Groups

Guide	11–17
Brownie	8–11

The first Girl Guide Company was opened in Curaçao on 31 May 1930 by the Het Nederlandse Padvindsters Gilde (NPG), one of the component associations of the Nationale Padfindstersraad of the Netherlands. Soon after this the Association became the Nederlandse Padfindstersgilde Curaçao (NPC). During the following years Girl Guiding continued to grow with assistance given by the Netherlands Association (NPG) in programme and training development.

In 1967 the Nederlandse Padvindsters Gilde, in the hope that the Association would benefit more from contact with National Organizations in the same geographical area, requested the World Association and the Western Hemisphere Committee to work directly with them. In 1972 the Nederlandse Padvindstersgilde Curaçao became a separate independent association. Since that time, they have been in close contact with the World Association and the Western Hemisphere Committee.

Girl Guiding has now spread to all areas of the island of Curaçao and to all sectors of the community. The name of the Association was changed to the Padvindstersvereniging van de Nederlandse Antillen in 1977 and they were recognized as an Associate Member of the World Association at the 23rd World Conference (Iran 1978).

PROGRAMME AND TRAINING

The programme for all age groups is planned to enable the girl to develop her character and mind, to attain a proficiency in her chosen activities and interests, to develop a willingness to help others and to gain a sense of fellowship. Those who wish to continue Girl Guiding after the age of seventeen are encouraged to take leadership training and become leaders.

Training is carried out by a team including the Commissioner for Training, and Trainers for the Brownies and Guides. Meetings for Leaders, usually held twice a month, include training as well.

SERVICE

Community service plays an important part in the life of the Association and each year a special programme is launched which involves all members. The project in 1977 was '1977 Konsiente Di Nos Ambiene' ('1977 Conscious of our Environment') aimed at making the public more civic minded.

PUBLIC RELATIONS

The annual projects undertaken by the Association have helped in making Girl Guiding known in the community. The Association is a member of the Federation for Youth Care in the Netherlands Antilles. Relations with the government are good and the Association has been granted use of the land on which many of their Troop Houses stand.

PARTICIPATION IN INTERNATIONAL EVENTS

During the past few years, the Association has participated in events organized by the Western Hemisphere Committee and also sent delegates to events organized by neighbouring countries.

Papua New Guinea

Girl Guides Association of Papua New Guinea

GUIDE

Promise

I promise that I will do my best
To do my duty to God and my Country,
To serve the Queen,
To help people at all times, and
To keep the Guide Law.

Law

1 A Guide is loyal and to be trusted.
2 A Guide is helpful.
3 A Guide is polite and considerate.
4 A Guide is friendly and a sister to all Guides.
5 A Guide is kind to animals and respects all living things.
6 A Guide is obedient.
7 A Guide has courage and is cheerful in all difficulties.
8 A Guide makes good use of her time.
9 A Guide takes care of her own possessions and those of other people.
10 A Guide is self-controlled in all she thinks, says and does.

Age Groups

Ranger	18–25
Ranger Guide	14–18
Guide	$10\frac{1}{2}$–$14\frac{1}{2}$
Brownie Guide	7–11

The first Girl Guide Company was started by Christian Chatterton (a missionary) near Port Moresby, Papua, in 1927. Soon after, other companies were established in the villages of Hula and Delena. In 1933 a Ranger Company was opened to allow Girl Guides to continue in the Movement. The first Girl Guide Company in New Guinea was begun in 1939. The membership at that time was 120. Between 1942 and 1945, Girl Guiding ceased to function but was restarted in 1946 with a Ranger Company for former Girl Guides. Soon after companies and packs were begun in several villages by former Girl Guides.

The Federal Council of the Girl Guides Association of Australia included the Girl Guides of Papua New Guinea as a division in 1948 and appointed Mrs. Murray, wife of the Australian Government Administrator, as president. A local Association was formed at that time and the following year a Territory Commissioner for Girl Guides was appointed. In 1955 the Association was recognized as a State branch of the Girl Guides Association of Australia. A Constitution was prepared and accepted the following year.

The first Chief Commissioner of the Girl Guides Association of Papua New Guinea, Mrs. Enny Moaitz, was appointed in 1972 and in 1976 a new Constitution was introduced and a Training course for Trainers was held. Girl Guiding has become a part of the life of the villages where it has been introduced and efforts are now being made to encourage village women to become leaders. The Association was recognized as an Associate Member of the World Association at the 23rd World Conference (Iran 1978).

PROGRAMME AND TRAINING

A new programme has recently been introduced which is designed to develop the Girl Guides of Papua New Guinea into self-reliant, able citizens. Detailed programmes have been prepared for the three branches based upon citizenship, cultural activities, Girl Guide craft and emergency preparedness. The citizenship section encourages service and involvement in the community. All handbooks are produced in the three major languages, Pidgin, Motu and English.

The Training Scheme brings selected Girl Guide Trainers to Port Moresby. After completion of the course, Trainers are employed in various parts of the country. The Cadet Trainers Scheme, introduced in 1975, provides a two-year training for girls (aged 16–18) who have completed a secondary education.

PUBLIC RELATIONS

The Girl Guides Association is one of the major youth organizations in the country and maintains good relations with government, both local and national, with churches and city councils. The Girl Guides participate in youth activities sponsored by the government and the churches.

Appendix A

Founder Members of WAGGGS

Founder Members of WAGGGS, as stated in the 5th World Conference Report, 1928, and confirmed in the 6th World Conference Report, 1930:

AUSTRALIA
BELGIUM
CANADA
CZECHOSLOVAKIA[1]
DENMARK
ESTHONIA[1]
FINLAND
FRANCE
HUNGARY[1]
ICELAND
INDIA[2]
JAPAN[3]
LATVIA[1]
LIBERIA[4]
LITHUANIA[1]
LUXEMBOURG
NETHERLANDS
NEW ZEALAND
NORWAY
POLAND[1]
SOUTH AFRICA
SWEDEN
SWITZERLAND
UNITED KINGDOM OF GREAT BRITAIN AND NORTHERN IRELAND
UNITED STATES OF AMERICA
YUGOSLAVIA[1]

[1] CZECHOSLOVAKIA, ESTHONIA, HUNGARY, LATVIA, LITHUANIA, POLAND, YUGOSLAVIA are no longer members of WAGGGS.

[2] INDIA – covering the areas known today as BANGLADESH, INDIA, PAKISTAN.

[3] JAPAN held membership only until 1939; on being reorganized was admitted in 1952 as an Associate Member and became a Full Member in 1960.

[4] LIBERIA held membership only until 1931; on being reorganized was admitted in 1966 as an Associate Member and became a Full Member in 1975.

Appendix B

Addresses of the World Centres

OUR CHALET

CH 3715, Adelboden, Switzerland
Telephone: 033 73 1226
Telegrams: WAGGGS Adelboden

OLAVE HOUSE

45 Longridge Road, London
SW5 9SD,
England
Telephone: 01–370 2574
Telegrams: 01–370 2574

OUR CABAÑA

Apartado 406, Cuernavaca, Morelos,
Mexico
Telephone: Cuernavaca 5–26–50
or 5–28–97
Telegrams: CabanaGuias Morelos

SANGAM

World Centre for the World
Association of Girl Guides and Girl
Scouts,
Alandi Road, Yerawada, Poona
411006, India
Telephone: 23252

How to apply to stay at a WAGGGS World Centre

Our Cabaña, Our Chalet, and Sangam – write first to your National Headquarters, who will give further details.

Olave House – write to the Guider-in-Charge, enclosing an International Reply Coupon (obtainable at any Post Office); those in the United Kingdom should send a stamped and self-addressed envelope.

Appendix C

Guide Houses

Compiled from information received from National Organizations. Groups and individuals wishing to visit these Guide Houses should write in the first place to their own National Organization.

Country	Address	Information
AUSTRALIA	'Glengarry', Corner Milton and Miowera Roads, North Turramurra, NEW SOUTH WALES, 2074 Tel. 44 2955	*Training centre with warden* *Correspondence to:* G.G.A., 201–203 Clarence Street, Sydney, NEW SOUTH WALES, 2000
	'Tara', Taylor's Road, Silverdale, NEW SOUTH WALES, 2750 Tel. Warragamba 74 1133	*Training centre with warden* *Correspondence to:* G.G.A., 201–203 Clarence Street, Sydney, NEW SOUTH WALES, 2000
	'Noonamena', Bargo, NEW SOUTH WALES, 2574	*Sleeps 20 people* *Situated in beautiful bush setting* Details from booking secretary 14 Elizabeth Street, Camden, NEW SOUTH WALES, 2570
	Rachel Cleland House, Port Moresby, PAPUA/NEW GUINEA	*Hostel with staff* *Correspondence to:* G.G.A., Box 2079, Konedobu, PAPUA/NEW GUINEA
	'Kindilan', Redland Bay, QUEENSLAND, 4165	*Training centre* *Correspondence to:* G.G.A., P.O. Box 56, North Brisbane, QUEENSLAND, 4001
	'Paxlease', Crafers, SOUTH AUSTRALIA, 5152	*Training centre*
	'Olave Hills', Olave Hills Road, Upper Sturt, SOUTH AUSTRALIA, 5156 Tel. 39 2781	*Correspondence to:* G.G.A., 278 South Terrace, Adelaide, SOUTH AUSTRALIA, 5000

Country	Address	Information
AUSTRALIA (*cont.*)	'Wongalere', Williamstown, SOUTH AUSTRALIA, 5351 Tel. 085 246347	
	'Tuckerway' Port Vincent, SOUTH AUSTRALIA, 5581	*Correspondence to:* Miss J. Tucker, Box 16 P.O., Port Vincent, SOUTH AUSTRALIA, 5581
	'Orana' Southern Regions Camp, Roches Beach Road, Lauderdale, TASMANIA, 7021 Tel. 48 6353	*Caretaker on site*
	'Nindethana', Deviot, West Tamar, TASMANIA, 7251	*Correspondence to:* G.G.A., 91 Davey Street, Hobart, TASMANIA, 7000
	'Myalla' Camp House, nr. Wynyard, TASMANIA, 7321	
	'Brittania Park', Yarra Junction, VICTORIA, 3797 Tel. 0596 71279	*Training centre* *Correspondence to:* G.G.A., 20 Russell Street, Melbourne, VICTORIA, 3000
	'Paxwold', Lesmurdie, WESTERN AUSTRALIA, 6076 Tel. 93 6417	*Training centre* *Correspondence to:* G.G.A., G.P.O. Box U 1895, Perth, WESTERN AUSTRALIA, 6001
BARBADOS	Pax Hill, Belmont Road, St. Michael, BARBADOS	
BELGIUM	Domaine des G.C.B., B. – 5132 Mozet, BELGIUM Tel. 081/58 84 04	*12 km from Namur – Ardennes* *Training centre* *Conference rooms, offices, bedrooms, kitchens* *Tents also available* *Correspondence to:* Guider-in-Charge

Country	Address	Information
BELGIUM *(cont.)*	'Trait d'Union' (G.C.B.), Lincé, B. – 4060 Sprimont, BELGIUM	*25 km from Liège* *Offices, bedrooms, kitchens* *Outdoor facilities* *Correspondence to:* Guider-in-Charge
	De Brink (V.V.K.M.), Bosbergen, 1, B. – 2410 Herentals, BELGIUM Tel. 014/21 15 33	*35 km from Antwerp* *Training centre* *Fully organized – 100 beds* *5 camping sites – tents available* *Correspondence to:* De Brink
	Woutershof (V.V.K.M.), Groot Broekstraat, 46, B. – 3688 Kinrooi, BELGIUM Tel. 011/86 48 25	*90 km from Brussels* *Holiday centre* *40 beds, 5 camping sites – tents available* *Correspondence to:* Woutershof
	Cul des Sarts (F.E.E.), Rue du Point de Vue, 2, B. – 6404 Cul des Sarts, BELGIUM	*30 beds* *Correspondence to:* M. André Dolphens, Grotewinkellaan, 95–97, B. – 1820 STROMBEEK
	Domaine de Rhisnes, Rue Bois des Broux, B. – 5840 Rhisnes, BELGIUM	*36 beds* *Camping site* *Correspondence to:* M. André Dolphens, Grotewinkellaan, 95–97, B. – 1820 STROMBEEK
	Domaine de Heure (F.E.E. – F.O.S.), B. – 5412 Heure-en-Famenne, BELGIUM	*60 beds* *Camping site* *Correspondence to:* Mme. D. Vermeylen, Hoge Aardstraat, 55, B. – 2610 WILRIJK Tel. 031/40 09 95
CHINA	Garden City, Yaipei Hsien, Taiwan, REP. OF CHINA	*Training centre*
CYPRUS	Volta Street, No. 1, P.O. Box 542, Famagusta, CYPRUS	*Hostel*
DENMARK	Jaegergården, Ørnholmvej. Rørtang Overdrev, 3070 Snekkersten, DENMARK	*Correspondence to:* Guider-in-Charge

Country	Address	Information
DOMINICAN REPUBLIC	Asociación Nacional de Guías Scouts Dominicanas, Inc., Calle El Sol 112, Santiago, REP. DOMINICANA	
EGYPT	Sharia Shanan, Galaa Street, P.O. Box 1446, Cairo, EGYPT	*Hostel with 36 beds*
FINLAND	Partiopoukama	*Seaside training centre and camp site near Helsinki* *No permanent staff* *Each group takes care of own cooking* *Correspondence to:* International Secretary, The Union of Finnish Girl Guides, Heikkilantie 10, 00210 Helsinki 21, FINLAND
	Rytilahti, North of Finland	*Camp site at peaceful lakeside* *Accommodation in tents* *Application as above*
FRANCE	La Goélette, Foyer International d'Accueil et de Culture, 39, rue du Maréchal de Lattre de Tassigny, 62600 Berck-Plage, FRANCE Tel. le 1 35 à Berck	*For handicapped persons but purpose is under revision* *Correspondence to:* Director
	Foyer International de Mélan, Haute Provence, FRANCE	*International centre*
	Domaine des Courmettes, 06490, Tourette sur Loup, FRANCE	*Situated in Provence* *20 km from the sea* *Open to girls and boys of France's National Organizations*
GHANA	Ghana Girl Guides Training Centre, P.O. Box 43, Achimota, GHANA Tel. 76551 Ext. 20	

Country	Address	Information
GREECE	'Marie-Laura Vretou' Brownie Home, Vari, GREECE	*30 km from Athens* *40 beds* *Any group of Brownies, Guides and members of the Movement welcomed* *Apply in good time to:* Guider-in-Charge of the Brownie Home, c/o The Association of Hellenic Girl Guides, 10 Odos Xenophontos, Athens 118, GREECE Tel. 3235794
INDIA	*World Association Centre,* Sangam, Alandi Road, Yerawada, Poona 41106, INDIA Tel. 23252	*Correspondence to:* Guider-in-Charge
IRAN	Maidan Kenedy, Nosrat Sharghy, District No. 1, Tehran, IRAN Tel. 930262 Khiban Kakh, Shah Avenue, District No. 2, Tehran, IRAN Tel. 43098 Farah Shomaly, Kuroosh Avenue, District No. 3, Tehran, IRAN Tel. 752075 Jalleh, Absardar, District No. 4, Tehran, IRAN Tel. 313377	*There are 11 Scout Houses in Tehran and also many more in other provinces and cities* *Correspondence to:* Iranian Scouting, Parke Shahr, Khiaban Behesht Avenue, Tehran, IRAN

Country	Address	Information
IRAN (*cont.*)	Shahbaz, Kharabat, District No. 5, Tehran, IRAN Tel. 353055	
	Shush, Janbe Sardkhaneh, District No. 6, Tehran, IRAN Tel. 536644	
	Nazy abad, District No. 7, Tehran, IRAN Tel. 531211	
	Rahahan, Solaiman Khani, District No. 8, Tehran, IRAN Tel. 27884	
	Narmak, Khiaban Bimeh, District No. 9, Tehran, IRAN Tel. 79745	
	Robatkarim, District No. 13, Tehran, IRAN Tel. 952607	
	Pamenar, Haiat Shahy, District No. 17, Tehran, IRAN Tel. 26526	
IRELAND	Leigh Dale Cottage, Carrigrohan, CORK	
	Girl Guide Memorial Cottage, Enniskerry, CO. WICKLOW	

Country	Address	Information
ISRAEL	Charat Hatzofim, Nr. Ramat Yocharan, Post Kfar Hamaccabi, ISRAEL	*Training centre*
JAPAN	Scouts Hut of Okinawa Girl Scouts Council, 280 Matsukawa, Naha-shi, Okinawa, JAPAN 902 Tel. Naha 32–4490	*20 beds* *Cooking facilities available* *Meals also obtainable*
	Togakushi National Camp Center, Togakushi, Kamiminochi-Gun, Nagano, JAPAN 381–41 Tel. Togakushi 104	*Open between 15 July and 31 August* *Conference room, offices, bedrooms, kitchen, storeroom, dispensary and indoor programme hall for 300 girls* *Also 2 camp cabins*
LIECHTENSTEIN	Guide House, Gapetschweg 608, FL–9494 Schaan, LIECHTENSTEIN	Accommodation for 30 people *Correspondence to:* Guider-in-Charge or Fürstlich Liechtensteinisches, Pfadfinderinnen-Korps Sta. Maria, P.O. Box 124, FL–9494 Vaduz, LIECHTENSTEIN
LUXEMBOURG	Centre International, Le Relais de l'Amitié, Bilsdorf par Arsdorf, LUXEMBOURG	*Correspondence to:* Quartier Général, 3 Place du Théâtre, LUXEMBOURG
	Centre International d'Accueil, 61 route de Trèves, LUXEMBOURG	
	Colpach-Bas, LUXEMBOURG	*Training centre* *Correspondence to:* 61 route de Trèves, LUXEMBOURG
	Chalet Guide, Esch-Alzette, LUXEMBOURG	*Correspondence to:* Mme. Irma Wagener, 2, rue Victor Hugo, Esch-Alzette, LUXEMBOURG
MALAYSIA	Wisma Pandu Putri, Jalan Pantai Baharu, Kuala Lumpur, N. BARAT	*National Guide House incorporating National Headquarters, Conference Hall, Hostel and guest rooms*

Country	Address	Information
MALAYSIA (*cont.*)	Wisma Pandu Putri N. Sembilan, 331D, Julan Rahang, Seremban, N. Sembilan, MALAYSIA BARAT	*State Guide House, Negeri Sembilan State*
	Persatuan Pandu Putri, Jalan Mahamood, Kota Bahru, Kelantan, MALAYSIA BARAT	*State Guide House, Kelantan State*
	Persatuan Pandu Putri, Jalan Abdul Jalil, Greentown, Ipoh, Perak, MALAYSIA BARAT	*State Guide House, Perak State*
	Persatuan Pemandu Perempuan, Jalan Abdul Samad, Brickfields, Kuala Lumpur, MALAYSIA BARAT	*State Guide House, Selangor State*
MEXICO	Ticalli, Guadalquivir 93, MEXICO 5, D.F. Tel. 5–33–64–12	
	World Association Centre Our Cabaña, Apartado Postal 406, Cuernavaca, Morelos, MEXICO Tel. Cuernavaca 2–30–98	*Correspondence to:* Guider-in-Charge
NETHERLANDS	Scout-centre, 'Buitenzorg', Amsterdamsestraatweg 51, BAARN Tel. 02154–2244	*For reservations:* Mr. B. van Dijk, 'Buitenzorg', Amsterdamsestraatweg 51, Baarn, THE NETHERLANDS
	Gilwell St. Walrick, St. Walrickweg 9, OVERASSELT	
	Gilwell Ada's Hoeve, Zwolseweg 17, OMMEN	

Country	Address	Information
PAKISTAN	Guide Headquarters, Strachen Road, Karachi I, SIND	
	Guide House, Nr. Government Girls High School, Hirabad, Hyderabad, SIND	
	Guide House, Anscomb Road, Quetta, BALUCHISTAN	
	Guide House, Model Town, Bahawalpur, PUNJAB	
	Guide House, Bagh Langay Khan, Multan, PUNJAB	
	Guide House, (Provincial Headquarters), 5 Habibullah Road, LAHORE	
	Guide House, Asghar Mall Road, RAWALPINDI	
	Guide House, G.T. Road, GUJRANWALA	
PANAMA	Casa 'Itabe', PANAMA CITY 'Nuestro Rancho', National Camp in El Barrero, COCLÉ PROVINCE	*Applications to:* Asociación Nacional, Muchachas Guías, Oficina Nacional, Apartado 7676, Panama 9, PANAMA
PERU	Godofredo Garcia 375, San Isidro, Lima, PERU	*International Guide House*

Country	Address	Information
PERU (*cont.*)	Parque El Retiro, La Castellana, Surco, Lima, PERU	*Training centre*
PHILIPPINES	Camp Concepcion R. Gonzalez, San Bartolome, Novaliches, Quezon City, PHILIPPINES	
	Ating Tahanan, 15 South Drive, Baguio City, PHILIPPINES	
RHODESIA	Pax Park, Lake MacIlwaine, MASHONALAND	*None of these centres has a resident staff, but anyone who wishes to use them can do so at nominal charges*
	Rowallan Park, Matopos, MATABELELAND	
	Kuchena-Gatooma, CENTRAL	
	Diamond Park, Fort Victoria, SOUTHERN	
	Chinziwa, Vumba, MANICALAND	
SRI LANKA	10 Sir Marcus Fernando Road, Colombo 7, SRI LANKA	*Training centre attached to Headquarters* *Two guest rooms*
SWITZERLAND	*World Association Centre* Our Chalet, 3715 Adelboden, SWITZERLAND Tel. 033–73–12–26	*Correspondence to:* Guider-in-Charge
	National Guide House, Casa del Pizzo, CH–6549 CAUCO	*Open during summertime* *Information:* Fédération des Eclaireuses Suisses, Secrétariat Central, Kramgasse 51, CH–3011 BERNE Tel. 031/ 22 07 24

Country	Address	Information
SWITZERLAND (*cont.*)	District Guide House, CH–4466 ORMALINGEN	*Information:* Frau V. Bächlin-Hofer Klosterreben 32, CH–400 BASEL Tel. 061/ 42 87 77
	District House, Sembrancher sur Martigny, SWITZERLAND	*Information:* Mlle Odile Saudan, Chemin de la Pierre à Voir 5, CH–1920 MARTIGNY 1 Tel. 026/ 2 20 97
TURKEY	National Camp Site, Gençlik ve Spor Bakanliği, İzcilik Daimi Tesisi, Manisa-KIRKAĞAC	
	İzcilik Egitim Merkezi, Hasanağa Bahcesi, Buca-İZMİR	*Training centre*
UNITED KINGDOM	*World Association Centre* Olave House, 45 Longridge Road, London SW5 9SD, ENGLAND Tel. 01–370 2574	*Correspondence to:* Guider-in-Charge

Appendix D

Since 1977, the following National Organizations have changed their titles. You will wish to amend your copy to be up to date:

Austria: Pfadfinder und Pfadfinderinnen Österreichs p. 24
Chile: Asociación de Guías y Scouts de Chile (sección femenina) p. 54
Costa Rica: Asociación de Guías y Scouts de Costa Rica (sección femenina) p. 60
Finland: Suomen Partiolaiset – Finlands Scouter r.y. p. 77
Jordan: Boy Scouts and Girl Guides of Jordan p. 129

Notes

Notes

Notes

Notes